DO YOU KNOW

that rays and signals are now being received from the center of our galaxy . . . that you can sensitize your mind to these messages and respond to faint impulses from far-away planets?

DO YOU KNOW

that you may well have an astro-twin, born under the same astrological sign, who lives a life almost exactly parallel to your own?

JOSEPH F. GOODAVAGE takes you from the sealed tombs of Egypt to Mars . . . and reveals the power of *ASTROLOGY: THE SPACE AGE SCIENCE.*

JOSEPH F. GOODAVAGE is a well-known writer and researcher who has investigated Astrology with an open mind. The author has worked as a reporter and tramp printer for at least half of the major dailies in the U.S. and has written hundreds of articles for the national magazines TRUE and FACT. Mr. Goodavage has also lectured widely before university groups on long-range weather forecasting with astrological principles

Other SIGNET Books of
Special Interest

ASTROLOGY
The Space Age Science

JOSEPH F. GOODAVAGE

A SIGNET BOOK from
NEW AMERICAN LIBRARY
TIMES MIRROR

Library of Congress Catalog Card Number 65-29333

*This is an authorized reprint of a hardcover edition
published by Parker Publishing Company, Inc.*

Ⓢ   SIGNET TRADEMARK REG. U.S. PAT. OFF. AND FOREIGN COUNTRIES
      REGISTERED TRADEMARK—MARCA REGISTRADA
      HECHO EN CHICAGO, U.S.A.

SIGNET, SIGNET CLASSICS, MENTOR, PLUME AND MERIDIAN BOOKS
*are published by The New American Library, Inc.,
1301 Avenue of the Americas, New York, New York 10019*

FIRST PRINTING, JUNE, 1967

9 10 11 12 13 14 15 16 17

PRINTED IN THE UNITED STATES OF AMERICA

DEDICATION

For Evelyn

Author's Acknowledgment

This book is designed to lead you into the often strange, always fascinating world of astrology—what it can do for you; how it may be used as a tool for understanding—by individuals, nations *and* scientific disciplines.

I have been privileged to know some of the truth-seekers who have preserved the ancient study of astrology and carried it through the ages for your present enlightenment and enrichment. Knowledge of the celestial forces that govern the terrestrial sphere is *true science*.

I cannot give a complete list of those who contributed to this work. Foremost in my mind of course, are all the great astrologers since ancient or antediluvian times. You'll learn about many of them here.

Oddly enough, a non-astrologer helped a great deal in making this book a reality. I owe a debt of gratitude to motion picture producer Max E. Youngstein, whose warmth and encouragement were invaluable.

America's official astrological organization, The American Federation of Astrologers, and many of its members have contributed greatly to research projects with no thought other than the advancement of their science. Paul R. Grell, the AFA's executive secretary, also helped more than he realizes. Ernest and Katherine Grant, of the National Astrological Library in Washington, D.C., have contributed a great deal.

Yet it was largely through the efforts of John W. Campbell, editor of ANALOG, and George J. McCormack, editor of ASTROTECH, that I was exposed to a finely discriminating scientific application of astrology.

In medical astrology and other branches I've gained valuable insight from Dr. Fred Sims Pounds and the late Dr. W. M. Davidson as well as Eugene Scheimann, M.D. Mathematician-astrologer Carl Payne Tobey and biologist-astrologer Al H. Morrison have also influenced these pages.

Without the suggestion and encouragement of Lionel Day, I may not have written this book at all. I'm grateful for the specialized assistance of B. V. Raman, Editor of *The Astrological Magazine,* Bangalore, India—and that of the Hon. Secretary of the Astrological Association of England, John M. Addey.

Special thanks is due the American Institute of Medical Climatology and Dr. Igho Kornblueh for their spirit of scientific cooperation in the Time-"Twins" research; this also applies to Dr. Forrest Speicher of Philco Corporation's science research department.

Many could profit by the example of Burton Browne, president and founder of the famous Gaslight key clubs, who used astrology as a springboard to a lucrative new career before anybody had ever thought of Gay Nineties-type key clubs.

On the distaff side, I owe a deep acknowledgment to Olive Adele Pryor, Doris Chase Doane, Hyacinthe Hill and Katherine de Jersey, all specializing astrologers of the national organization, the AFA.

A special note of thanks is due Frances Jacoby and Dorothy Rice for their selfless assistance in the preparation of the manuscript.

Medals ought to be given to those who do the "infantry work" for such a book. In this case, I refer to all those dedicated people who contributed unstintingly in calculating charts for earthquakes, volcanic eruptions and severe weather anomalies: Nora Forrest, Frances Conyers, Carl Rauser, Mrs. Charles J. Bennett, Dwight D. Williamson, K. Barbara Dunn, Mrs. Earl Riblet, Mrs. Cordelia E. Coull, A. C. Kirn, and Dorothy B. Hughes. I'm also indebted to Dr. Regina Lorr, Frances Aldred and Harmony Pearl for invaluable assistance in various aspects of medical and mundane astrology.

These people are a mere handful of the astrologers who assisted in my attempt to show what astrology really is—and what it can mean to you.

In large measure, this is their book, not mine.

JOSEPH F. GOODAVAGE

What Astrology
Can Do For You

Over many thousands of years astrologers have deduced a connection between the motions of the planets and positions of the stars with every kind of terrestrial activity. Their ability to predict future trends—even actual events—has been repeatedly demonstrated.

ASTROLOGY'S VALIDITY HAS NEVER BEEN DISPROVED

Yet, as a skeptical newspaperman, reporter and free-lance writer, I have spent the better part of a decade trying to disprove the validity of astrology. Admittedly, I began these investigations with the preconceived notion that astrology was a "phony" science—that, in fact, there was nothing at all scientific about it. I was driven to disprove it on any ground that seemed likely: "superstition," "ignorance," "stupidity," "trickery," or just "sloppy, unscientific thinking." This proved to be impossible. In fact, this book stands as a complete reversal of my former attitude.

Some of history's greatest minds have attempted the same thing—only to become convinced of astrology's validity. No one can disprove astrology without altering facts—the same unvarnished, unadulterated facts you will find in these pages. As months of investigation stretched into years of research, I was forced to concede (*quite literally against my will*) that this ancient science was extremely valuable in *timing* important moves, in understanding what makes people tick. I found astrology remarkably dependable when used to determine the outcome of any venture. I learned how to cast horoscopes, and so can you, but it was several years before I learned how to interpret a birth chart.

ASTROLOGY IS THE MOST VALUABLE AID TO PSYCHOLOGY

I discovered that all the "in-depth" psychological studies, all the psychiatric know-how and all the aptitude testing ever devised can't compare with the answers a good astrologer can obtain from an exact horoscope.

I learned about people with wasted talents (some of them potential millionaires) who lead a humdrum 9-to-5 life because they have never investigated their true "Birthright." I saw people who considered themselves failures at lower-echelon jobs but who could have been magnificently successful *at the head* of an important enterprise (and vice versa). I've written articles about people who have used the advice of astrologers in timing their key moves—people who became rich by working in harmony with cosmic tides!

As these investigations continued, I deviated from my original course and determined to write the *truth* about astrology—*whichever* way the factual evidence led.

What I discovered amazed me! It *still* astonishes me each time I see a Sagittarian, a Virgoan (or someone strongly affected by *any* astrological Sign) doing precisely what he or she *should* be doing. The more you observe this, the more uncanny it seems.

Astrology is invaluable as a system for discovering your innate talents, for anticipating your life pattern and enabling you to experience a happier, fuller, richer, more meaningful existence. Here are the facts—what astrology is—how it can help you—how it can lift your sights, or even revolutionize your life!

Once you have turned the sharply defined light of incisive reasoning on *true* astrology, your entire outlook is bound to change. And with it, quite likely, the course of your life.

In a very broad sense, astrology may succeed where both science and religion have failed: that is, to give each human being a true picture of his own uniqueness and worthwhileness in what seems to be a vast, chaotic and often hostile universe.

THE GREATEST KNOWLEDGE IN HISTORY

Having become an astrologer in the course of my investigations, I can predict with reasonable accuracy that this ancient study will be standard fare in most of our colleges and universities within a decade.

It definitely will *not* be called "astrology," but the rules will remain the same as they were in the remote past. Astrology has survived all the ages because it magnificently reflects Nature. It is the greatest body of knowledge in human history —*bar none*.

There are many branches in astrology. Some practitioners specialize in only one or two: medical astrology, astrometeorology, horary astrology, natal astrology, mundane or "state" astrology and so on. The simplest, most immediately useful branch is called "horary" meaning *the hour* of the question asked. A chart is calculated for the hour, minute, and location —a few simple rules of interpretation will give you a better than 90%-accurate answer to any question. This is considered the easiest branch, yet it is the most remarkable use of astrological prediction I've ever seen.

Five astrologers who set up *"event"* charts for the time and place of the launching of the *nuclear submarine U.S.S. Thresher* independently predicted that it would meet with disaster through *sabotage!* Three of these astrologers agreed on the section of the vessel that would be tampered with. One of them went so far as to describe the saboteur as a foreign-speaking workman, probably a technician—possibly an espionage agent posing as an exile.

Could we have saved the *Thresher* and its 129-man crew from a watery grave through astrological means? It would have been worth a try.

One large insurance company in the East is now concluding a vast horoscopic study of 30,000 cases of longevity that astrology could have predicted. At least two major airlines are investigating the possibility that certain flights might be doomed as soon as their wheels leave the runway. With computers analyzing all the astronomical influences (at light-speed) before each flight, it may soon be possible to completely eliminate the danger of air disasters.

THE GREAT BIBLICAL PROPHETS WERE ASTROLOGERS

Timing is the all-important element for everything you undertake. This simple fact of Nature has been recognized by the greatest minds of all ages, including the Seers who wrote the Bible:

"All things have their season, and in their times all things pass under Heaven. A time to be born and a time to die. A time to plant, and a time to pluck up that which is planted. A time to kill, and a time to heal. A time to destroy, and a time to build. A time to weep, and a time to laugh . . ." (ECCLESIASTICS: 3:1–8).

This is pure philosophical astrology. The Bible is full of it.

Nothing can happen until the *time* for it to happen is right. When you observe this over a long period, it won't make you fatalistic, as some may think. Knowing the right and wrong times to act—*in advance*—gives you an enormous advantage. Astrology can broaden your choice. It's like having tomorrow's paper today. It gives you a tremendous edge. This is why astrology is called *Occultism*. "Occult" simply means *hidden* (as during an eclipse).

Long ago, certain corrupt astrologers kept their knowledge of the heavens secret so that they could use it to their own advantage. In time, they took to wearing foolish robes and dunce caps and pretending they were *causing* the things they predicted. As a Prince of Egypt, Moses was an Adept in astrology—and was thus able to beat the Priests and Magicians of Pharaoh's Court at their own game. They selfishly hid their knowledge from "profane eyes," formed groups with Secret Rites in order to perpetuate the myth of mystical-magical powers, and pass it on to those they selected, their apprentices, the new *Initiates*.

Thus, "occultism" came to mean things like "witchcraft," "black magic" *and* "demonism"—and these nefarious activities came to be associated with astrology. But when 19th Century materialism came into vogue, everyone stopped believing in demons, witches, magic—*and astrology*.

THE SPACE-AGE REBIRTH OF ANCIENT ASTROLOGY

Space-age science however, is throwing the clear light of objective reasoning into new areas of human knowledge. Many have already concluded that phenomena like dowsing, ESP and astrology will not yield to strictly physical probing. These scientists are discarding many outmoded scientific methods to meet the great adventure of totally unexpected knowledge.

This spirit of adventure is opposed to the idea of a cellophane-wrapped, cradle-to-grave security. And the subject of this book IS a great adventure—in the sense that Time Travel would be an adventure if it existed . . . and there is no proof that it doesn't already exist (in some remote future).

Light from inconceivably immense Quasars has been flashing through intergalactic space at 186,000 miles a second for billions of years. These Quasars (a contraction of Quasi-Stellar Radio Sources) are said to be millions of times as big as the largest stars in our galaxy, but too compact to be galaxies. They're so distant that we're actually looking at a part of our universe as it appeared seven or eight billion years ago before man was created—*even before the Earth existed*.

YOUR PERSONAL CYCLES AND HOW THEY CONTROL YOUR LIFE

Your personal cycles are as individual as your finger-prints. There are broad, general cycles that affect *everyone*—cycles of war and peace, cycles of famine and abundance, prosperity and depression, for example. Directly or indirectly, we live our personal cycles against the background of world and national cycles. As a backdrop, there are galactic cycles—and universal cycles.

Women know monthly cycles. So do hospitals, veteran policemen and fishermen. Ask any newspaperman about the night of the Full Moon; if he had a choice he would pick this as his night off. Mostly, we are unaware of such things. Possibly this is because you can't study any kind of cycle without noticing a strange tendency for a planetary cycle to recur at about the same time.

This is called astrology.

A general restlessness occurs with the Full Moon; patients on operating tables tend to hemorrhage as though the tides of the body were affected by lunar force just as the tides of the oceans.

LUNAR PHASE AND EXTROVERSION

Scientists are beginning to learn that the season, even the month of birth, can make a dramatic difference in physique, mental and emotional attitudes. Lunar phase at birth often makes the difference between introversion and extroversion.

According to your personal lunar cycle, there are times when you cannot succeed at any undertaking, regardless of detailed planning or positive thinking. On the other hand, if you choose the *right time* to act, you are virtually assured of success.

PREDICTING FUTURE TRENDS IN YOUR LIFE IS A SCIENCE

This book probes a complex system, through the use of which logical, rational predictions may be made for individuals, for governments, for the world.

There is no longer any doubt that extraterrestrial forces have a powerful, unseen effect in all areas of existence—individual and collective. There are biological cycles, industrial cycles, emotional cycles which affect the stock market, agricultural cycles, weather and earthquake cycles, economic and financial cycles, cycles of revolution, style and fad cycles, cycles of art and science, intellectual cycles and cycles of world destruction.

Our Earth does not rotate at a regular, eternal rate of motion. Neither does Jupiter, which is larger than all other planets combined. Quite possibly *none* of the planets do. There is abundant evidence that planets sometimes leave their orbits or stop rotating, that they even slip over, reverse their axes and magnetic poles—and that this occurs with cyclic regularity, but that humanity doesn't remember such catastrophic events because they occur so far apart in time and are therefore historically remote.

So we prefer to deny that it happens at all. *But look!* It snows all the time in the Antarctic, a place bigger than the continental United States. Several thousand years' accumulation of never-melting water vapor from the oceans of the world—hundreds of thousands of square miles of billions of tons of ice and snow—must eventually have *some* effect on this spinning Earth!

Like causing a slight wobble. Scientific cooperation in dealing with this problem on an international scale could result in a long period of fairly stable peace.

HOW TO TIME YOUR ACTIVITIES WITH LUNAR PHASE

Farmers have sown and harvested in harmony with the Moon from time immemorial. You can plant a garden, mow your lawn, trim your shrubs or even have your hair cut at the proper phase of the Moon. It results in thicker growth. At the wrong time during the lunar phase, such activities have the opposite effect. Barbers and scalp specialists know nothing about it.

Nevertheless, it works. Any activity has a greater chance of success when undertaken as the Moon *increases* in light (from New to Full Moon). With every Full Moon, Nature reaches a *crescendo* of activity. It's a regular cycle.

In our smog-laden, artificially lighted cities, we rarely see the stars and planets. We spend most of our time indoors, protected from the elements. We do not observe the invariability with which certain celestial patterns coincide with terrestrial events. From this invariability, ancient astronomers deduced *the necessity for one to occur with the other.*

HOW PLANETARY FORCES ENABLE YOU TO FORESEE YOUR FUTURE

The Science of Celestial Correspondences—or whatever you choose to call it—is the best of all known tools with which to open the door to the future. Unlike extrasensory talents, it is a skill that can be acquired by reasonably intelligent people. Like mathematics, it works whenever it is applied, not just when *it* wants to.

During the next decade the predictions ventured in the final pages of this book will provide the most dramatic evidence that the trends of the world can be anticipated with a high incidence of direct hits. Since most of us are curious to know what will happen, you'll probably read this part first.

But come back and discover how we got this way. It's a great adventure—the biggest I know—as eternal as time and as broad as the galactic universe. You may develop a few symptoms of insecurity or insignificance, but like everything else, that, too, shall pass.

Contents

2. YOUR MESSAGE FROM THE STARS (Continued)

3. THE WORLD'S OLDEST SCIENCE . . . 47

4. CAN ASTROLOGY PREDICT FUTURE DISASTERS? 66

Your Astro-Twin
Can Revolutionize Your Life

I

Almost everyone has a "Time-Twin" somewhere. These are people who have the same birthdate, the same hour of birth, and were born of the same longitude and latitude. It often happens that dozens of babies are born in big cities at *exactly the same moment!* And, as big as modern cities are, they represent only the tiniest dot on the global map. People born at the same instant anywhere in any city must, therefore, share virtually the same horoscope.

For centuries, astrologers have been saying that people with identical horoscopes live parallel lives, with occasional differences explained by genetics and the station or position into which they were born.

Until now, no one has ever proved it.

The fact is that if powerful forces from the surrounding universe have a predictable effect on human life, the action of these forces in *your* life can be dramatically demonstrated by locating people who were born at almost the same time and place and then comparing their life histories with yours. The entire structure of astrology must stand or fall on such evidence.

I decided to look into the matter and "prove" how fraudulent astrology really was.

Here is what I learned:

In 100 percent of the cases investigated, such "astro-twins" do indeed show parallelism. They tend to become ill simultaneously, and of the same disease—to suffer identical injuries at the same times and to the same parts of the body. The injuries often leave identical scars. They tend to get married, to have accidents, receive promotions, and have the same number of children at the same times and

*of the same sex—and they even die at the same times and
of the same causes!*

We regard these things as little more than curious coincidences. But there does seem to be a pattern in them, and
our evidence must come from Nature rather than opinions.
If the evidence for or against anything continually appears
in Nature, our conclusions *must* be influenced by the weight
of the facts, not by our preconceived notions.

THERE ARE GENETIC DIFFERENCES

Naturally, heredity must be taken into account—and also,
to a lesser extent, environment. But such explanations not
only leave many questions unanswered, they leave wide
open the possibility of exogenous forces at work in the
shaping of individual character or destiny. The prince and
the pauper may have identical horoscopes, but their station
in life prevents them from operating at the same levels. If
two individuals have the same horoscope and one becomes
a concert pianist, the other would find this career impossible—*if he happens to be a horse!*

A curious fact emerged during a Llewellyn Research
Foundation report: There are more twins and other
multiple-births when the Sun transits Gemini (The Twins)
than at any other time of the year.

In the October, 1964 issue of the *Archives of General
Psychiatry*, Ian C. Wilson and John C. Reece reported on
"Simultaneous Death in Schizophrenic Twins," concerning
two young women who seem to have "willed" themselves
to death. Such studies have been going on for centuries.
We all *know* twins often live strangely similar lives, and we
attribute this (in the cases of identical twins) to development
from the same egg.

But what about fraternal twins? And what about brothers
and sisters who share the same heredity and environment
but do *not* show similarity in their lives?

THE STRANGE COINCIDENCE OF SIMULTANEOUS DEATH

There are many studies indicating that the time of birth
has a great deal to do with the way we think, feel, and
behave. Unfortunately, most of the evidence for this is in
the realm of *abnormal* psychology.

The twins studied by the Drs. Wilson and Reece were Bobby Jean and Betty Jo Ellen, who were born on August 19, 1930, in Purlear, North Carolina. After a lifetime of similar incidents—accidents, injuries and sickness of amazing "parallelism" in all areas of their lives—both women became mentally ill and reached identical plateaus simultaneously.

On April 11, 1962 in Broughton State Mental Hospital in Morgantown, N.C., a night attendant found Bobby dead. Knowing of the strange affinity each had for the other, she called another ward where Betty was sleeping. The second twin was found lying dead on the floor. Autopsies could not determine the cause of death in either case.

A "strange coincidence" indeed!

Dr. Franz J. Kallmann of the N.Y. Psychiatric Institute, in a monumental report on schizophrenia in identical twins, said his study "abounds in cases in which both partners developed similar types of schizophrenia at practically the same time and with the same outcome of the disease."

Why?

PARALLELISM AMONG COMMONERS AND KINGS

We will avoid abnormalities and concentrate instead on some actual anomalies. The following four cases properly belong in the "Prince and Pauper" department:

On June 4th, 1738, two completely unrelated babies were born at almost the same minute in the English parish of St. Martin's-in-the-Fields.

One child was Samuel Hemmings, a commoner. The other was King George III.

Hemmings became an ironmonger; he went into business for himself on the same October date in 1760 that George III ascended to the throne of England.

Hemmings was married on September 8th, 1761.

King George was also married on September 8th, 1761.

Each became ill and had accidents at the same times. Every major event in Hemmings' life was mirrored in the life of the king, and vice versa. The scope and importance of their activities varied in keeping with their respective positions in life.

One always suspects that twins *deliberately* synchronize their activities, wear the same clothes, etc., from a rather morbid compulsion to merge their identities. Conceivably, this might also be the case with the commoner who wanted to ape the king, so we can't dismiss this possibility—yet.

But on January 29th, 1820, King George died.

On January 29th, 1820, Samuel Hemmings, a prosperous ironmonger, also died. In the same hour and of the same cause.

George IV, the Prince of Wales, was not so affectionately regarded. He was born in the same year, month, date and hour as a commoner who became a chimney sweep. When the commoner's parents learned of the Prince's birth, they promptly christened him "Prince George."

In "Shadow Land, or The Seer" (1852, Fowler and Wells), E. Oakes-Smith wrote, "Of the career of the Prince of Wales it is unnecessary to speak—his vices, his follies, his perjuries were all royal, and his fellow, the sweep, was not a jot behind him. The broom and scraper were as ill-adapted to the hands of one as the sceptre to the hands of the other.

"The parents of 'Prince George,' tired and ashamed of his profligacy, finally established him as a tallow chandler."

On the same date, George IV was put on a royal allowance and both men embarked on separate but similarly notorious careers as gamblers, philanderers and spendthrifts—but on entirely different financial and social levels. The commoner "Prince" acquired a stable of asses and ran the best donkey races of the day. George IV kept the best blooded ponies and ran the finest horse races in the country.

INJURED IN THE SAME WAY

On the day that "Prince George" was kicked in the hip by a donkey, George IV was kicked in the ribs by a horse. Both were injured and incapacitated for the same amount of time.

When the Prince of Wales lost everything and went bankrupt, so did the commoner "prince." And when all the King's horses were sold by the royal horseseller, the ex-chimney sweep lost his asses under the auctioneer's hammer. However much he wanted to imitate royalty, it seems unlikely that the commoner would choose to lose everything he had to serve that end.

Edward VII was born in the same year, month, date and hour as yet another commoner. Both displayed parallelism in their respective levels of life. And both died on May 6th, 1910—within an hour.

Kaiser William II of Germany was born at the same time and in the same locality as a lowly artisan. Each had the same number of children, of the same age and the same sex.

Each experienced identical illnesses and accidents at the same times. Except for the difference in their respective environments, the children of these men also showed many similarities.

When the Kaiser eventually learned of his "double," he "bestowed the royal bounty upon him." The Kaiser and his "twin" died at the same time.

SCIENTIFIC AWARENESS OF PARALLELISM

Historical researchers have cited many remarkable incidents of parallelism between royalty and commoners—possibly because such incidents were well recorded and are dramatic.

In our modern age of accurate record-keeping and fast communications, many more outstanding incidents should be available.

Dr. William A. Horwitz, who reported his in-depth studies of a pair of retarded "genius" twins to the American Psychiatric Association, said, "All previous explanations must again be questioned. We hope to indicate that other factors, *probably beyond our present knowledge* (author's italics), *must be better understood before we have a better explanation of these phenomena.*"

TWINS AND "STENCIL" FRACTURES

On December 1, 1961, twin sisters Sue and Mary Arnold of Lubbock, Texas, fell from their bicycles and broke their left arms. X-ray pictures showed the fractures to be identical. Sue fell first. Startled and frightened by her sister's cries, Mary peddled off at top speed to get help. Within 45 seconds her bicycle skidded; she too fell and fractured her left arm in the same place as had her sister.

These young girls often have the same experiences at the same times. Six months before their arm fractures, when they were separated by a distance of several miles, each girl got out of a car in a different neighborhood, and each closed a car door on her left hand—they suffered identical injuries. These accidents occurred less than 10 seconds apart.

The odds against two people having the same injuries to the same parts of the body in an automobile accident are exceedingly high. But it happened on October 4, 1964, in Trier, Germany, when 21-year-old twin daughters of a

Washington physician, Karen Ann and Shirley Ann Peterson
were instantly killed when their sports car crashed into another in which three American Air Force men were riding.
    None of the soldiers were killed.

Another "Impossible Coincidence"—That Happened!

In April, 1958, another strange incident involving variations on the name "Peterson" occurred outside Miami,
Florida.
    Three cars were stopped at a red light when a young
woman rammed the last car from behind. Here was the line-
up:

    Car No. 1 was driven by Cecil H. Peterson.
    Car No. 2 was driven by Harry C. Petterson.
    Car No. 3 was driven by Arthur H. Pettersen.
    All three cars suffered similar damages. The Petersons,
Pettersons and Pettersens were reported to be born in dif-
ferent years—but all within four days of the same month.
None were related to any of the others.

Birth and Death at the Same Moment

The bizarre and unexplainable case of Donald Chapman
and Donald Brazill is representative of about ten others of
its kind. They were born at the same hour and minute in
neighboring towns in California on September 5, 1933.
    Five days after their 23rd birthday—on Sept. 10, 1956—
Mr. Brazill of Ferndale and Mr. Chapman of Eureka met for
the first and last time in this life as they drove in opposite
directions on U.S. highway 101, south of Eureka, early on
a Sunday morning. They crashed head-on, and both were
killed instantly.
    Don Brazill and Don Chapman, who were born in the
same moment and lived nearly identical lives, held the
same kind of jobs and dated girls in each other's home town,
also died at the same moment—each causing the other's
death.
    Just another meaningless coincidence?
    Astrologers claim the planetary patterns in the horoscopes
of parents and grandparents are reflected in the charts of
their offspring.
    In this particular case, it's worthy of note that Donald

Brazill's father was killed in an automobile accident at the same place on the same road on September 10th, 1954 (See AP report—Sept. 10, 1956, Eureka, Calif.)

THE FANTASTIC "COINCIDENCE" IN IRELAND

Shortly before Christmas, about three months after the deaths of Don Brazill and Don Chapman in 1956, Jack Smith and his wife were driving along a road in Dublin next to the river Liffey that flows through the Irish capital. In a rare accident, their car somehow flipped off the road and toppled into the river.

Mr. and Mrs. Jack Smith were drowned. Their children, 11-year-old Vicky and 8-year-old Peter Smith (who were not with them) became orphans—but not for long.

John Shannon and his wife, close friends of the Smiths, adopted the children.

Four years from the date on which the Smiths had drowned, John Shannon was driving along the same road. Somehow, his car slipped off the road and toppled into the river Liffey at the exact spot the Smiths' car had gone down.

Shannon was also drowned. He left a widow and two orphans—Peter and Vicky. John Shannon was born in the same year and month, and only four days after Jack Smith!

FIREMEN, POLICEMEN—AND MARS

On July 19, 1913, Michael J. Murphy and Edward Thompson were born in Queens County, New York. Unknown to the other, each boy had similar interests and ambitions. Each graduated from Brooklyn Law School in the class of 1936, but future events transpired with about a year's difference in their lives.

Since astrology claims Mars to be associated with firemen and policemen, and since Mars happens to be prominent in their horoscopes, it is interesting to note that Michael J. Murphy rose through the ranks to become Police Commissioner of the world's greatest city, while Edward Thompson became the same city's Fire Commissioner.

ANOTHER CALIFORNIA TRAGEDY

Thirty-one years after Murphy and Thompson were born,

two other boys came into the world at the same time on the
West Coast. The common birthdate of Fred Schokley Jr.
and Barrett Woodruff was July 19, 1944. They were close
friends through elementary and high school, and they had
identical grades, identical interests, hobbies, likes and
dislikes. They did the same things at the same time and
entered Oakland City College together.

On March 23, 1964, after taking their dates home they
headed for Oakland for a late snack.

Neither boy made it. Each smashed into a trailer truck,
each was thrown from his car, and each suffered identical
fatal injuries—each died at the same moment.

Some "coincidence"!

THE FUGITIVE "TWINS"

On February 27, 1964, another remarkable coincidence
occurred in two different states at the same time. In Hacketts-
town, N.J., a 17-year-old escapee from Annandale Reforma-
tory held off state and local police from the attic of an
abandoned house during a two-hour gun battle. The fugitive
fired away with a .22-calibre rifle, but had a shotgun and
some pistols as well. Troopers brought in tear gas, but the
boy's father managed to talk him into surrendering.

On the same date and hour in Syracuse, N.Y. another 17-
year-old boy was holding off police and state troopers from
another attic retreat—also with a .22-calibre rifle. He too
had other weapons. This boy's father tried to talk him down
—unsuccessfully. He was smoked out with a barrage of
tear gas.

Both boys were born in the same year, same month, and
same date.

THE "ASTRO-TWIN" FAMILIES

In 1939 two unrelated women met for the first time in a
hospital room in Hackensack, N.J. Their last names were
Hanna and Osborne, but they had the same first name—
Edna. Each woman had a baby at the same time; the babies
weighed the same and were given the same name—Patricia
Edna.

Just another coincidence? Maybe, but here's what their
conversation revealed: both their husbands were named
Harold. Each Harold was in the same business and owned

the same make, model, and color car. The Hannas and the Osbornes had been married exactly three and a half years and had the same anniversary. The babies were their first. Both fathers were born in the same year, month, and day. The mothers too had the same birthdate—and the same number of brothers and sisters. Each Edna was a blue-eyed brunette—same height, same weight—and wore the same size clothes. Their husbands were of the same religion—a different one than that of the wives, which was also the same. Each family owned a dog named Spot—same mixed breed, same size, and same age. Both "Spots" were bought at the same time and were of the same sex.

THE OBVIOUS IS MOST DIFFICULT TO SEE

On March 30, 1964, a doctor and his wife were sentenced to two years in prison in Tucson, Arizona, for extreme cruelty to their five-year-old adopted daughter, Tina. The child was found by the housekeeper—beaten, bloody, and half-starved. Her hands were tightly roped behind her back and she cowered behind the furnace room in the basement. The shocked housekeeper released the child and called police, who were obliged to protect their prisoners against a mob of outraged neighbors.

At almost the same time, but in another state, an identical story unfolded. A dentist and his wife had beaten and brutalized their five-year-old adopted daughter and kept her tied up in the basement of their home. They too were sentenced.

The second child was Tina's twin sister from whom she had been separated since infancy!

Was this coincidence—or Law? And if it is the result of a Law, what *kind* of Law? It's at least conceivable that some kind of connection could exist between the people who adopted these children.

W. I. B. Beveridge, in *The Art of Scientific Investigation*, says "It is often curiously difficult to recognize a new, unexpected fact, even when obvious. Only people who have never found themselves face to face with a new fact laugh at the inability of medieval observers to believe their own eyes."

A closer examination of tens of thousands of like coincidences might reveal this new, "unexpected fact." In New Jersey, for example, twin sisters gave birth to sets of twins at

Chilton Memorial Hospital in Pompton Plains on July 31, 1962.

July 31 was the 30th birthday of the two mothers. The babies were born in the same hour as their parents—about 7 minutes apart.

WHY THE GENERATIONS ARE DIFFERENT

An ex-government official with degrees in two disciplines spent several years investigating the claims of astrologers, and eventually became one himself. "The mind of man," he said, "is a pattern-seeking entity. If the disciplined mind of an astronomer tries comparing a thousand people with Mars and Saturn, in adverse aspect at birth, against a control group —or against a thousand with these planets beneficially aspected—he'll never rest until he finds out why one group is so solidly different from the other. It has happened, and astrology has gained a new convert—or at least a silenced heckler. The outer planets—Uranus, Neptune and Pluto— move so slowly that they affect entire generations in the same way."

Professor Lars Friberg of Karelinska Institute of Stockholm, Sweden, who is currently directing a study on smoking, says, "Early results in a massive study of smoking habits among twins indicated that people may be *born* with a constitutional predisposition to smoking. The study shows that even though twins who live far apart in different environments, and may even not have known each other because of separation in infancy, still grew up to adopt similar smoking patterns."

WHEN IDENTICAL TWINS ARE "COMPLETELY DIFFERENT"

There could be all kinds of "predisposition" at birth— among "time-twins" as well as related twins. It is a well-known and universally recognized fact among astrologers that even identical twins who are born 45 minutes apart are not as alike as fraternal twins who are born within five minutes.

On September 12, 1963, for example, Mrs. Anne Powell gave birth to twins several miles and almost an hour apart in Brentwood, England. The first baby, a girl, was delivered at Brentwood Maternity Hospital, but Mrs. Powell developed serious complications and was rushed to St. Andrews

Hospital's Special Maternity Unit. The other twin, a boy, was born normally. Considering the difference in time, location and sex, astrologers anticipate that these identical twins will have no more in common than most ordinary brothers and sisters.

THE "BIOLOGICAL CLOCK" AT BIRTH

Some coincidences have nothing to do with twins or "time twins," but they're worth mentioning because they just might reveal something about genetics or the process that triggers our entrance into this life.

Louis J. Cacace, for example, is a New York Police sergeant who was born Janauary 26, 1915 at 3:52 A.M. He became a grandfather on January 26, 1959 at 3:52 A.M.

Mr. & Mrs. James E. Brown of Brownsburg, Indiana, have three children, all of whom were born at the same time on January 28 over a three-year period.

November 2, 1959 at Colorado Springs, Mr. & Mrs. John Le Croys had their third child. *Exactly* like the previous two, the third was born on November 2nd at 3:13 A.M.

And on February 24, 1959 at Indianapolis, Donald Duane Carter became the fourth generation of his family to be born at the same hour and minute on the same month and date.

At Salt Lake City on March 23, 1959, another pair of identical twins, who have a habit of synchronizing their activities, gave birth to their fourth child, a daughter, on the same date of the same month, in the same hour and minute as their other three children.

At Manhattan's Lenox Hill Hospital on November 4, 1966 Evan Kaliner was born on the same date and same hour as his father, Edward Kaliner and his paternal grandfather, Fred Kaliner. The baby was exactly six pounds, the same weight as his father and grandfather at birth.

COINCIDENCE—OR COSMIC LAW?

Probability, chance, or coincidence might explain such cases. But there must be a better answer for the many curious parallelisms found so often among twins. Especially the coincidence of death.

On December 24, 1960, at 3:58 P.M., Arthur Bruce Cochrane died in the U.S. Marine Hospital at Staten Island,

N.Y. Within two hours, his sister received a telgram from a hospital in California, saying that Arthur's twin brother, Albert, whom he had not seen in over ten years, had died, at 7:03 P.M. Pacific Standard Time—less than six minutes apart.

An 84-year-old woman in Lancaster, Pennsylvania, walked into the bedroom of her farmhouse on April 8, 1964 and discovered that her twin sister, Mary Burnheimer, had just died in bed. Annie K. Burnheimer notified a neighbor and walked into the barn—where the neighbor found her dead a short time later.

On July 19, 1958, a 21-year-old laborer from New Rochelle, N.Y., was arraigned in the death of a 36-year-old drifter. At the same time in Mount Vernon, N.Y., his twin brother was arrested for killing a 36-year-old junk yard operator in an argument over a dog.

Identical twins Reggie and Ray Wicks were wrestling on their school teams in LaCrosse, Wisconsin on March 13, 1964—each against a different opponent. Within seconds of each other, both wrestlers cried out in pain. Each had torn a cartilage in his left knee.

On August 11, 1962, 3-year-old Steve Cox fell off a sliding board and fractured his right collarbone. A short time later, his identical twin Stanley fell out of bed and fractured his right collarbone. According to amazed X-ray technicians, if the broken bones had been transposed, they would have fitted together perfectly.

Two poultry trucks collided outside Miami in June, 1961. It turned out the drivers were identical twins, separated at birth, who had somehow gotten into the same business about 45 miles apart, and married girls with the same first names. Each had a dog of the same breed and age—and with the same name. The twins had the same number of children, who were born at the same times. Both men were driving the same make and model truck at the time of the accident. The damage to each vehicle was identical.

THE UNRELATED "MARTIAN TWINS"

The contestant who walked off with $26,000 on the now-defunct "$64,000 Question" TV show was New York City policeman Redmond O'Hanlon. His brother-in-law, Vincent Murphy, was a former classmate at Manhattan College, and is now a New York City *fireman*. They are unrelated, but happen to have married twin sisters Teresa and

Marguerite O'Connell. At last count, each family had six children in identical order, both in the month of their birth and their gender. O'Hanlon and Murphy strongly resemble each other, and their careers show many close parallels.

A DOUBLE-TWIN "COINCIDENCE"

Plenty of curiosities, oddities, and coincidences are reported at the International Twins Convention. At the 1950 convention in St. Louis, Elvin and Melvin Dameier were elected joint presidents of the association, and Margaret and Elizabeth Finch were chosen the Most Nearly Identical Twins in attendance. Thus, the Dameiers and Finches met. One thing led to another and they were married on June 29, 1952. Both families took up residence in twin houses on a farm at Lena, Illinois. The wives gave birth to their first children, girls, at the same time. Later, each had a boy—also at the same time.

Then both sets of twins began having trouble about the same things at the same time. In their adjoining domiciles, Elvin and Melvin clouted Margaret and Elizabeth—presumably about the same thing. The girls sued for divorces at the same time, and on the same charge. The judge went along and granted twin divorces, giving each wife custody of their children—and possession of two 1960 sedans, which were same make and color.

A "senseless and motiveless" double tragedy occurred in New York on April 29, 1964. Two highly respected and seemingly well-adjusted married men shot and killed their children; one was a girl, the other a boy. The girl was shot several times in the back. The boy was shot several times in the back of the head. Each father then turned the gun on himself and committed suicide. The men were born in different years, but in the same month, date, and hour.

HOW WE FIND THE "ASTRO-TWINS"

Hospital records have yielded thousands of cases of Time Twins. Elaborate questionnaires were sent out, but only a fraction replied. The major part of that fraction's responses didn't match with a Time Twin. When one would reply, quite often the other would not. Yet, in 100 percent of the lives of those who were born within a few minutes of each other, the same tendency kept reappearing. The major events in the lives of these people paralleled one another as though they were perfectly synchronized.

That a thing like this exists at all is beyond anything that conventional science has thus far anticipated. A completely new and unexpected "Fact of Nature" is implied.

In finding the "time twins," one major problem is the elimination of inaccurate birth data, which occurs more often than suspected. Few people are certain of the exact time of their birth.

Since the Earth rotates at the rate of one degree every four minutes, the difference of a half-hour or forty-five minutes in time of birth results in a somewhat altered horoscope, and, theoretically, in the timing of the events of the life—*if* astrological ideas are valid. And, according to horoscopic interpretation, if the fast-moving Moon changes Signs during that interval, a subtle but completely different influence on the personality and outlook will result—even in the case of identical twins.

This ancient study rests its claims about your physical attributes not only on the Sun-Sign, but also on the Sign that happens to be rising on the Eastern horizon at the exact moment you took your first breath. Each element in your horoscope tends to modify the others. In the case of the Ascending Sign—if the given time of birth is only four minutes off—a different degree may be ascending, and sometimes an entirely different Sign.

Your Own "Time Twin" May Be Nearby

Comparing your life pattern—the major events of your life—with that of someone born at or close to the same time and place, is likely to reveal this startling and almost incredible fact of nature. A simple but sometimes expensive method used in our research was the "personal" columns of various newspapers.

We ran an ad requesting that those born at a certain time and place respond to a box number. The immediate results were disappointing—and expensive. No replies.

The same procedure was tried in different cities, but only a small percentage responded. In that small percentage, however, the questionnaires which matched could almost have been taken as carbon copies if not for the allowed difference in genetics (hereditary characteristics).

Attitudes of progressivism or conservatism seemed basically oriented to various Sun-Signs; the liberal attitude was represented by the *fire* and *air* Signs and the conservatives were found mostly with strong *water* and *earth* characteristics.

Comparative studies of much wider samples of twins and Time Twins will certainly reveal many more completely unsuspected facts about homo sapiens. These facts may not be entirely pleasant; they may, in fact, conflict with some of our most cherished notions.

But unless a much better explanation than the time-wearied "coincidence" is forthcoming for the cases we've presented here (which is only a random sampling of that gathered), it stands to reason that astrology's claims of planetary and stellar influence can and must be considered a respectable area for scientific investigation. It happens to be a perfectly beautiful set-up for the scientific investigator—whichever way it turns out.

He must either find positive results and discover a brand-new Law—or become the first scientist in history to prove that Copernicus, Galileo, Brahe, Kepler and Newton were utter fools for believing in astrology, because each of these great men were astrologers.

Such a negative finding would also show that the greatest minds in human history were taken in by a simple superstition!

From an eternal, boundless darkness, densely packed points of brightness resolve into billions of tiny glowing clouds. These galactic clouds are *themselves* composed of billions of intensely radiant points of light—the stars. Here and there a star flares into supernova brilliance, expanding, engulfing, and consuming all its planets. For some mysterious reason, an entire galaxy of stars sometimes explodes at once.

Inside other galaxies the novae wink on and off, lighting up the whirling discs like sparkling Christmas trees. Far off at incredible distances there are great Quasars, whose mass and volume are often greater than entire galaxies such as the Milky Way.

ORIENTING YOURSELF

Within this cloud-like galaxy called the Milky Way, there is a medium-sized star-sun with nine cool dark beads, or "planetismals," of different sizes spinning around the nucleus of this huge "Atom," the solar system.

Third out from the star is Terra, a tiny blue-green globule with a transparent envelope of gas in which vapors coalesce into clouds and livings things fly. Beneath this there is a hard surface on which other entities crawl and walk upright. Three quarters of this globe is covered with a sheen of liquid hardly deeper than eight miles, in which other creatures swim and crawl, some of them still unknown to the inhabitants of the surface.

The Moon of Terra has no appreciable atmosphere. Mercury, closest to the Sun, may have none either. Venus is hidden beneath a thick, opaque cloud of gas and hydrocarbons. The atmospheres of Jupiter and Saturn are 8000 and 12,000 miles deep, respectively. Both are seas of hydrogen, methane, and ammonia beneath which, astronomers tell us, are shells of ice many more thousands of miles thick. Mars is red and seems more moon-like than earth-like; its volume is 0.15 that of the Earth. It is 9000 times smaller than Jupiter.

The atmosphere of Venus has the reflective power of a snow-covered Earth. The surface characteristics of Mars are its changing polar caps, its red color, craters and its "canals." Like Mars, the Moon's craters bear mute testimony of cosmic or internal cataclysm. Three quarters of the Earth's surface is covered by reflecting oceans. Jupiter is brilliantly striped and has a moving red spot into which many Earth-sized planets could be dropped. Saturn has perfect rings of tiny asteroids, or ice; they are more than 40,000 miles across; astronomers say they are anywhere between eight inches and ten miles in thickness.

Uranus has a north pole where its equator should be. Neptune is banded like Jupiter and Saturn; it is four times as large as the Earth and 17 times as heavy. It has two moons, one of which is almost the size of the Earth and considerably larger than our Moon. In fact, it's the largest satellite in the solar system. Its name is Triton and it may be even larger than Pluto, our outermost (known) planet, which has an atmosphere that lays frozen on the dead rocks of the surface. Pluto is probably an escaped moon of Neptune.

The orbital velocities of the spheres increase as you move in closer to the Sun. Pluto takes 248 Earth years to make one solar orbit. Mercury 88 days.

All these planets whirling in counterclockwise direction when seen from "above" the Sun (North) exert an invisible, powerful effect upon each other and upon Terra, causing mutual planetary perturbations.

AN ANCIENT SCIENCE RE-EMERGES

Man, the species which considers itself dominant upon Earth, has all but conquered this third planet, and yet understands nothing of its origin or his own, let alone how or why the celestial environment was formed, how it interacts, or his place in it.

He believes he has nearly mastered space, but at this writing no man has even been completely outside the Earth's atmosphere. God-like, he has almost deciphered the ultra-microscopic Code of Life, yet hasn't the faintest idea where the oil which runs his mighty techno-industrial society came from or how it was formed. He has measured the speed of light, and is deeply concerned about the cosmic signifi-cance of fantastically huge Super-stars billions of light years from his home galaxy; yet he doesn't understand how the nearby Moon can affect his life and affairs. He busies him-self with questions about the cores of the great stars, but has no conception of the profound influence the Sun may have on his life and times. He cannot understand what comets are, how they are formed, or where they come from, but he measures the sizes of infinitely remote galaxies.

The Destruction of a Planet

He believes his universe is orderly and changeless, yet he cannot solve the mystery of the Moon's craters or the ex-istence of the asteroid belt between Jupiter and Mars where, in all probability, there once existed another great planet.

He sees evidence of something he calls gravity; he realizes the Sun is a giant electro-magnet and that the Earth and other planets produce magnetic fields. He knows that he also generates an electro-magnetic charge, but he cannot con-ceive any relationship because he is so tiny and so far from the planets.

Modern man credits himself with more knowledge and wisdom than all the ages of his ancestors. But his science cannot explain the remnants of vast, highly-developed, ex-tinct civilizations, some of which are dismissed as legends and myths. He knows his species has existed in its present form for at least two million years, but sees no mystery in the fact that his recorded history is only a few thousand years old. He subscribes to the idea of evolution, although no new species have appeared during his entire history. He knows his domestic cat could not have existed in the car-boniferous jungles of prehistoric times, yet the cat has al-ways been with him, small and domesticated. Modern man does not consider that the cat may have been artificially mu-tated.

The Character of Man

His science and technology are the diamond-hard drills

with which he plans to probe all the mysteries of physical nature. Yet he is surrounded by an ocean of evidence indicating a Non-Material Cause. He has worshiped and rejected more than 10,000 gods. He plots cycles on graphs to predict economic events and other material-physical phenomena, but ignores the corresponding celestial events. He propagates himself almost beyond the physical capacity of his planet to support him, but does not consider this, too, as a cycle.

He is characterized both by rapaciousness—the lust to kill with a weapon—and by self-sacrificing devotion to protect and preserve the most helpless of creatures. He does not think his own species can be graphed to show peaks and troughs, or that today's abundance of humanity may be insurance against future dearth. He is convinced that lower animals react instinctively, but that his own choices are completely free of all exogenous influence.

Whatever we learn or discover here must, of necessity, be viewed through the consciousness of this unique creature, who sought to learn the mystery of creation by evolving a rational system which came to be called astrology.

How to Use Celestial Forces

The largest long-distance communications network on Earth has a branch which calculates planetary influences on the Sun to predict great sunspots which cause storms in the high reaches of the Earth's atmosphere. They don't call it astrology. The scientist who heads the National Center for Atmospheric Research and coordinates investigations of celestial influences on the atmosphere with 14 corporate universities (all underwritten by National Science Foundation grants) once studied astrology and knows how to erect horoscopes.

Astro-weathermen can predict, with almost 100 percent accuracy, when and where the next blizzard, drought, or hurricane will strike. Certain planets relate to specific diseases, and this enables astrologers to predict—sometimes years in advance—when and where big epidemics will strike; they often specify the symptoms and the exact duration of the outbreak.

The chief value of astro-meteorology lies in its ability to pick out the times and locations of truly big anomalies—the devastating natural occurrences that strike with little or no advance warning. Astrological weather experts have been doing this since the time of Kepler—even since Democritus

of ancient Greece, and the prophets and seers of the Bible
—and other peoples whose histories have been forgotten.

Every scientist or fair-minded layman who ever studied
the system and experimented with it has ruled in favor of
astrology.

And yet Max Planck discovered a remarkable fact: "A
new scientific truth," he wrote, "does not triumph by convincing its opponents and making them see the light, but
rather because its opponents eventually die, and a new generation grows up that is familiar with it."

Astrology cannot be called "new," but it has gradually
been recognized in this space age as a demonstrable scientific
truth, or series of truths. It seems to encompass the entire
electromagnetic spectrum, and the growing awareness of
scientists that Man is a responsive element in the cosmos is
a very ancient astrological truism.

THE MYSTERIOUS "PRAYER PLANTS"

Dr. Franklin Loehr, a minister of the Religious Research
Foundation, discovered that plants, when "prayed over" by
his congregation, grew 75 times faster than an equally tended and nourished plant that was *not* prayed over. "Intense,
concentrated thought has the same effect as prayer," the
minister said.

These prayer plants are evidence of Life's interdependence. Doctors at various universities and hospitals learned
that the human brain has a positive and a negative magnetic polarization. The center of the forehead is negative
and the base of the brain at the back of the head is positive. By suddenly reversing the polarity of the brains of test
animals, they have succeeded in rendering the animals un-
conscious.

ALL LIFE FORMS ARE AFFECTED

Our brains seem to have the characteristics of radio receivers, the magnetic field they generate acting as invisible
response-receptors (antennae) which pick up signals from
somewhere and translate them into emotional attitudes,
moods, etc.

Fish, animals, insects, and plants also generate magnetic
changes and are subject to invisible biological influences
from somewhere. Oysters, for example, open and close their

shells in perfect synchronization with the rise and fall of the tides.

We find the same sort of data in police reports, firemen's and hospital records—peaks and troughs at the time of New and Full Moon.

No astrologer knows precisely what the connecting link is between celestial bodies and the terrestrial phenomena with which they correlate. So far, not even the scientists who are interested in these observations have postulated a theory on the intermediate force.

YOUR BIOLOGICAL RHYTHMS

Every plant, animal, fish, and insect responds to exogenous forces—for the most part, forces unseen and unknown. Man, too, is influenced by many biological cycles. Mood, temperature, blood pressure—all rise and fall at regular intervals; and so does accident-proneness, intellectual force, emotional attitude, and physical energy. These cycles are variable. They start at birth when the human entity begins to function independently of its parent.

"INSTINCT" OR "FREE WILL"?

The so-called "lower" life forms on our planet are excellent clues to the study of the effects of cosmic influences. If science generally accepts the overwhelming evidence of stellar and planetary forces acting on the flora and fauna of our planet (phototropism and magnetotropism are fairly well established), only a few final hurdles remain. It has always been known that animals respond to external stimuli; it's called "instinct."

But what exactly is instinct? And is man, by virtue of his complexity, immune to it? Considering the highly-developed human brain and nervous system, it would seem that he is even more likely to react to exogenous forces than the less sensitive animals.

That the solar system is an interdependent unit in this universe of galaxies, and that man interacts with his terrestrial and celestial environment (as a completely responsive element), is the essence of our expression here.

Astrology is indeed a legitimate and attractive field for scientific research and study.

On October 5, 1963, United Press International reported:

"WASHINGTON—Science has come to the support of farmers who for centuries have insisted it was best to plant crops during a New Moon.

"Dr. Geoffrey Keller, assistant director for the National Science Foundation, told a House Appropriations subcommittee that research at New York University indicated farmers might be right in believing crops grow better if planted during a New Moon.

"Researchers, after poring over weather records going back 91 years, discovered that chances for a heavy rainfall in the week after New Moon and Full Moon were up to three times greater than for the week preceding the New Moon."

A few hundred years ago, before astronomy and astrology diverged, a handful of scientists tried to learn something about the interaction of the cosmos. They revolutionized astronomy and created a whole new cosmology. These men were astrologers.

John Flamstead, the first astronomer-royal, was a prolific astrologer. He built the internationally renowned Greenwich Observatory in 1675—by order of King Charles II. Flamstead set up a series of horoscopes for the observatory and chose a special moment as being the most propitious.

He had some difficulty with the masons of his day because of the delay in laying the foundation stone at Greenwich. Flamstead finally decided that the correct astrological moment had arrived, and work began on the building. The horoscope for this moment is still there, preserved with Flamstead's other documents. The opponents of astrology claim he did it as a joke—but did he? Consider that Flamstead wanted the Greenwich Observatory to last a long time and to be recognized for ages throughout the entire world. Then, notice that the world agrees to reckon time based on the calculations at Greenwich, which is more famous than Mts. Wilson or Palomar.

Flamstead's astrology worked!

The World's
Oldest Science

3

Astrology has influenced all men of all ages. It is a fact of historical record that it is the foremost intellectual movement of all time. It predates all other sciences, all political systems, and all religions. It is older than the Great Wall of China, the Egyptian Pyramids, the Dead Sea Scrolls, the temples of Greece, the tablets of ancient Babylon or the Ark of the Covenant.

Astrology crosses every intellectual level of every society of every age, and it attracts the greatest minds of all cultures, regardless of the prevailing religion or the incumbent political system. It is the cornerstone upon which education, religion, law, and science—in short, civilization—are built.

THE WORLD'S GREATEST KNOWLEDGE

Astrology influenced the Arabs, the Greeks, the Hindus, the Romans, the Chinese, and the Egyptians. It influenced the believers in Mohammed, the followers of Christ, and all the ancient Americans (the Aztecs, Toltecs, Incas and Mayans) the believers in the Platonic Eros, and those who subscribed to the mores and manners of Confucius.

Astrology fascinated Stoics in togas and Mystics in robes —the Popes of the Middle Ages and contemplative Buddhists—the prophets and holy men who wrote the Old and New Testaments, as well as Hippocrates, the Father of Medicine. It influenced Catholic Saints and Jewish Seers—the Caesars of the Second Century and the Arabs of the Sixth— the founders of Rome and the intellectuals of Greece—totalitarian dictators and American presidents—Wall Street brokers and space-age scientists.

Critics like to claim astrology is "discredited." But they can't explain why the founders of the New Cosmology "believed in" astrology. The real reasons have no relation at all to those we usually hear.

Fact vs. Fancy

1. *"They were not really believers in astrology. It was only an amusing sideline—a hobby."*

Not so. They were neither dabblers nor hobbyists, but dedicated, full-time practitioners of the ancient system. It was the life work of Kepler; he labored over his laws in order to perfect his astrological predictions. Newton's primary interest was astrology. It was the problems posed by astrological "influence" which caused him to investigate light and gravity.

2. *"They were living in a superstitious age; therefore they were superstitious men."*

Wrong again. These men broke with all traditional natural philosophy and established their own on the basis of scientific truths they discovered and proved. They were not superstitious in any ordinary sense.

3. *"They were religious. You can't be religious and objective. Religion weakened their intellectual discipline."*

This doesn't work either. They were devout Christians, but modern astronomy and physics also includes devout Christians who, without study or investigation, do not "believe in" astrology.

4. *"They were forced by the wealthy and titled to cast horoscopes in order to make a living and continue their astronomical researches."*

Wrong. They were financially solvent. The uncle of Copernicus was a sovereign bishop who provided him with a generous lifelong allowance. Kepler was married to a landed and wealthy widow. Galileo was a well-to-do professor of mathematics. Newton lived in a London palace and made philanthropic contributions at the time he worked out his final views on astrology. Unfortunately, it has taken over

300 years for his astrological ideas to receive the serious scientific consideration they are now receiving.

How the Discoveries of Copernicus Affect You

By the time he was 39, the great astronomer Nicholas Copernicus was learned in medicine, theology, mathematics, astronomy, and Greek. He was personal physician to his uncle, the Bishop-Prince of Ermeland diocese. When the Bishop died, Copernicus took over the diocese during several emergencies, and personally supervised the defenses which drove off hordes of Teutonic knights, and, later, Polish occupation troops. He was nothing if not versatile. His use of the cannon and strategic warfare made him famous as a soldier, commandant, and mathematician.

When peace returned, Copernicus was a hero. Like veterans of later campaigns, he resumed his education and studied medicine, astronomy, and history, for he was intrigued by the great minds of the Greek and Egyptian era. He was fascinated by their astronomical knowledge and use of astrology, but he did not blindly accept the theories of men like Meton, Pythagoras, Aristotle, and Ptolemy—all of whom were astrologers. Skeptical, doubting, but always inquiring, he questioned their astrological conclusions every step of the way.

Medical Astrology

Pythagoras, the Greek philosopher-astrologer, born in 572 B.C., lived a century before Meton and was generally credited for discovering that the Earth is a sphere. By the time of Aristotle (384–322 B.C.) this concept was not only well established among the scholars of that period, but also was known long before this to the most ancient peoples on the planet, as we'll show later.

Copernicus, as a doctor, was stimulated by the ideas of Hippocrates, the Father of Medicine, who stressed purposeful creation. Hippocrates was an authority on diagnoses and treatments of disease deduced from astronomical correlations. In fact, the famous Hippocratic Crises are based on the hexagon angles of the moon's monthly motion in the case of fevers, diseases, and even surgical operations. Copernicus confirmed these crises by his own medical experience.

This timing is still observed by modern medical men, who seem to have forgotten their celestial origin.

Hippocrates taught that there was an astronomical correspondence for every known rhythm, periodicity, or cycle of time, whether applied to the Earth or to the life upon it.

Between 800 to 2,000 years before the Greeks, the Egyptians already knew of the connection between the different parts of the body and the "Signs" of the zodiac. The Babylonians and Chaldeans knew it before the Egyptians, and the Sumerians knew it before the Chaldeans or Phoenicians.

KNOWLEDGE OF INCREDIBLE ANTIQUITY

It was then a matter of established record that the Egyptians, the Babylonians, the Chaldeans, and the Sumerians possessed superior skills in the sciences, medicine, and philosophy, than the Greeks, who themselves admitted this by the fact that their most distinguished philosophers traveled to Memphis and Babylon to study geometry, astrology, and astronomy. Those fragments of science and wisdom gathered by Thales, Pythagoras, and Democrates, which were absorbed by the Greek culture, belonged to a once-mighty system. The truth is that astrology, the pariah of modern science, was the keystone of this system.

The Chaldeans deduced a cycle in the affairs of men and nations called "Saros," which consisted of 3,600 years. This is the time taken by a "fixed star" to move through one degree of a 360 degree circle. They inherited this from the Sumerians, who presumably had observed many Saros cycles, thus attesting to their knowledge of astronomy.

The Alexandrian Library and School of Mathematics and Astronomy was then formed, and the Greeks surpassed the fame of their predecessors. Yet this institution knew no more than Pythagoras had brought back from Chaldea and Egypt. Democritus, Plato, and Eudoxus also gathered remnants of wisdom from this people of a great past.

HOW ECLIPSES AFFECT WORLD CHANGE

Spurred by these studies, Copernicus added his voice to the demands of astrologers in the Middle Ages for facts and experiments. He contended from his study of eclipses that these phenomena preceded radical change. He found that after total solar eclipses, troops were shifted along lines delineating the path of totality, and that European rulers who were born during an eclipse while Mars was within five degrees of the midheaven usually died a violent death.

It happened that on November 2, 878 A.D., a total annular eclipse's path traversed what is now called Old Wapping Road—from Chester to London. King Alfred stopped the invading Vikings dead in their tracks along a line defined by the edge of the eclipse path. There were Vikings on one side and Britons on the other; the country was thus divided.

Charles A. Jayne, Jr., editor of "In Search," reported that during World War II Allied military observers and strategists noticed mass troop movements immediately following eclipses.

Directly after one of these solar eclipses, five divisions of the American First Army crossed the Rhine in 1945. Following Presidential instructions, General Omar Bradley ordered his forces to withdraw (behind the eclipse's path) as Russian troops marched in to occupy East German territory. After two decades the country is still divided this way.

While commanding his lonely fortress, Copernicus was able to repulse both Polish occupation troops and the attacking hordes of Teutonic knights because he knew in advance of the eclipse, when and where they would move to strike. But, of course, he also had cannon, a fact not generally known.

This great Polish astrologer seemed almost destined to formulate a rational scientific concept of the universe.

THE DISCOVERIES OF TYCHO BRAHE

Tycho Brahe provided the exact planetary figures which enabled his most promising pupil, Johannes Kepler, to work out his great Laws of Motion. Yet Tycho practiced and defended astrology with all of his intellectual and emotional power.

In one of his many duels as a young student, the fiery Dane's nose was sliced off. The resourceful Tycho created a copper proboscis, painted it flesh color, and attached it each morning. The disfigurement drove him into a common-law marriage with a peasant woman who eventually bore him seven children. No noblewoman would have him.

Nevertheless, it did not prevent the King of Denmark from presenting Tycho with an island where Brahe built the first astronomical observatory in the Western World—solely for the purpose of expanding and perfecting his astrological work.

In order to do this, Tycho worked out a system of figuring the exact timing of the solar system. The planetary tables of King Alfonso then in use were off by days, sometimes even weeks. In order to plot the exact courses and positions of the planets, *minutes* were of prime importance to Tycho.

When young Kepler came to work as the Dane's assistant, he was not only unacquainted with astrology, he scoffed openly at such superstitious nonsense.

"To deny astrology," the noseless Dane thundered, "is to deny the glory of God!"

TYCHO'S STAR

Brahe could predict social prominence from horoscopic data, and claimed that Jupiter's position on the midheaven (near the upper meridian at birth) indicated success and fame, because Jupiter was the "great benefic"—the planet of good fortune, expansiveness, and prominence.

It happened that one of the reasons Brahe chose Kepler to succeed him was because of Jupiter's placement in the young man's horoscope. The Dane said that Kepler would carry on his own work and become a world-famous astrologer. Although Kepler *did* become an astrologer, and also became famous, it was his three laws of motion which made his name great in the annals of science.

In November, 1572, a brilliant new star appeared in the heavens—a true supernova, the rarest of astronomical events. It was so bright it could be seen in full daylight, and it lasted for 18 months.

Pressed for an astrological interpretation of this event (actually a supernova in Cassiopeia), Tycho published two heavy velvet-bound volumes in which he concluded that a great soldier and humanitarian would arise in Finland and would reign from 1593 and die a violent death in 1632. (*Gustavus Adolphus was born in Stockholm in 1594, when Finland was a Swedish province, and was killed in battle with Wallenstein's mercenaries in 1632. Gustavus was a great humanitarian, soldier, and patriot, which seemed convincing testimony to Tycho's accuracy.*)

The Dane was remarkably clever, resourceful, and inventive. He devised all kinds of precise instruments to measure angular stellar distances, longitude, declination, and latitude. He trained more than 40 astrologers and astronomers and lived in luxury. Counts, dukes, and even kings from all over Europe came to visit his "court" and stayed for months, awed by the astrologer's forceful personality and broad knowledge.

He was also remarkably objective. During 14 years of hard work he made literally thousands of precise measurements, and finally experienced the crowning achievement of his life—a catalogue of 777 stars, every one of them a completely new determination. This was the first star catalogue since the days of Hipparchus, the early Greek astrologer-astronomer.

THE WIND OF EVIL

Through these efforts Tycho provided the figures which enabled Kepler to create his new celestial mechanics. Without them, astronomy would now be centuries behind its current progress. There is no doubt that before he succeeded his Danish teacher, Kepler was powerfully influenced by him. Within the two years he spent as Tycho's assistant, Kepler became thoroughly acquainted with the older man's interpretation of every event as the effect of celestial influence. For example, he predicted outbreaks of seemingly motiveless murders, attacks, and crimes, and held these events to be caused by the 27⅓ day Lunar cycle.

The Twentieth Century Nobel Prize-winning chemist, Svante Arrhenius of Sweden, upheld Tycho by proving that the ion conductivity in the atmosphere increases the rate of violent crime every 27⅓ days.

The relationship between Kepler and Brahe was a volatile combination, often flaring into violent quarrels and ending in deep remorse. They were like father and son. But young Kepler was more interested in the "pure theory" of the time, astronomy, than the "applied science" aspect, astrology. With the avowed purpose of discrediting it once and for all, Kepler began a serious study of astrology.

THE MARS' BUSINESS CYCLE

He started by evaluating the effects of the apogean and perigean passages of Mars (farthest from and closest to the Earth respectively), and was forced to conclude that these transits have an important connection with business activity, as there were always peaks or rises in the German markets at these times. Some modern-day security analysts and cycle researchers seem to have come upon the same idea; several prominent New York brokers abide by it in stock transactions. The simple 22½ month cycle of Mars is probably connected with the so-called "real estate cycle" of the same approximate duration.

But Kepler plunged into deeper researches. He decided that the 7½ month heliocentric period of Venus was vitally significant in the incidence of disease epidemics and in the recurrence of critical phases in the known forms of insanity.

The only similar study in modern times was made by a Dr. Webster in England. He arrived at the same general conclusions as Kepler.

From his diligent researches, Kepler concluded that astrology was the study of the "laws of correspondence" which seemed to exist between celestial and terrestrial phenomena and man. He was the first of his time to notice that the attraction of the Moon caused the tides in the oceans. Considering the times, this alone was something of a heresy.

Astronomic Weather Forecasters

His earliest work, *"Mysterium Cosmographicum,"* was born as a result of his astrological studies and truly launched his career. In 1602 he published *"De Fundamentis Astrologiae"* in Prague. Someone managed to destroy half of his work, but the other half was hidden in the observatory of Pulkowa. Early in the nineteenth century a German physicist found it, made a translation, and had it reprinted in Frankfort in 1858. This is why many modern astrologers consider Germany as the best source of modern scientific astrological material.

Johannes Kepler published the first two of his now famous Laws in 1609, but it was his weather forecasts that originally brought him fame. He predicted the bitterly cold winter in Styermark and the revolutionary disturbances among the Austrian peasantry in 1593. The publication of his *"Mysterium Cosmographicum"* established and stabilized his career. He maintained an "astro-weather" diary from 1617 to 1629 which included his notes, rules, formulae, and planetary configurations. The diary was published by Dr. J. Goad in 1686 in his book, *"Astro Meteorologica,"* fifty-six years after Kepler's death.

Actually, it was Aristotle who wrote the first known

treatise on astronomic weather. On the publication of *"Astro Meteorologica,"* Dr. Goad's book was immediately recognized as *the* world authority on weather prediction, until modern scientists discarded the idea of planetary influence on the weather two hundred years later.

MODERN WEATHER ASTROLOGERS

RCA Communications, Inc., now uses a form of Keplerian astrology to predict storms in the ionosphere which garble and destroy shortwave radio communications. These storms are caused by sunspots and solar flares, which RCA's chief weatherman, John H. Nelson, predicts with 93 percent accuracy. He sets up charts (in effect, horoscopes) of the planets' positions in relation to the Sun.

For thousands of years astrologers have referred to certain angles between planets as being favorable, and others as unfavorable. The 90-degree or "square" angle is generally considered adverse. On the other hand, 120° has always been considered the most "beneficient aspect" (trine). The 60° "sextile" aspect is considered good, but not as beneficial as a trine of 120°.

Astrologers consider each planet as a special indicator which operates through the astrological "Sign" or constellation, and is further modified by the degree of the "house" which marks the divisions of the zodiacal wheel.

After 50 years of hard, objective research, during which he went through mountains of data, astro-meteorologist George J. McCormack crystallized the essence of a completely new approach to weather forecasting. He made the first formal scientific presentation of weather astrology to the American Meteorological Society in January, 1964.

MAGNETIC ANGLES

Several centuries previously, his early predecessor, Johannes Kepler, reasoned that primary weather patterns in eastward transit are continually changing in intensity, latitude, and character around the globe in response to planetary and luni-solar phenomena affecting magnetic fields over various terrestrial areas. These fields, he said, remain dormant until "sparked" or "triggered" by conjunctions or "magnetic angles" to sensitized points in space.

Reversing his original position on pure theory, Kepler

attempted to convert astrology into an experimental and practical science. He kept statistics of the highest possible objectivity. Using his own findings as the basis, he found and recalculated more than 1000 years of astronomical and mathematical error.

That which he discovered through his astronomical studies went into the correction of his astrological data. With his horoscopes as a basis, he wrote descriptions of relatives, friends, and of himself with great insight and detail. *"In me, Saturn and the Sun work together in their sextile aspect . . . to toil up mountains, to stumble over fields and rocky slopes —these things delight me. My destiny is similar; where others despair, money and fame come to me, though in modest measure. I meet opposition . . . True astrology,"* he asserted, *"is a holy testimony to God's glorious works, and I, for my part, do not wish to dishonor it."* Note that he stressed *"true"* astrology!

He devised a different astrology from that which was used by the traditionalists of his day: *"Observe this; if today two planets stand at 89 degrees from one another nothing will happen in the air. But tomorrow, when the full square of 90 degrees is reached, a thunderstorm will suddenly arise. The effect, therefore, does not come from a single star, but from the angle, from the harmonious segment of the circle."*

The Music of the Spheres

Kepler had formerly tried to fit the five regular solids in between the spheres of the planets. Now he pointed out that the regular polygons which could be constructed within a circle yielded the astrologically important planetary angles: square, trine, conjunction, opposition, quadrature, sextile, etc. Kepler demonstrated that these angles were related to the total number of degrees in a circle in the proportions of 1/2, 2/3, 3/4, 4/5, 5/6, 3/5 and 5/8. If he straightened his circle into a violin string, the astrological angles would correspond to the different divisions upon which harmonics are based.

"The music God made during the Creation," he stated. *"He also taught nature to play; indeed, she repeats what He played to her."*

"I have touched mountains," he said when he finally succeeded in demonstrating the mathematical relationship between the distances of the planets and their velocities. *"It is tremendous, what smoke they belch forth!"*

Kepler recalculated Ptolemy's orbit of Mars and found an error of a mere eight minutes of arc. *"Those eight minutes,"* he claimed afterward, *"opened the way for me to renew the whole of astronomy."*

The most amazing thing about his discovery of the Law of Areas is the fact that he totally lacked the mathematical tools which could finally prove his findings—or even *demonstrate* this law! But, credit to him, it worked. Only a master astrologer could have made such a remarkable deduction.

INTERSECTING "WORLD LINES"

As astrologer to Emperor Rudolph II Kepler cast the horoscopes of Augustus, Mohammed, and the Sultan of Turkey, and he corresponded with Galileo. After acquiring a telescope of his own, he studied the surface of the Moon for weeks, and went into ecstasies of joy. He even fulfilled a boyhood dream by writing one of the first science-fiction stories in history, of a voyage to the Moon and back. The grandiose title of this little book was, *"Somnium Sive Opus Posthumum de Astronomia Sublunari."*

More than two generations before Newton, he simply took for granted that both the Earth and the Moon had gravitational fields. Years later, Sir Isaac Newton proved this theory, and then attempted to formulate the link between planetary forces and terrestrial events.

In 1907 an American scientist, George Sutcliffe, also became interested in the idea. He advanced the notion that the planets affected the earth by electrodynamic induction. He predicted several large earthquakes, and received a great deal of publicity and attention, but then was forgotten.

Isaac Newton, who followed in Kepler's footsteps, believed there was profound logic in the latter's correlations. He was convinced that because points of intersection of certain "world lines" *did* change (due to precession, orbital, and diurnal revolutions) and because man, by reason of his geographic location, altered the couplings of his "personal field" (this is a scientific fact, see chapter 7) with that of the Earth, planets, and stars, there occurred all the changes men designated as events. This was extraordinary reasoning in view of the fact that electricity was then virtually unknown, while the *human* electrical field was merely a "fiction."

MORE "WINDS OF EVIL"

Galileo shared his enthusiasm for telescopes and experimental physics in his correspondence with Kepler. He lived in Florence, which was then the heart of European culture, so his early environment was far better than that of his Bavarian friend. As professor of mathematics at the University of Padua, Galileo began seeking the truth in nature. He rebelled at dogmatic ideas and at those who believed that truth could be found in dusty old manuscripts. It isn't clear just where he began probing into ancient prophecies and astrology, but at the birth of each of his children Galileo cast their horoscopes. He was consulted regularly by relatives, friends, and colleagues for interpretations of their horoscopes, and wrote a great deal of astrology under a pen name.

Like Copernicus, he believed that something in the air changed with the geometric relationships of the Earth and the planets. This "something" caused changes in the behavior and emotions of all living creatures, and especially man.

Justification for his idea is found in the example of the "Foehn" in Switzerland, a warm, dry wind that brings an explosion of extreme restlessness and senseless crime. And along the northern Mediterranean, broadminded courts impose exceptionally light sentences for crimes that take place during the "Sirocco," a wind that blows from the Libyan desert and brings in its wake a sharp upswing in the crime rate.

SCIENCE VALIDATES ASTROLOGY

There is some indication that the violent disturbing effects of such "evil winds" are directly attributable to fluctuations in the ion count, which are caused by lunar and solar effects on the atmosphere.

Galileo would have been delighted to see this theory confirmed by the three-year study of ionization effects concluded in Philadelphia in 1961. The American Institute of Medical Climatology, which sponsored the city-wide survey, flatly stated that electrical charges in the atmosphere affect the way we think, feel, and behave. In the ionosphere, these are influenced by solar flares.

Dr. William Peterson, a professor at the University of Illinois, in an epic tome, *The Patient and the Weather,* also found positive and negative ionization of the air to be very significant to health and psychosomatic function.

Dr. Peterson and a large number of other independent investigators, found that the sunspot cycle, which John H. Nelson of RCA has shown to correlate to planetary positions, has "important effects" on human beings.

Galileo would have been delighted. But in 1642, the Prisoner of the Inquisition closed his blind old eyes forever and a baby named Isaac Newton first saw the light of the world. By the time young Newton began to study mathematics, the schism between astrology and astronomy was complete.

Still, young Newton chose astrology as his life work.

MATHEMATICAL POINTS IN SPACE

But eventually, like his predecessors, he was virtually forced to take up the study of astronomy. It was the nerve fiber, tissue, heart, and brain—the physical body—without which the more abstract study of astrology could not exist.

"I do not believe in a universe of accidents," Newton said. Today he towers above all other scientists, but he also admitted a great debt to his predecessors. "If I have seen farther than others, it is because I have stood upon the shoulders of giants." Those giants were *all* astrologers.

Kepler was successful in predicting weather and earthquakes, but Newton outdid him in the number and accuracy of his predictions. He employed some ancient Arabian mathematical points in his calculations which "did not exist in reality."

Newton explored the possibility of the Moon's influence on weather, crops, and mental illness as well as mass psychology—and found positive correlations.

His experiments and studies are now being duplicated in modern science by space-age scientists. "The Journal of Mental Disease" reported that the solar-lunar or synodic cycle of 29½ days has a marked effect on mental illness.

Drs. Leinex and Gibbs reported in the "Journal of Heredity" that brain wave cycles actually do correlate with the phases of the Moon. And Dr. Leonard J. Ravitz of the Veterans Bureau Hospital in Downey, Illinois, detected mood changes in people synchronizing with the Moon's phases. On the distaff side, Dr. Hannah Hendrick of the U.S. Naval Observatory, in her study of mental institutions, noticed that women were more likely to enter a mental hospital during a Full Moon; men on the second day after the New Moon.

A complete report on the scientific studies which validate ancient astrological beliefs and practices would cover a volume for the titles alone. There is a veritable avalanche of new discovery indicating that astrology bids fair to become the number one science of the space age.

Crystallizing the rapidly growing scientific interest in astrology as a science was a 1965 issue of "Hospital Focus," a professional publication. The last paragraph of an article titled "Astrology and Biology" read:

> Some fundamental questions arise that bear directly on health and disease. Consider one: If there is an effect on the human nervous system by a geomagnetic field, and if this effect is mediated by the relative orientation of nervous system and external field, how much of man's history is a consequence of his erect posture? Other questions arise with rather prickling significance for epistemology. If it is verified that human processes are affected by the magnetic field interactions among celestial bodies, and if the Babylonians and Harappans knew nothing at all (sic) about wave mechanics or the solid state, *how were they able to conceive of astrology?*" (author's italics).

The evidence is that ancient humans on this planet were far, far more advanced than we have yet begun to realize, that whole areas of human knowledge and wisdom were lost during the periods of global cataclysm when the human race was decimated, and that advanced mathematics, wave mechanics, and solid state physics may well have been known to them.

This will be detailed in later chapters, with the evidence that a new kind of non-physical science heralds the New Age.

THE SCIENTIST-MYSTIC

Sir Isaac Newton violently disagreed with the then growing belief of lesser astronomers that the Copernican theory had finally killed astrology simply because astrologers used the Earth as the central focus of the system. Newton also used the Earth as a point of perspective in his astrological work—a fact that until recently was very little known. He insisted that Ptolemy's astrological rules, which used the

Earth as a central point (in 155 A.D.), were merely his way of dealing with the problem of relativity.

It certainly is a paradox that the ancient Greeks and Egyptians recognized that the Earth was a planet which, like the other celestial "wanderers," orbited the Sun, which in turn was recognized as the physical center of the system —*while people living three thousand years later were completely ignorant of the fact!*

This intrigued Newton, who sought knowledge in many strange places. He studied Hermes and collected an entire library on alchemy. He was intrigued by Greek mythology and once suggested that the gods of ancient Greece were in fact living people, legendary figures of an incredibly ancient civilization. Newton wrote over a million words on theology and ancient mysticism as well as 500,000 words on other esoteric subjects.

He had some ideas of the phase change cycle of civilization; a subtle but powerful influence which occurred about every 250 years. His basis for this seems to have been the mathematical points of the ancient Arabs. In truth, the ancient Arabs from whom we inherited algebra possessed a far superior mathematical science than anything existing in Newton's time. And their system included the astrology of mathematical points, the true origin of which remains a mystery even to this day.

It is curious that in Spengler's *Cycle of Culture and Civilization,* he cites the 248-year anomalistic cycle of Pluto as being most significant. Pluto's perihelion (closest approach to the Sun) cycle correlates to and defines psycho-cultural phase changes that happen at intervals of 250 years, both A.D. and B.C. Two other investigators, Lamprecht and Bradford, support Spengler's idea.

Could Newton have deduced the existence of a tiny planet as far out as Pluto?

His Jupiter-Saturn cycle hypothesis was detected in history by two independent investigators, Arnold J. Toynbee and Dr. J. S. Lee of China. Dr. Lee's collaboration with Lin Yutang and Hu Shih showed that his study was a quantitative one of Chinese internal warfare of 2150 years: from the Ch'in and early Han Dynasties of 221 B.C. to 1930 A.D. He traced nearly three full cycles whose mean length was 794 years.

Toynbee established his cycle from empirical studies of many societies. In his *Regional Civilizations* and in *A Study of History,* the average length of his tables is about 795 years. Traditionally, astrologers hold that the cycles and con-

junctions of the two largest planets are the primary in-
dicators of political and dynastic changes.

THE SLAUGHTER OF OUR PRESIDENTS

During the past 125 years, there has been a 20-year recurrence of a Jupiter-Saturn conjunction in one of the
astrological "earth" signs. Is it merely *coincidental* that each
American president in office at the times of these conjunctions
either died or was assassinated before leaving the Presi-
dency?

William H. Harrison, elected in 1840, held office at the
time of a Jupiter-Saturn conjunction in Capricorn and died
of pneumonia in 1841.

Abraham Lincoln, elected in 1860, held office during the
following Jupiter-Saturn conjunction in Virgo, another "earth"
sign. He won a second term in 1864 and was assassinated
in 1865.

James A. Garfield, elected in 1880, held office during a
Jupiter-Saturn conjunction in Taurus and was assassinated
in 1881.

William McKinley won his second term in 1900 during
a conjunction of Jupiter and Saturn in Capricorn. He was
assassinated in 1901.

Warren G. Harding, elected in 1920 at the following
Jupiter-Saturn conjunction in Virgo, died in office in 1923.

Franklin Delano Roosevelt, elected to his third term in
1940 during a Jupiter-Saturn conjunction in Taurus, went on
to win his fourth term in 1944, but died in office in 1945.

John F. Kennedy was elected in 1960 at the time of a
Jupiter-Saturn conjunction in Capricorn.

HOW YOU INTERACT WITH THE COSMOS

Admiral Dewey, General Nelson, and President Grover
Cleveland consulted astrologers regularly. Mark Twain swore
by astrology all his life. He said he was born under Halley's
comet and expected to die with its return. He died according
to his own prediction.

The great Swiss psychiatrist, Carl G. Jung, was intrigued by
astrology. He used it as a tool in making certain determina-
tions, and to predict harmony or conflict between personali
ties. He used horoscopes to examine the planetary patterns in
the charts of 483 married couples, or 966 individuals. As a

control group he used a similar number of unacquainted, unmarried couples.

Here are Jung's conclusions: "The statistical material shows that a practically as well as a theoretically improbable chance combination occurred, which coincides in the most remarkable way with traditional astrological expectations.

"That such a coincidence could occur at all is so improbable and so incredible that nobody could have dared predict anything like it. It really does look as if the statistical material had been manipulated and arranged to give the appearance of a positive result."

Modern physiologists now realize that man is a completely responsive element in the cosmos, that he interacts with his environment, both terrestrial and celestial.

TESTIMONY OF A SKEPTIC

John J. O'Neill, the first science writer ever to win a Pulitzer Prize for his work, once condemned astrology as totally unscientific and completely irrational. As science editor of the New York Herald Tribune, O'Neill deviated from his main interest, astronomy, to avail himself of the heavy anti-astrological ammunition within the study of astrology itself. In so doing, rather like Kepler, he came to believe in it.

In a letter supporting Sydney Omarr, an astrologer, in a radio debate with Roy K. Marshall, then director of the Fels Planetarium in Philadelphia, astronomer O'Neill is reported to have said, "I speak as a scientist who does not deviate from the most rigorous adherence to the highest standards of evidence in support of truth. I *do* deviate from the average attitude of scientists in that I place far more reliance on direct observation of nature than I place on textbooks and human authorities . . . Astrology is one of the most important fields for scientific research today, and one of the most neglected. Astrology, properly defined, is the science of the relationship of man and his celestial environment; it is the accumulated and organized knowledge of the effect on man of the forces reaching the Earth from surrounding space.

"There is absolutely nothing unscientific about engaging in research in this field, and no stigma of any kind should be associated with it in the mind of any scientist or laymen . . . Scientists today cannot look down on astrology;

instead, they must raise their eyes to take in the higher horizons that astrologers have preserved for them.

"Attacks on astrology, without previous extensive investigations by competent individuals must, from now on, be regarded as a very antiquated, unscientific practice closely related to witch hunting, and must be correctly diagnosed as a symptom of professional paranoia on the part of the individual doing the attacking."

YOUR POWER OF REASON

Let's see if we can build a case, based on factual data, step by step. Let's try to determine, logically, whether the planets *could* have some unknown effect upon human beings.

1—Sunspots and solar flares have a powerful effect on the Earth's weather, particularly on the ion concentration in the atmosphere.

2—Electrical atmospheric charges, geomagnetism, and electromagnetism all affect plant, animal, and human health and disease conditions.

3—It has been proven that positive and negative ions in the atmosphere definitely affect the way we think, feel, and behave.

4—Lunar influence has an important, direct effect on climate, atmospheric moisture, plants, animals, and humans.

5—Oxygen has certain magnetic properties, so solar magnetic fields and sunspots can affect the Earth's atmosphere magnetically as well as thermally.

6—Geomagnetism affects animal and human organisms, which respond to geomagnetic changes.

7—Cosmic radiation is known to alter DNA and RNA, the nucleic acids in all living things.

8—The ever-changing angles formed by the planets trigger solar flares and spots. There is some evidence that they are also responsible for seismic and volcanic disturbances due to the shifting center of gravity of the solar system.

Since these harmonic planetary positions affect solar magnetic field phenomena and the magnetic field patterns of the Earth, they also cause some reactions among the creatures of the Earth. It is indisputable scientific fact that affected solar phenomena affects the Earth, its atmosphere, its oceans, and all its inhabitants.

Therefore, as all the great minds of ancient and modern scientific history believed, the harmonic angles formed by the planets do indeed affect all of mankind, individually as well as collectively!

Can Astrology Predict
Future Disasters?

4

In the scientific search for ways to foresee an approaching catastrophe, a 100 percent reliable rule may be used: *Major earthquakes always closely follow solar eclipses and often coincide with major planetary conjunctions!*

This is completely dependable as a general guide, but it does not indicate *where* the catastrophe will occur, or the exact date it will happen. Large-scale earth shocks also strike at other times—unexpectedly. Despite substantial progress in methods of detecting and reporting earthquakes, no true theory has been evolved in over two hundred years of seismic investigations. Isaac Newton developed a theory with which he successfully predicted not only weather, but earthquakes and other natural phenomena. His calculations may have included some as-yet-unformulated laws governing the center of gravity of the solar system and the interrelationship of all the celestial bodies.

How Isaac Newton Predicted
England's Greatest Natural Disaster

The solar system, in some scientific quarters, is being considered as an interdependent unit—at least as far as interplanetary action is concerned. This gradually emerging view is gaining the support of the best scientific minds and is perfectly compatible with the statements of scientists like Einstein, Johndro, Steinmetz, Kepler, and Newton.

In one of his astro-forecasts, Newton predicted the most unique series of natural occurrences ever experienced in England. It was scheduled to begin with the startling appearance of the Aurora Borealis during the first three months of 1750, twenty-three years *after* his death!

The Northern Lights, he said, would culminate in a series of mighty storms with unusually destructive gales. As if that weren't enough to stir up his contemporaries, many of whom regarded him as a slightly eccentric genius, he further warned that sharp earthquakes would follow these storms and cause widespread damage and death throughout London.

His precision calculations indicated that the great planet Jupiter would be near enough to the Earth on the date of an eclipse and that the Moon would be closest to the Earth. These and other celestial conditions, he theorized, would be the cause of tremendous atmospheric and seismic activity, beginning in February, 1750.

Nearly a quarter of a century later, the skies and Earth opened almost at the same time. It was the first case on record of an "air quake," and began with the Northern Lights flickering over the peaceful English countryside. Then came the death-dealing storms with winds up to 100 miles per hour. A roaring series of earthquakes toppled remaining steeples and chimneys, collapsed walls, and buried screaming Londoners alive in their homes and beds.

There is simply no experience from the hand of God or man to equal an earthquake. But more than two centuries after Newton's pioneering experiment, we know of these disasters only *after* they occur.

What happened to Newton's theories on the cause of earthquakes?

How Ancient Biblical Disasters Were Foreseen

Many earthquakes *have* been predicted regularly, with respectable accuracy. Following Newton's accomplishments, Commander Morrison of the Royal Navy duplicated them. Dr. Alfred J. Pearce did it again in 1886, and an American followed suit in 1933.

In part, the system used by these men is based on the early work of an ancient scientist named Anaximander, who erected the first *gnomon* for astronomical observations in Lacedaemon, Greece. He then predicted in detail the earthquakes which ultimately destroyed that city.

Democritus, an astrologer of classical Greek antiquity, formulated the atomic theory and conceived the idea of atomic energy; he also predicted earthquakes. It has taken more than 2,000 years to prove that Democritus had also advanced the correct explanation for the whiteness of the Milky Way and the fact that additional planets existed beyond Saturn.

Because astro-weathermen often noticed volcanic eruptions and earthquakes recurring with or directly after planetary conjunctions and eclipses, these phenomena were included in long-range forecasts.

When Joseph made his prophecies to Pharoah, he was using astrology. Isaiah, Daniel, Moses, and many other Biblical prophets were astrologers.

THE EARTHQUAKE YEARS

In 1953, Dr. Rudolf Tomaschek, a geophysicist from the University of Munich, published his celestial data with coincidental seismological occurrences. After checking the places of all the planets during 134 severe earthquakes, he discovered that Uranus was close to the overhead (midheaven) position at the times and places of the major disasters.

Since the discovery of Uranus in 1781, Tomaschek and other investigators have consistently reported a relationship between the position of this planet and upheavals of the Earth. The German scientist learned that in five cases out of six, Uranus was directly or almost directly overhead when the earth shook. Twenty-three major quakes during the 1903–1906 period showed the best correlation.

During these four years the two slowest moving planets, Neptune and Pluto, were aligned across the solar system (as shown in Illustration "A") in opposition to Uranus.

Throughout this period, our planet expended about four times as much energy on earthquakes as in most other years. Tomaschek later discovered that Uranus by itself looked significant in regard to earthquakes.

At the second largest quake of this century for instance, Uranus was 30 minutes of arc shy of its meridian passage. In the great Assam earthquake of 1950, Uranus was 25 minutes of arc from the overhead position (this is less than one-thousandth of the circumference of a circle).

At the devastating Yokohama-Tokyo quake of 1923 in which 100,000 people were killed, Uranus was a mere 16 minutes of arc past the meridian of Tokyo.

In the San Francisco disaster of 1906, Uranus was then just six minutes short of its overhead position. Neptune was directly *beneath* the Earth (the nadir) at San Francisco, and in exact opposition to Uranus across the solar system when the quake struck.

A statistical check of the critical earthquake years produced odds of 10,000 to one *against* the quakes occurring when Uranus was directly over the stricken areas! If it were a matter of pure chance, then each time a quake occurred it had only one chance in 10,000 of happening!

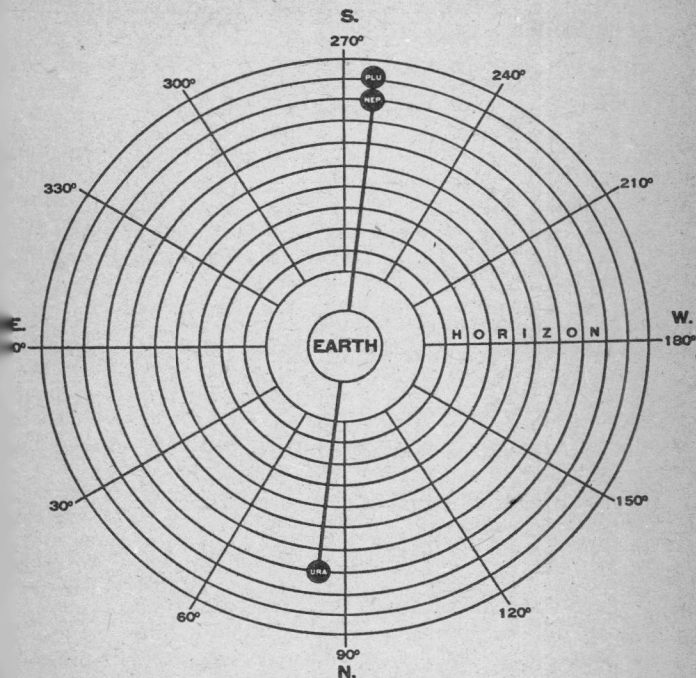

Illustration "A": Uranus in opposition to Neptune and Pluto during Earthquake years 1904–1906.

It has since been learned that more earthquakes occur when two or more planets are in line to the Earth (as during an eclipse). This also happens during the critical period when Neptune opposes Uranus.

DELAYED REACTION EFFECTS

When pressure is applied to one end of a steel bar, it will cause a compression wave of molecules to race to the other end of the bar. But the bar will not move until the molecular wave returns to meet the applying pressure. This is an oversimplification of the 4th Law of Motion discovered by Dr. William O. Davis, which states that it is possible to side-step the reaction-effect of the pressure by withdrawing it *before* the molecules return to meet the applying force.

Planetary conjunctions and eclipses of the Sun and Moon seem to set up powerful magnetic fields in space which are triggered by *future* transits of the planets to that point.

An intriguing but unexplained relationship exists between cycles of weather—earthquakes and volcanic eruptions—in general phase with the changing positions of the celestial bodies and the rotation of the Earth on its axis.

The timing of weather patterns once was a complex problem. The time-lag is now correlated to planetary triggering of sensitive points in space where a recent eclipse or conjunction took place.

The same factors also produce the "forces" which create a pregnant condition for the production of an earthquake. Apparently, it takes a *series* of crucial planetary aspects to trigger seismic shocks; one alone will not do it.

HOW AN EARTHQUAKE IS PREDICTED

Here is a detailed example of how a disaster was predicted nearly seven months before it happened:

While studying the elements of a planetary weather map for the solar eclipse of August 31, 1932, astro-meteorologist George J. McCormack noted that Neptune would be in conjunction with the Sun and Moon at eclipse time. Neptune, a planet of large mass, would also be close to conjunction with Jupiter, the planet of *largest* mass.

The weatherman, who was familiar with some of the elements used by previous earthquake forecasters, decided to experiment with the theory that the Sun-Moon-Neptune-Jupiter conjunction had seismic implications.

This rare bunching together of celestial bodies at eclipse time, he theorized, would set up a magnetic field of *unusual* intensity in that area of space, to be "triggered" at a later date by the orbital passage of yet another planet (the timing element). The eclipse path, a long narrow band, happened to fall directly over the longitude of Los Angeles at the moment of greatest totality. This "meridian" or midheaven position is considered of utmost importance in astronomic weather forecasting. Los Angeles, therefore, was the calculated area for future seismic activity.

McCormack now had to determine which planet might trigger an earthquake. If correct, this would provide the timing element.

The eclipse would occur at 158° of celestial longitude. This is measured by a circle of 360° around the belt of the ecliptic beginning at 0° of the sign Aries. Since each Sign is 30° of the circle, the eclipse would take place at 8° of the Sign Leo.

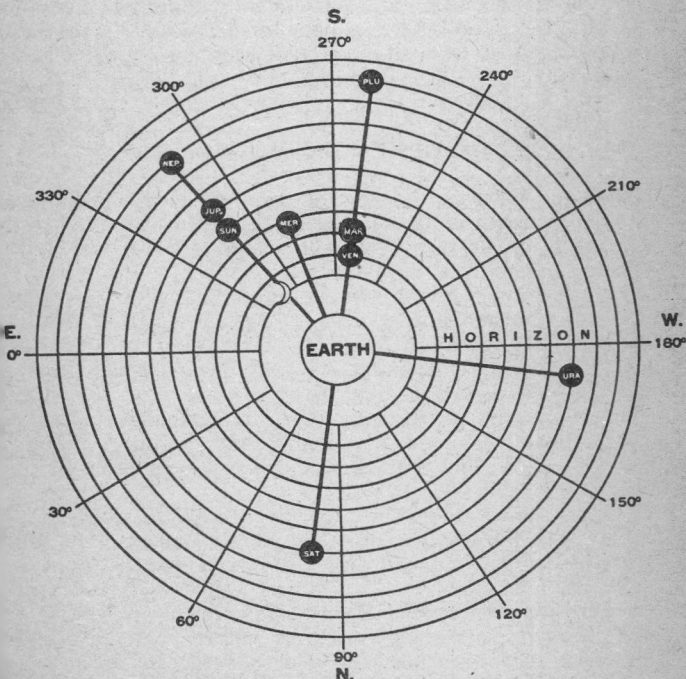

Illustration "B": Planetary pattern at Long Beach, California on August 3, 1932.

Mars, he observed, would be orbiting close to conjunction of this area between March 8th and 12th, 1933, and Mars has always been considered the catalyst or energizer in the celestial scheme.

Choosing March 10 as the date and Mars as the planet, McCormack then published the eclipse maps, including the set-up at Mars' transit of the place of the previous eclipse (with his prediction of an earthquake) in "Astro-Weather Guide."

On March 10, 1933 at 5:54 P.M. Mars swung to within one degree of the previous eclipse area, 158° from 0° Aries. The faster-moving Moon approached within 2° from conjunction with Mars.

The more ponderous Neptune was still at 158° when the disastrous Long Beach earthquake struck, killing 115 people, injuring a thousand others and resulting in $50,000,000 damage. It registered 9 on the Modified Mercalli Intensity Scale of 12.

MYSTERIOUS EARTHQUAKE WEATHER

Professor Charles C. Conroy, who cooperated with the Weather Bureau office at Los Angeles, described March 10 as an unusually hazy day with temperatures in the upper 70s and above-normal humidity.

"In the late afternoon the air was filled with a peculiar bluish haze resembling a veil of smoke. At 4:30 P.M. I called the attention of Mark H. Stanley of the Weather Bureau to this phenomenon. At 4:45 P.M. a sheet of altostratus cloud moved rapidly from the West and at 5:10 P.M. had already covered the sky. The earthquake occurred at 5:54 P.M. This cloud sheet persisted but thinned gradually after 6:45 P.M., and the Moon shone with increasing brightness in the evening."

Weather observations and reports, both official and private, indicate peculiar weather or other phenomena of some kind either preceding or occurring during seismic phenomena. There often seems to be a kind of "earthquake weather" preceding the first shocks. Birds and animals are known to vacate the premises sometimes days before a quake occurs. This seems to confirm the idea that subtle, powerful changes are building up in the geomagnetic field as a result of magnetic conjunctions of planets. It is now established that most, if not all animals are able to "tune in" on the Earth's magnetic field.

THE EARTHQUAKE METEORS

Many strange occurrences have been reported by eye-witnesses during earth upheavals and volcanic eruptions: meteors shooting into erupting volcanoes in Italy, for example. But we tend to ignore Nature's warnings.

"A dense, mountain-like cloud" appeared at Callao, Peru, on Sept. 4, 1868. Meteors "like fire balls" were seen. Then an earthquake shook the land. August 31, 1886: "Just before the Sun dipped behind the horizon, it was eclipsed by a mass of inky, black clouds." There followed a display of luminous clouds such as those seen during a volcanic eruption. People watching the phenomenon were merely curious and amused.

Then the meteors streaked in, and Charleston, South Carolina, lay devasted by a massive earthquake that covered millions of square miles. On Sept. 4, the ground was still shaking. The New York World reported "volcanic dust" falling at Wilmington, N.C.

Every paper of the time reported another severe shock on Sept. 5 at Charleston. Minutes later a large brilliant meteor followed by a long trail of fire streaked into Charleston. At Columbia, S.C., at the same time, two brilliant meteors were seen.

The September 8th, Charleston News & Courier reported: a "strange, dark, and heavy cloud hung off the South Carolina coast. Meteors continued falling throughout September and October as the Charleston area continued quaking." On October 22 about 50 meteors fell at Charleston during a particularly severe quake. At midnight on Oct. 23, a meteor exploded over Atlanta, Ga. Its light cast shadows and it was bright enough to read newspapers by. The same happened on October 28th. One Professor Oswald, a teacher of physics, observed an entire series of meteors shoot out from "an apparent radiant near Leo." On August 27th, the date of the first shock in Charleston, there was a violent quake in Greece. Tremendous torrents, literally "rivers from the sky," carried off people, cattle, homes, and bridges. There were shocks at Srinagar, Kashmir, Italy, and Malta. Vesuvius increased her activity. An inky cloud was seen in the Mediterranean, at the time of the Greek catastrophe, reported by the captain and crew of the steamship LaValette on Sept. 2: "A mass of thick black smoke, changing into reddish color. The sea was perfectly calm at the time."

A vivid glare, like the light from a volcano, was seen in the skies over Greece.

On Oct. 20th, meteors fell profusely at Srinagar, Kashmir. An earthquake followed, then meteors and earthquakes together. No meteors were reported elsewhere.

SOLAR AND LUNAR CAUSES

According to astro-weather correlations, the planet Neptune augurs depressing atmospheric conditions unless in positive aspect to either Jupiter or Venus.

In describing his investigations of Neptune in 1924, Walter Gorn Old said, "The mythology of Neptune seems to support the notion that it has much to do with earthquakes. It is a fact that some of the more recent great earthquakes have happened at or immediately after the conjunctions or oppositions of Uranus, Mars, and Neptune."

John J. O'Neill, the Pulitzer Prize-winning Science Editor of the N.Y. Herald Tribune, wrote in his column: "The Sun and Moon exert maximum forces when they are on a line with the Earth at New and Full Moon which take place alternately at 14-day intervals. The Sierra region is more sensitive to the New Moon combination. The San Andreas and other parallel fault regions respond to the Full Moon situation."

His observations lend support to certain astrological ideas about the Sun's entry into the solstices and equinoxes. (In winter and summer the Sun is at the *solstices:* in spring and fall, at the *equinoxes.*)

"As the Sun starts changing its altitude in the solstices of June 21 and December 21," he reported, "new strains seen to activate the full length of the great mountain ranges. This strain, plus the maximum forces of the Sun and Moon at the New and Full Moon which follows, provides a most likely situation for the release of an earthquake."

Ancient astronomers were more intrigued by such relationships than modern seismologists. Their first correlations were quite naturally, atmospheric. But eventually all agreed that "When an eclipse of the Sun or Moon takes place in conjunction with Mercury, it will generate in the atmosphere turbulent, sharp, and variable winds, together with thunder and lightning accompanied by *sudden chasms in the Earth and earthquakes.*"

Barthelemy St. Hilaire, a French physicist, after years of studying soli-lunar coincidence to Earth shocks, concluded

"The dates of many great earthquakes which compare with eclipses of the Sun and Moon indicate that they are *en rapport.*"

Less than 24 hours after an eclipse of the Sun, the great Riviera earthquake struck on Feb. 22, 1887. On June 1, 1883, following a total lunar eclipse when the Moon was in *perigee,* an earthquake in Manila killed over 10,000 people. The perigee station of the Moon has been observed and reported in more than half the quakes that occur. We can propose, then, that "if the Moon is in *perigee* during an eclipse or other conjunction, the likelihood of an earthquake in the calculated area is increased."

The Full Moon on Good Friday following the Vernal Equinox of March 21, 1964, was exactly conjunct Mars. Venus, Uranus, Neptune, and Pluto were in signs associated with earthquakes when the great disaster at Anchorage, Alaska occurred.

Sir Isaac Newton experimented with Kepler's theory that the New or Full Moon in configuration with certain planets that "take place in the first degrees of *Taurus,* and especially the *Pleiades,* will produce earthquakes . . ."

SEISMIC BREAKING POINTS

Dr. J. Goad, who listed many major earthquakes which happened while Jupiter was transiting through *Taurus,* wrote: "I am sure that this phenomenon depends on the conjunction of Venus or Mercury with Jupiter."

The triple conjunction of Jupiter, Saturn, and Uranus at 60 to 90 degrees of celestial longitude during the spring of 1941 coincided with the greatest series of earthquakes in thirty years.

Where Saturn is directly beneath the Earth at the point of observation (during the times the Sun is at the equinoxes or solstices), that point is significant in locating *future* seismic breaking points. This position seems to pinpoint the place of weakest resistance to earth shocks. It is called the *nadir.*

The difference between celestial conditions that coincide with earthquakes and those which equate to volcanic eruptions is subtle. The precise locations of earth faults as opposed to active volcanoes must be known in order to deliver an accurate forecast.

There are unexplained cases, for example, when a predicted earthquake has failed to materialize at Uranus' meridian transit. Instead, a building, a wall, or a mine has collapsed at the predicted area.

The Moon's influence on atmospheric moisture and rainfall, as shown by an NYU computer study in 1962, is in perfect phase with the conjunction, opposition, and quadrature of the Moon to the Sun as seen from the Earth.

Since we are not living on the Sun the calculations of astrologers must consider the Earth as a focal point. Longitudinal and latitudinal coordinates provide the geographic location of future events.

"Spokes" in the Magnetic Wheel

According to exhaustive observations, a conjunction of Jupiter and Mars seems to influence earthquakes by expansion. Saturn operates exactly in the opposite way—by *contraction.* Uranus is more erratic; its keyword is "abruptness," and its overhead position coincides with unexpected volcanic and seismic activity. Where Jupiter or Saturn-influenced quakes would be preceded by ominous rumbling, the Uranus-type earthquake strikes without warning.

The timing factor of earthquakes, therefore, is related to eclipses, conjunctions, and the planetary patterns formed at the moment of seasonal change (the equinoxes and solstices).

In certain cases, such celestial events may have occurred months before an earthquake. In an extremely rare eclipse when many planets are in line with the Earth (as on Feb. 4, 1962) the terrestrial effects are felt for a long time afterward.

It's as though each conjunction or eclipse develops extremely long "spokes" or concentrated lines of energy which radiate from the point of an eclipse or conjunction throughout the solar system—each spoke being 15° apart. When the first planet swinging around in its orbit contacts one of these invisible "spokes," the charge it had accrued at the time of the conjunction or eclipse is suddenly set off.

The Electromagnetic "Mold" for All Matter

This may be illustrated by snowflakes, which always form their patterns with the basic hexagon design.

"As above, so below," claimed the early astronomers. The 60° angle between planets, especially Uranus and Venus, is the most "crystallizing" aspect. It always coincides with a sparkling clear atmosphere and cool weather at the point of observation. The hexagon angles in a snowflake are, of course, 60° apart.

Other natural phenomena also conform to this pattern. Responding to some unknown "instinct," bees all over the world build hexagonal honeycombs. Many crystals found in the Earth also form hexagonal structures. So do many minerals; basalt rock formations, for example. Diamonds and other pizeo-electric crystals always form with twelve axes or sides, and diamonds must always be cut along their natural axes. It could be that minerals, crystals, snowflakes, and honeycombs have something to do with the Sun, Moon and planets as well as the electromagnetic field of the Earth. It's conceivable that a certain arrangement of planets can build up a charge which is felt in the Earth when another planet forms a critical angle to the overall pattern.

When a planet touches a spoke of pent-up energy at a predetermined point in space, it releases its charge, then remains neutral until the next conjunction or eclipse, when the aspecting planets are "charged" again. If two or three major celestial events occur before a slower-moving planet makes the first contact and discharges its pent-up energy, the force-potential seems to be that much greater.

EARTHQUAKE CRYSTALS

In July, 1963, F. F. Evison, Ph.D., a member of the American Geophysical Union, announced the discovery of a new theory on the cause of earthquakes. Dr. Evison detected a change in the angular structure of crystals deep inside the Earth's crust. Many of the known fault areas, he claimed, have large amounts of agate and garnet. A change in the angular growth of these minerals can (a) change them from one form of crystal to another, (b) cause a three percent change in the volume of the crystals, and (c) occur in a period of several seconds!

If millions or even thousands of tons of garnet deep in the Earth's mantle suddenly gains or loses three percent of its volume, tremendous physical changes are bound to occur at the surface. This *expansion* (Jupiter) or *contraction* (Saturn) may occur many miles within the Earth's interior.

Dr. Evison may have supplied the final clue on the true cause of earthquakes. A remarkable correspondence exists between the angles formed between the planets and those of complex crystalline structures beneath the Earth's surface—

quartz, graphite, diamond, agate, and garnet.

If an electro-magnetic effect occurs in space during a conjunction or eclipse, only the faster-moving bodies such as the Moon, Mercury, or Venus would contact one of the 15° angles to that point within a short time.

The outer planets take longer to come around; they move progressively slower as you go out from the sun. This could account for the time lag between eclipses and earthquakes. It may be as close to a description of what happens as we'll be able to get until teams of specialists begin an intensive investigation of the phenomenon.

Dr. Pearce's Amazing Almanac

In 1885, Dr. A. J. Pearce, one of the most accurate astrologers of the 19th Century, cited the conjunction of Mars and Jupiter on June 27th, 1886, and ventured this forecast:

"The conjunction takes place at 5:30 P.M., at 177° of celestial longitude (27° Virgo) and on the nadir (beneath the Earth) at Washington, D.C. . . . severe earth shocks near the 78th degree of West Longitude may, therefore, be expected . . ."

Pearce also predicted that on the day following a total eclipse of the Sun on August 29th, 1886—during which the Moon would be in *perigee* at 156° of celestial longitude— there would be "a great quake on the Italian peninsula."

At 11 P.M. on the day following this eclipse, the severest earthquake in 29 years struck Naples, Italy.

Then on August 31, 1886, the second greatest earthquake in American history occurred at 9:51 P.M. at 78 degrees west longitude. This was the great catastrophe at Charleston, South Carolina. Its occurrence underscored just one of Pearce's many accurate earthquake forecasts that appeared each year in his *Almanac*.

The epicenter of the disaster was located 15 miles northwest of Charleston, and the area of almost total devastation encompassed a radius of 100 miles. The affected area had an 800-mile radius. This series of shocks, therefore, was felt across a staggering 2,000,000 square miles of the Earth's surface!

Three subsequent quakes of somewhat lesser intensity occurred in the same place on October 22nd and November 5th of the same year. Flashing meteors were seen in every case.

The affected cities, each of which felt the jolts, ranged

from as far west as Omaha, Nebraska; as far north as Augusta, Maine; south to Mobile, Alabama; and east to New York City.

A Scientific Astrological Prediction

At the epicenter and especially in and around Charleston, large gouts appeared in the earth; millions of tons of sand and mud were forcibly erupted from these fissures; geysers of hot water and sulphur sprang up everywhere. Two hundred people were killed and 40,000 left homeless—a remarkably small toll in view of the magnitude of the convulsions. This was due to the fact that large areas near the epicenter were sparsely populated.

Pearce also foresaw a severe quake in the ocean's floor at the equator—30° west longitude; a Japanese quake on July 23; a submarine volcanic eruption west of Malta on August 18; an earthquake in southern India on August 25; a series of American quakes beginning on the same date.

This is how accurate he was: Directly following the Jupiter-Mars conjunction (as predicted) a submarine earthquake was recorded by the captain and crew of the steamer *Thessaly* at 0° S. Lat., 29° W. Long., as the Moon transited the midheaven. The ship seemed to crash four times as if against hard rock; her hull was battered, shaken, and bumped severely as loud rumbling noises rose from the depths of the ocean.

On July 23 another earthquake destroyed scores of homes in Japan; deep fissures yawned, and houses tilted and slid into the chasms. A famous hot spring near Nozawa abruptly stopped flowing.

On August 17th, 200 miles west of Malta, one of the most remarkable natural events ever witnessed occurred. Less than 100 feet from the startled eyes of the crew and passengers of the steamship *Transition,* a searing wall of fire leaped from the water; the ocean bubbled and boiled. The fiery column was 30 feet wide and roared to a height of 100 feet. Deep groaning rumbles came from the floor of the sea as the bodies of marine life bobbed around on churning waters, thoroughly cooked.

On August 25th there was a sharp earthquake at Srinagar. These were merely previews of a devastating series of earthquakes in two different parts of the world. South Carolina and Peloponnesus in Greece were the centers.

DEATH AND DESTRUCTION FORECAST

During the night of August 27th (again as predicted) nine Greek towns were laid in ruins by earthquakes; 500 people were killed, 1000 seriously injured, and many more thousands made homeless. At exactly the same time, Mount Vesuvius erupted with renewed vigor.

On August 30th, the eastern (and highest) peak of Galita erupted violently and unexpectedly. In the United States, a series of earthquakes began, as Dr. Pearce had forewarned, on August 27th. These quakes continued almost without interruption throughout September, and afterward at longer intervals until November 5th.

Pearce concluded that, "The close approach to Earth of the most massive planets as well as their approach to the celestial equator and their passage through the signs *Taurus* and *Scorpio,* coincide with earthquakes and volcanic eruptions . . ."

In 1783, massive earthquakes in Calabria killed 40,000 Italians. These quakes occurred when Jupiter, Saturn, and Neptune formed a "T-square" across the solar system from 90° and 270° of celestial longitude. Neptune, of course was at 180°—at *right angles* to both bodies.

Ancient astrologers called these points of the zodiac the "cardinal" signs because the Sun at these positions marked the beginning of the new seasons. At the solstices, the Sun begins to change direction North or South of the equator.

Earthquakes are exceptionally likely when planetary stress is applied across the 90°-270° sectors, or at quadrature to either point, as shown in Illustration "C."

On December 28, 1908, more than 78,000 people were killed in an earthquake at Messina, Italy. The Sun, Mercury, and Uranus were in the "cardinal" sign, Capricorn, at 270°, and in quadrature to Saturn, a planet of large mass.

Saturn was then only 3° from the Spring Equinox point, 0° Aries. Uranus, at 270°, was in exact opposition to Neptune at 90°. The Moon was making its closest approach to the Earth (*perigee*) and was in opposition to Jupiter, the planet of largest mass. Tremendous forces may have been applying to a point about 700 miles beneath the surface of the Earth. The catastrophe happened at a time when the Earth's orbital inertia carried it along at right angles to the line of force, theoretically subjecting the planet to a sudden, powerful torque.

ECLIPSES AS A BASIC CAUSE

Some researchers have found that the combined effect of the Sun and Moon of the syzygies (conjunction and opposition) is approximately three times as great as the effect produced at quadrature.

Alexis Perrey of Dijon, France, compared soli-lunar positions of almost 24,000 earthquakes between 1751 and 1852.

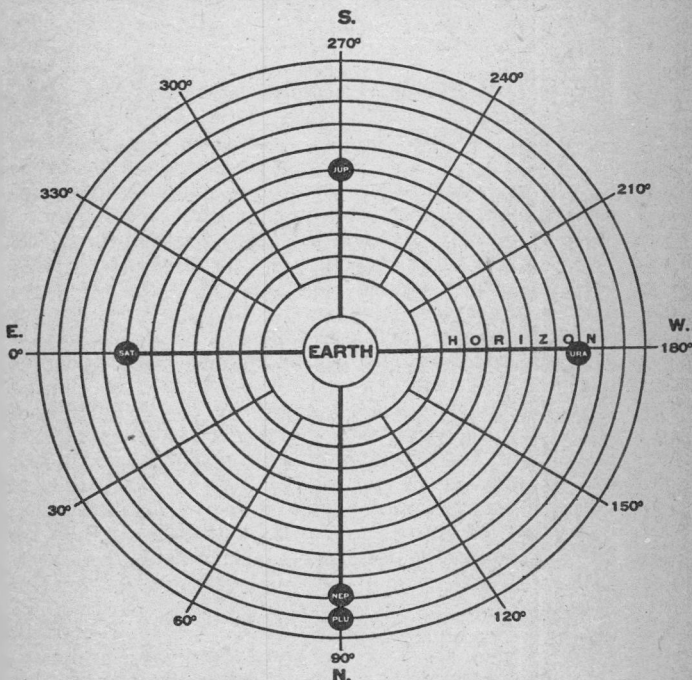

Illustration "C": Planetary stress pattern at 90° to 270° sectors.

He also learned that quakes of large magnitude often take place soon after the Sun and Moon are in line to the Earth, and when the Moon is in *perigee*. 12,347 earthquakes occurred in syzygy weeks, compared to 11,601 at quadrature.

"They are also more frequent," he said, "when the action

of the Sun and Moon on the Earth is in the same direction, and shocks are more numerous when the Moon is overhead than when near the horizon."

A research group from the French Academy later used Perrey's data to discover something they never expected to find.

"There is a maximum of earthquake activity," one spokesman said, "when Jupiter and Saturn are close to conjunction in the same mean longitudes—265° and 135°." Why this should occur in the signs Leo and Sagittarius more so than in Jupiter-Saturn conjunctions in any other sector of space is still a complete mystery.

CONCLUSIVE EVIDENCE OF CELESTIAL CAUSE

C. G. Knott, another seismic researcher, examined the soli-lunar data of 7,000 Japanese earthquakes over an eight-year period. His conclusions supported Perrey's syzygy hypothesis. He found a 12 percent increase in the liability for an earthquake to occur at the syzygies than at quadrature. This led him to several other conclusions, one of which (again) was that earthquakes are at their greatest frequency when the Moon is in *perigee*. Another was that the frequency of earthquakes increases when the Moon is *directly overhead* at the site of the disturbance. Both findings generally agree with those of all other independent researchers.

In his book, *Eclipses in Theory and Practice,* Walter Gorn Old noted that Neptune was closely related to volcanic activity and that Mars' conjunctions, oppositions, and quadratures to Neptune often triggered them.

The British scientist and astrologer, Wm. J. Tucker, D. Sc., Ph.D., one of the most thorough investigators in the field, has independently confirmed these data in his book, *Forecasting World Events*.

ASTROLOGY IS A RELIABLE SCIENCE

On July 20, 1963, people all over the United States, Canada, and even Mexico were watching the spectacle of a total solar eclipse taking place at 109° of celestial longitude. American scientists and astronauts in high flying planes racing the Moon's shadow across the Earth, took pictures and made a multitude of tests while the fast-moving Moon seemed to remain at 19° of the sign Cancer.

A few days later, the celestial event was forgotten. The Moon, meanwhile, was moving an average of 13° a day through the signs Leo and Virgo, entering Libra seven days later. It happened to be directly overhead at the meridian of Skopje, Yugoslavia, at 5:17 A.M. just as it reached 19° of Libra—exactly *quadrature* the celestial longitude of the eclipse.

In recent years, the increased number of observations have yielded another fact that became important in regard to earthquakes and volcanic eruptions in the dark, silent depths of the oceans. "When a planet is in *perigee* (closest to Earth), *perihelion* (close to the Sun), or stationary, it acts with greater potency than at other times."

ANATOMY OF A HEMISPHERIC DISASTER

The quakes which hammered the coast of Chile in May, 1960, spawned the dreaded *tsunami,* Japanese for seismic wave. Many of the shocks felt along this coastline are known to originate close to the continental shelf or even a few miles offshore where the great invisible faults lie 15 to 30 miles beneath the bed of the ocean. Some of these faults are almost constantly active.

Tsunami are divided into two phases. The first manifests immediately after the quake, causing a sudden withdrawal of water from the shoreline "as if a huge plug had been pulled from the floor of the ocean."

In Chile, the seismic waves tear over coastlines north, east and south of the epicenter. In the second phase, the waves are unimpeded by any shoreline; they rip freely into the open sea and damage ports thousands of miles from the starting point.

In such a case, the sudden disappearance of the shoreline is followed by a fast succession of very high waves, some of which merely roll back to the former marks; others smash a destructive swath hundreds of yards inland. Chile's quakes of 1960 resulted in seismic waves which caused tremendous damage through the entire Pacific area. But the shock on May 22 was the most spectacularly violent one since the advent of official world records in 1881. Here is its actual description, given at 1961's world earthquake conference in Helsinki:

"The shock was so severe that the whole body of the planet, down to its core, rang like a bell. For a considerable time afterward, regular slow impulses like the deep breathing of a

wounded man were recorded independently at various sta-tions . . ."

The entire planet "rang" again during the Anchorage, Alas-ka, quake of March 27, 1964. This great disaster was pre-dicted 18 months before it happened. Huset Forecasts (Wil-liston, North Dakota), an annual astro-weather almanac, printed the probable date as between "the 27th to 31st" on page 16 of the 28th edition.

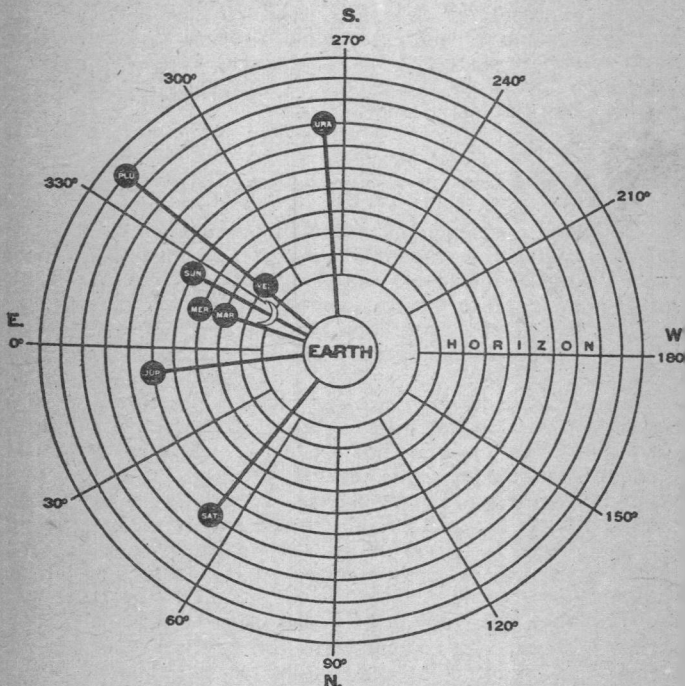

Illustration "D": Eclipse pattern of October 2, 1959 at Concepcion, Chile.

On October 2, 1959, a total solar eclipse took place at 188° 45′ of celestial longitude at Concepcion, Chile. Mer-cury and Mars were within 1° of conjunction. Saturn at 270° was in quadrature to the eclipse, and Uranus (on the midheaven, incidentally) also squared the Sun and Moon.

In a cosmic frame of reference, this was a powerful celestial setup for possible future release the next time a planet would contact one of the imaginary "spokes" emanating from the eclipse point. At such a time, theoretically, the entire eclipse pattern of squares, conjunctions, and oppositions would be set off, "releasing" the stored-up energy.

THE EARTH RUPTURED

On May 22, 1960, Mars contacted a "spoke" of the eclipse

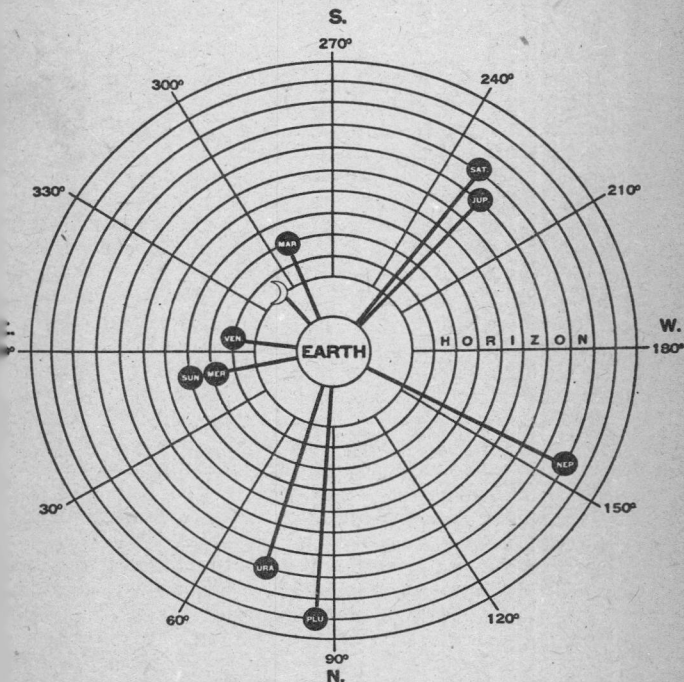

Illustration "E": Celestial pattern for earthquake, May 21, 1960, Concepcion, Chile.

at 8° 34′ of celestial longitude, in exact *opposition* (180°) to the 1959 eclipse. Though the first tremors were felt a day before as Mars swung into *near* contact with that point, the exact aspect corresponded with the mighty rupture deep in the bowels of the Earth which caused the whole planet to "ring like a bell."

As Mars, Uranus and Jupiter reached their critical positions, a series of intense quakes reverberated throughout Chile for the rest of the month. The immediate result of the Martian contact to that sensitive point in space was nothing less than spectacular!

Within 30 hours a great series of waves swept into the far northwesterly corners of the ocean; within fourteen hours they reached the coast of California and ripped through all harbors from San Diego to Crescent City in a succession of 20-minute rises. 300 boats were torn from moorings; three bridges closed down. Thousands of gallons of gas from smashed fuel tanks covered the whole harbor, making it virtually impossible to operate ferries to Long Beach.

Twelve-knot currents sped their way up and down the inland waterways and channels. At Santa Monica, the water withdrew far beyond low tide level before the great spates began. The main surge tore northward past British Columbia and arrived at the Alaskan coast two hours later. It rolled against Montague Island near Cordova at the entrance to Prince William Sound—a 45 foot wave!

Here, against the jagged shores of the Aleutians, this part of the *tsunami* smashed itself to death. These were merely the Northern effects of the great undersea quake!

In Hawaii, 12 tidal stations and 10 seismological observatories began sending out warnings before the *tsunami* arrived. For three hours sirens screamed throughout the islands after the warnings were broadcast. The whole population raced to the hills in buses, cars, and on foot until the entire coastline had been evacuated.

A reporter who watched the destruction of Waikiki Beach —from a safe height—said: "As far as the eye could see, the waterline began receding, moving back to expose thousands of acres of glittering sand. And then it started to rush back. Softly at first, then with a deafening roar that swept everything before wave after boiling wave of total destruction."

Hilo, on the eastern coast, took the full force of the spates from start to finish. When the onslaught was over, the town was utterly devastated. Homes had been dragged nearly half a mile inland; concrete buildings were shoved across streets. Some people were killed, others seriously injured; some were trapped inside homes and buildings, crying out for help.

Within one hour, four huge waves had destroyed the entire sea front. Rows of parking meters were twisted like tortured flowers or torn out of their concrete moorings. Thousands of trees were ripped out of the earth, and thousands of acres of garden vegetables were snatched from their roots and lay scattered to rot all over the devastated landscape.

Just when the first handful of survivors came down to see what they could save, one of the worst tropical cyclones on record smashed into Hilo and finished the job. Torrential rains whipped by gale force winds raised floods and killed what little hope there was left.

There was total destruction. Washington declared the Islands a disaster area. The final score: 5,700 killed; 8,000 injured; 2,000,000 homeless; $550 million damage to Southern Chile, where seismic waves killed 2,161 people; $75 million damage in Hawaii; $50 million damage and 118 drowned in Japan; 32 drowned and missing in the Philippines; $1,000,000 damage to the west coast of the United States.

Such is the terrible power of a single submarine earthquake. This one could have been predicted years in advance —with astrology.

THE ERUPTION THAT EXCEEDED THOUSANDS OF 100-MEGATON H-BOMBS

Those volcanoes that cough, rattle, and spew up the insides of the planet were known to man long before Pompeii and Herculaneum (which, until recently, were considered "myths"). The heat of one erupting volcano is in itself a most remarkable phenomenon. Yet, in tightly concentrated areas of time and space, man has created conditions surpassing those on the Sun! The detonation of a 100-megaton H-bomb is an awesome spectacle, especially so when a mountain of TNT weighing a hundred million tons is visualized as its equivalent in explosive power.

But 80 years ago, with no assistance whatever from puny man, Nature unleashed the most colossal series of blasts ever known in the record of post-Biblical man.

On August 27, 1883, the volcano *Karang* on the island of Krakatoa in the Sunda Strait, belched up fire, ash, and lava in preparation for a series of eruptions that would affect the entire planet for years to come. Each of these mighty explosions were to surpass in fury thousands of 100-megaton H-bombs all going off at once!

This story has a particularly interesting celestial background, beginning with the rising of the Sun at Java on

November 10, 1882, more than eight months before the main event.

At sunrise, there was a solar eclipse which occurred at 218° 30′ (the middle of the sign *Scorpio*).

Eight of the planets were in those areas of space long associated with earthquakes and volcanic eruptions. In addition, the Sun and Moon were 180° (in opposition) to

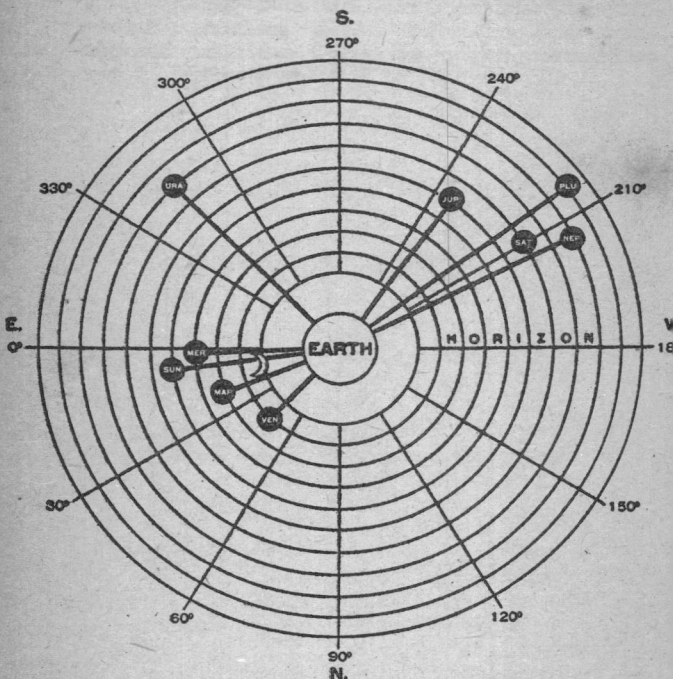

Illustration "F": Eclipse pattern preceding Krakatoa eruption of November 10, 1882.

Neptune, within a few degrees of opposition to Saturn, and a slightly wider orb of opposition to Pluto (as yet undiscovered). The Mars-Pluto opposition lacked only two degrees to be exact. Mercury was in trine (120°) aspect with Jupiter.

Thus, on November 10 at 11:19 P.M., G.M.T. (sunrise, Java time) the Moon and Mars were *rising* with the Sun in

Scorpio; Saturn, Neptune and Pluto were *setting* in *Taurus*.

Three days later, a series of world-wide earthquakes and volcanic eruptions began, as the orbiting planets formed a closer series of "triggering" aspects with each other and with sensitized points in space. These natural events lasted throughout 1883 and took an enormous toll of human life.

Panama and Colon caught it first. The November shock ruptured a telegraph cable 30 miles away. On December 8th, as the Moon transited the place of the eclipse, the earth shook in Romania; volcanoes erupted on the island of Santorin and a new submarine volcano suddenly formed near Missolonghi. Meteors were seen in all cases. On February 1, 1883, when the Moon was quadrature to the eclipse point, Iquique and several other places in South America were rocked again by earthquakes; these shocks extended to Colon on the 4th and 5th, and the cable was torn apart once more.

In the middle of February, when the Sun was exactly quadrature to Saturn, Vesuvius and Etna erupted. On the 21st, an earthquake shook South Australia.

On March 5th, as Mars moved into 90° aspect with Saturn, the severest shocks in years rocked Cyprus, and Etna erupted anew.

THE CELESTIAL SYSTEM BUILDS UP PRESSURE

On May 12, when the Sun conjoined Saturn and both bodies opposed the place of the November 10th eclipse, the volcano *Karang*, after 200 years of slumber, stirred, belched, and darkened the sky with dust, smoke, and fine ash. From May 20th to 22nd, the violence of these eruptions intensified; they were felt as far away as Anjer and Batavia.

Seven days after a Mars-Saturn conjunction, when the Moon was 90° from the point of the previous conjunction, Venus, Mars, and Jupiter were at exactly the same degree south of the celestial equator and Mercury was in conjunction with the Sun when a great quake opened chasms at Ischia and killed 5000 people.

Before the pent-up charge of the eclipse and opposition pattern was entirely set off, however, another important celestial event took place, "loading" the system even more.

On May 6, 1883, a total eclipse of the Sun occurred at 45° of celestial longitude (15° *Taurus*). Saturn was at 27° *Taurus* and Jupiter was at 90° celestial longitude. The Moon was in *perigee* at 8 P.M. just before the eclipse.

Shortly afterward, when the Moon conjoined Saturn, a devastating earthquake occurred in Central America. Every coastal city and village suffered enormous damage.

A Mountain Blasted into Space

Then on August 27th, 1883, as Mars (the trigger) and the Moon, in conjunction, reached the place held by Jupiter (expansion) at the eclipse, the awesome climax was reached: With a release of energy exceeding that of scores of H-bombs, Krakatoa erupted like nothing known in man's memory. In a series of unimaginably violent explosions, the island volcano blasted four and a half cubic miles of itself into the thinnest reaches of the upper atmosphere on four consecutive 80,000 foot towers of flaming violence!

Each convulsive earth-shattering roar was felt and heard 2,750 miles away. Huge walls of water rose to a height of 100 feet and roared off at unbelievable speeds into the South China Sea and the Pacific and Indian Oceans. They destroyed everything in their paths. Tidal registers in every part of the world recorded it.

On the coast of Java, three towns and every living creature within them were literally erased from the face of the planet. A great hole 1,000 feet deep was ripped out of the floor of the ocean. Thirty-five thousand people met instant death, and thousands more died in the aftermath. An island 3,000 feet high was totally submerged. High noon for thousands of miles surrounding Sunda Strait was as black as a Moonless, starless, midnight for almost two weeks.

Several years later, due to atmospheric debris from the eruptions, the world's sunsets were still weirdly beautiful red and scarlet panoramas—like a view from an alien world. Ten years afterward the dust and ashes of Krakatoa, carried by the trade winds and jet streams, was still settling all over the globe.

Krakatoa, now considered dormant, still synchronizes its activity with celestial events. It erupted ten times during the 1950s.

Computers using celestial data could provide the seismic warning systems of the future, months, or even years, before the first ominous rumblings or ruptures in the Earth's crust.

Ancient people learned the catastrophic nature of Mars
at the cost of unbelievable agony, hardship, and depri-
vation, the intensity of which cannot be imagined—not even by
the survivors of Hiroshima and Nagasaki! Because of their suffering, modern astrology knows the tremendous power and
energy of Mars, and how to use this Martian energy in our
lives.

Despite humanity's avowed love of peace, harmony,
brotherhood, and tranquility, the harsh fact is that, historically, homo sapiens have fallen upon violence, due to the
negative influence of Mars. The exprience of astrologers for
thousands of years has equated this influence to obstacles,
to friction, to conflict, and to warfare. It may be that
violence is part of natural evolution, built into the Universal System as a prime requirement to the very existence of
things; Mars may be equated to the spark plug or fire in-
jector of the solar system, or as a symbol of the Darwinian
idea of the survival of species. Once survival is secured,
Saturn represents organization and status quo. But Mars'
strife, conflict, and violence are inherently a part of the
survival mechanism.

YOUR BODY—A MASS OF ELECTROMAGNETIC ENERGY

One of the latest discoveries in physical medicine is
that the human body may be considered as a mass of electrical energy which, in necessarily simplified terms, has
"pressed" into what we consider "solid" matter through the
concentration of electromagnetic light waves. In fact, electromagnetic energy vibration is now considered an accurate scientific description of all matter in the universe.

Such discoveries are leading scientists out of the muddle of 19th Century materialistic thinking. They have nearly reached a point where many seemingly non-physical ideas will be re-discovered.

The opposite polarities of electromagnetic energy, symbolized respectively by Mars and Saturn, were illustrated in a recent medical article by Dr. Lloyd Graham of Grants Pass, Oregon: "In a concentrated energy field, there is an increase of the hydrogen ions which make the cell acid, with all the cardinal symptoms of inflammation (redness, heat, and swelling). In a decentrated energy field, there is an increase in the hydroxyl ions which make the cell alkaline, cold, constricted, and dehydrated."

Dr. Graham is one of a growing number of medical men who apply electromagnetic energy to restore a normal balance in the body's biomagnetic field. A concentrated electromagnetic energy field and its consequent heat, redness, swelling, and inflammation is quite definitely connected to the observed high incidence of acute, eruptive diseases coincident with Mars' perigee approach every couple of years.

The character of Mars, like that of Saturn, only *seems* to be malefic. An imbalance between these extremes of Mars and Saturn may be the stumbling block to moderation.

The Roman God of War was Mars, almost indisputably accepted as the ruler of the sign Aries and possibly of Scorpio as well. The *Greek* name for the same War-God Planet was *Ares!* In the constellation of Scorpius there is a great red supergiant of a star called Antares, meaning "of the nature of Mars," which was known by the ancients.

What is a Mars-like star doing in the constellation of the Scorpion? Were these ancients deceived by a similarity of color or was there another as yet undetected connection between the great Red Star and the Red Planet which was claimed to be the ruler of the sign of which Antares was part?

THE CELESTIAL SCORPION

What direct connection could there have been between the Planet Mars and the Signs Aries and Scorpio which it is said to rule? The ancient Mayan astrologers called Scorpio by the name we now know it. Yet the outlines of the constellation of Scorpius do not and did not then look anything like a Scorpion. This is a highly remarkable coincidence, if it is a coincidence.

Despite the fact that the Scorpion of the ancients was

farther south then the modern constellation, we can account for this discrepancy by the shifting of the terrestrial poles in the time of historical man (not billions or millions of years ago). Both the ancient and modern constellations are the same, even though in seemingly different locations.

That the Earth has shifted its poles and changed its magnetic orientation is an established and proven geological fact. In his *Worlds in Collision*, Dr. Immanuel Velikovsky attributes this to the incredibly close passage of Mars to the Earth-Moon system, which causes untold catastrophe and violence on this planet.

One of the Babylonian astrological tablets reports that a great star flared out with supernova violence and its light turned night into day. As it blazed, it lashed its tail "like an angry scorpion."

Modern x-ray astronomers seeking the source of extremely powerful radiations coming from Scorpius have postulated that the great red supergiant, Antares, was once a supernova which flared forth with the brilliance of twenty million suns. This is probably an understatement, supernovae are known to outshine the combined brilliance of all other stars in the galaxy. In our Milky Way Galaxy, this is more than ten billion stars.

WHEN PLANETS WERE MOVED FROM THEIR ORBITS

Judging from its present condition, Antares was probably one of the stars that expanded in a mighty blast billions of times larger than our Sun and outshone our entire Galaxy of stars combined. There is increasing evidence that shortly thereafter a great comet was expelled from Jupiter's huge bulk and Mars extended its orbit into a fantastically elongated perigee passage toward the Earth. Other astronomical records of ancient times clearly agree that something happened to the solar system.

Whether this was real or merely apparent, it is reported that the planets left their orbits. In the observations and records of these ancient astronomers, a connection was made between the supernova blast of Antares and the *global* destruction caused by Mars—as well as the peculiar behavior of the planets.

There is evidence in the real universe to indicate *why* the ancient scientists made the correlation between Mars and Scorpio, particularly Antares.

On June 16, 1962, an instrumented rocket launch from

White Sands, New Mexico, detected an extremely powerful source of x-rays in the general direction of the center of our Galaxy. In a joint effort of the American Scientific & Engineering Corporation and Massachusetts Institute of Technology, subsequent rocket flights confirmed this remarkable x-ray astronomical discovery.

X-Ray Intensity from Scorpius

About a year later, the Naval Research Laboratory launched an Aerobee rocket from White Sands equipped with an x-ray counter ten times more sensitive than the previous one. The detector recorded one outstanding x-ray source in the Constellation of Scorpius about 20° off center of the galactic hub.

Eight subsequent sweeps of the galaxy each revealed the same powerful x-ray broadcaster, with a secondary center in the Crab Nebula in Taurus!

In the June, 1964 issue of *Scientific American*, Dr. Herbert Friedman wrote, "The intensity of the x-radiation from the Scorpius source is remarkable. It is comparable to that emitted by the quiet Sun in the same wavelength range. Yet the entire neighborhood around the source is devoid of any visibly bright star, nebulosity, or radio emission. What kind of celestial object could produce such intense x-ray emission and still remain invisible in the optical and radio wavelengths?

"A neutron star seems to meet all the requirements," Friedman concluded.

Our star, the Sun, is a neutron star at its core; this neutrino core is about 1/100th the size of the visible Sun. A diagram of the Neutrino Sun is a circle with a small dot in the center. This symbol for the Sun has been used by astrologers for thousands of years.

A neutron star is all core; that is, almost all its neutrons are stripped of their electrons and compressed by a gravitational field so colossal that the neutrons actually touch. This is like jamming several thousand billion Earth-sized planets into a huge lump. A neutron star only ten miles in diameter (the Sun is close to a million) can have a core temperature of several hundred billion degrees—so dense that if one cubic inch of it were brought to Earth it would weigh several billion tons!

X-rays produced in the core of a neutron star at these pressures and temperatures match the measured intensity of

the Scorpius source, and Antares could once have been a
neutron star before exploding into supernova brilliance.
Oriental astrological records also indicate several great star
explosions in the immediate neighborhood of the Scorpius
x-ray source in 827 A.D. One of these was as bright as the
quarter moon and remained visible for four months, even in
broad daylight.

THE CELESTIAL "SPARKPLUG"

Such violence and intensity is unparalleled in this part of
the Galaxy. It happened at a time when Scorpius the constellation and Scorpio the Sign were one and the same.

Why is Mars the planet of strife, action, energy, and
violence? How was this first discovered? In seeking the
answer, we run into another mystery. In pre-Babylonian
times the orbit of Mars was plotted and its nature and effect
well understood. Mars was *not* then considered either
malefic or a planet of war, violence, or destruction. We
must examine the records of these ancient astrological
observations in the light of modern science and technology.

During fairly recent geological and historical epochs, mankind witnessed the awful power of Mars action, Mars energy,
and Mars violence. He actually responded and participated
in it, as though his ignorance made him more vulnerable
to its negative aspects. I will attempt, here, to show the
evidence for this conviction.

The red planet's two moons, Phobos and Diemos, were discovered by an American astronomer named Asaph Hall in
1877. Nearly a century and a quarter before Hall's discovery, Dean Jonathan Swift, author of "Gulliver's Travels,"
described these two moons in uncanny detail and even gave
them the very names used by Asaph Hall.

How could Swift have known that Phobos was five miles
in diameter and Diemos ten? How could he have anticipated
the exact names Hall would give them a century later?

And how could he have guessed at something so utterly
fantastic in those days—that the orbital periods of these
satellites were measured in *hours* rather than months or
years? Diemos orbits Mars in less than 8 hours and
Phobos in little over 30 hours. In other words, Diemos
revolves around the Red Planet in less than one-third the
time it takes for Mars to rotate only once on its axis. This,
according to the known laws of astrophysics, is impossible.

Yet these are astronomical facts and Swift anticipated them. The question is *how?*

ANCIENT ASTROLOGERS HAD TELESCOPES

His information was derived from several extremely ancient astrological tomes which are no longer in existence. The original facts were probably standard knowledge among astrologers thousands of years ago.

Now, there are only two ways in which this could have been possible: (1) the Biblical and pre-Biblical astrologers had powerful telescopes, or (2) the theory expounded in Dr. Velikovsky's *Worlds in Collision* is correct—that Mars swung into a remarkable perigee (closest approach to Earth) 27 centuries ago and was close enough for the two moons of Mars to be seen either with the naked eye *or with telescopes!* Curiously enough, Aztec pictographs found by archeologists along with planetary ephemerides, show an Aztec astrologer looking through a long tubular instrument at the stars and planets; the time: B.C.

There seems to be no other explanation for the fact that ancient Hebrew, Egyptian, Chinese, Babylonian, and Indian astrologers could have known Mars had two moons, not to mention their sizes, orbital velocities, and distances from the parent body, as was indicated by Jonathan Swift, the Dean of Canterbury.

In 1724, here's what he wrote in his fictional narrative titled "Travels into Several Remote Nations of the World": "Certain astrologers have discovered two lesser stars or satellites which revolve about Mars, whereof the innermost is distant from the center of the primary planet exactly three of its diameters and the outermost five; the former revolves in the space of ten hours . . ."

ALL ANCIENTS HAD "MODERN" KNOWLEDGE

Both Homer and Virgil were aware of the existence of the two moons of Mars, and their knowledge was also derived from ancient astrological texts. Yet modern astronomers have only known of them for 87 years. Isaac Newton, Halley Herschel, and Leverrier had pretty good telescopes and couldn't see the Martian moons, so what instruments could these ancient astrologers have had? Even if Mars approached as close to the Earth as Velikovsky says it did during its last Great Perigee passage, causing terrible devastation to the Earth, its moons would *still* have been too distant to see without telescopes.

Possibly because he read Dean Swift's stories, Asaph Hall gave the Martian Moons the identical names by which they were known to the ancients: Phobos (terror) and Diemos (rout). What reason could these ancient people have had for giving the Martian moons such names unless they were associated with the very things for which they were named?

An object five miles in diameter would have to approach much closer than our Moon to be visible from the Earth by the unaided eye. If this actually happened, then Mars itself would have been *many* times closer to the Earth than the Moon is today!

WHEN MARS "ATTACKED" THE EARTH

Here's what astrophysics has to say about this possibility: According to the law of Roche's Limit, a celestial body may come slightly closer than 2½ times its radius to another without breaking up. Thus, Mars *could* have approached well within 24,000 miles of the Earth *without* being destroyed by the great magnetic-gravitational stress of such a close approach.

If Mars actually did approach this close to the Earth in the time of historical man, the astrologers of the world would have noted the fact, recorded the event and predicted world-wide catastrophe.

What does ancient history reveal? Great catastrophes actually did rend the lands and seas. Sennacherib's astrologers warned him to speed up the war and finish off the Israelites before the catastrophe struck. The Babylonian king ignored his astrologers, and he lost 180,000 soldiers in natural disasters and was himself killed.

Isaiah, the Hebrew astrologer and Biblical chronicler, also foresaw the great natural disasters coming in the year of the Martian superperigee. He advised King Hezekiah to muster his strength against Sennacherib at the same time.

Men everywhere were doing their best to annihilate each other even as violent earthquakes, floods, meteors, and volcanic eruptions devastated the surface of the land. A large part of all life was wiped out, including millions of animals strewn across the American continent; the bones of whales have been found embedded in the topmost peaks of the highest mountains on Earth.

The Satellite "Cities" Orbiting Mars

All the ancient records say that Mars destroyed most of the world. "The heavens he makes dark; he moves the Earth off its hinges," wrote the ancient Indians. "Nergal (Mars) causes the Earth to shudder . . ." said the Babylonians. "His body fills the heavens with the color of blood," wrote the ancient Peruvians. Mars *must* have come terrifyingly close to the Earth in those days—close enough perhaps for living men to have seen its so-called "moons." I say "so-called" because these two moons are not natural satellites.

On the authority of the studies and conclusions of some of the world's finest scientific minds, we can be reasonably certain that intelligent beings on Mars must have constructed and placed these objects into orbit more than 2700 years ago.

Dr. Fred S. Singer, a top American astronomer, is in agreement with Dr. Fred Hoyle, the world's most prominent astrophysicist, in that Mars' satellites are artificial. Dr. Hoyle, a kind of modern Isaac Newton, and Leonardo da Vinci, combined, commutes between Cambridge University and the Mts. Palomar and Wilson observatories in America.

On Jan. 23, 1963, Raymond E. Wilson, Chief of Applied Mathematics of our own National Aeronautics and Space Administration said, "Space probes are now being prepared to determine if Phobos is actually a huge orbiting space base." NASA is siphoning off $60 million, and this project is now well under way.

Back in 1959, Dr. I. S. Shklovsky, Russia's most learned planetary physicist, told the Soviet Academy of Sciences that Phobos was actually an artificial satellite, probably made of aluminum or magnesium. "We have to assume that Phobos is hollow inside," he said, "something like a tin can from which the contents have been removed. It is an artificial satellite of Mars."

Ancient Martian Scientists and Astronauts

Shklovsky's evidence is based on five peculiar properties of Phobos:

(a) No other planet has natural satellites as small as those of Mars.

   (b) Phobos is only 5,000 miles from the surface of Mars; Diemos is also much too close.

   (c) Phobos orbits the red planet at three times the speed of Mars' rotation. This is something no natural satellite is known to do. A natural satellite cannot move faster than the planet around which it orbits because both the planet and its satellite "were originally made from the same materials, traveling at the same speed."

   (d) Phobos, like all orbiting Russian and American space vehicles, is slowing down and falling toward Mars.

   (e) The satellites contain aluminum; aluminum is "unnatural" in that it does not exist in a natural state. A highly advanced science (metallurgy) and technology is necessary to produce aluminum.

Spurred on by these data, scientists and astronomers the world over undertook independent studies. Dr. H. M. Sinton, an astronomer at Yerkes Observatory in Wisconsin, told the American National Academy of Sciences: "Phobos may be a huge orbiting city filled with men, women, and children. The other moon, Diemos, might be one, too."

As one of the NASA Mars Probe scientists, Dr. S. Fred Singer, Professor of Astronomy at the University of Maryland, said, "If Shklovsky's figures are accurate, then Phobos could be artificial, hollow, and, therefore, made by living creatures."

Astrophysicist Dr. Fred Hoyle, who completely dominates the New Cosmology and is recognized throughout the world as the father of the Steady State theory of Creation, agrees with Singer: "This is the only theory I have heard that covers the mystery of these two moons," he declared.

Critics who say it is physically impossible to orbit such huge satellites completely overlook the fact that our own National Aeronautics and Space Administration has been planning for years to orbit platforms bigger than several of the world's biggest ocean liners combined.

How Lunar Craters Were Formed

Let's assume the satellites are artificial and that they've been in orbit around Mars for thousands of years. The question that arises is: *Why were they built and put into space?*

Dr. Singer says, "Their purpose naturally would be to sweep up the radiation belts around Mars to enable the

Martians to operate in space without radiation hazards." Another scientist suggested that they could be huge lifeboats into which a carefully controlled population can escape during times of violent natural cataclysms on the surface of Mars.

There are several good solid reasons for suspecting that Mars came into extremely close contact with the Earth—and caused violent catastrophe.

The Old Testament astrologer-prophet Isaiah (29:5–6) told that "a multitude of terrible ones" (meteors) bombarded the Earth with "thunder, and with earthquake, and great noise, the storm and tempest and the flame of devouring fire."

From his observatory-watchtower in Jerusalem, Isaiah became the astrologer who warned the Jewish world of impending disaster. When he spoke of "stones falling from the sky," it is clear he meant exactly that and was not merely speaking in subjective flowery phrases peculiar to the Biblical Jews.

METEORS RAIN ON THE EARTH AND MOON

Isaiah foretold of a darkened Sun, of brimstone and pitch and a scorching blast of fire from the blackened heavens, of storm and tempest and a change of time and seasons. One must remember that until 1803 scientists were certain that stones falling from the sky were absolute nonsense, yet ancient literature and history abounds with such reports.

The Chinese "Bamboo Books" state that during Emperor Kwei's tenth year, "the five planets went out of their courses. In the night, the stars fell like rain (meteorites). The Earth shook." We find a curious chronological coincidence between the event recorded by the Chinese and the date of the catastrophe according to the calendar of the ancient Hebrews. Immanuel Velikovsky places this date as March 23, 687 B.C.

In the prophecies of all ancient astrologers of the time, Mars is clearly recognizable: in Greece, Mars was *Ares;* the Romans called him *Mars;* in Babylon, *Nergal*; to the Aztecs and Toltecs, he was *Huitzilopochtli;* the Chinese called Mars the *Wolf Star;* the Slavic peoples, *Vukadlak;* the Germanics, *Skoll;* in the Icelandic Edda, Mars was *Fenris Wolf;* in Hebrew *Maadim;* in ancient India, he was *Taraka.*

To *all* peoples, Mars was feared as the bringer of wars, violence, catastrophe and devastation—but *not* before the

9th or 8th century, B.C. There is hardly any mention of Mars as a malefic planet among the Assyro-Babylonians, the Chinese, Indian, Hebrew, or among ancient American astrologers before this time.

But after 687 B.C., Mars suddenly loomed among the legends of all peoples as the most dreaded planet, the frightful storm and war god, the planet of strife, conflict, violence and often destruction. This is the Mars astrologers recognize today. Even the astronomical symbol for the red planet is the same, a symbol or glyph for a spear and shield. If Mars did indeed make a remarkably close contact with the Earth, the question is: *What caused it?*

HISTORY AND MYTHOLOGY OF MARS

Here again, Dr. Velikovsky resurrects volumes from ancient legendary Biblical and astrological sources to indicate the following: that Venus was ejected from the gaseous body of the great planet Jupiter, that the comet Venus orbited the solar system many times between 3600 and 2700 years ago, and that, through Venus' intercession, the Earth was spared even greater destruction from Mars. Thereafter, Venus eventually settled into its peaceful orbit between Mercury and the Earth. It is curious that no astrological ephemerides prior to 3600 B.C. record any planet in the present orbit of Venus. Somehow, the Greeks came to look upon this brilliant body (which rivaled the Sun in brilliance) as something of a goddess. They called her *Pallas Athena,* and Jupiter was *Zeus.* According to Greek mythology, Athene was born out of the head of her father, Zeus.

If, in some cataclysmic celestial imbalance, a planet-sized chunk of matter was torn from Jupiter to orbit the solar system as a comet for several centuries, then the scar of this colossal event should still be visible in or beneath the surface of Jupiter's atmosphere. We here note mighty Jupiter's great Red Spot, an enigma which may eventually provide the explanation for this mystery.

It should be pointed out that everything Velikovsky predicted about Venus—that is, the chemical composition of its atmosphere and even its exact temperature—was ultimately proven on all counts by the voyage of America's Mariner II Venus Probe.

The Earth "Saved" by Venus

Long before the general adoption of the Copernican theory, ancient astrologers knew the Earth was spherical, another planet that orbited the Sun, the latter being the center of the solar system. In "The Soochow Astronomical Chart" by Rufus and Ksing-chih tien (about 1193 A.D.), it was reported that the planets did indeed veer from their courses. The ancients stated that Venus ran off her cometary orbit around the Zodiac and attacked the Wolf-Star. This ancient Oriental belief clearly recognized that the Earth was a body suspended in space, moving in an easterly direction.

If Mars came that close to the Earth-Moon system and was deflected by Venus, then the reports of multitudes of meteorites should be visible on an airless body such as the Moon. This was clearly demonstrated by the instrumented rocket shots to our satellite.

But there would also have been a terrible discharge of interplanetary electricity as the two planets were cushioned in each other's gigantic magnetic field. Pliny, on the authority of the Tuscan writings (the Etruscan books) said a great bolt of lightning totally destroyed Bolsena, the richest area in Tuscany. The entire ancient city and its environs was apparently burned to a crisp by this terrible bolt, and the carnage surpassed that of Hiroshima and Nagasaki combined. Similar destructions took place all over the world as earthquakes, volcanoes, and seismic waves bombarded the population.

How the Seasons Were Changed

Geologists tell us that the geomagnetic poles did indeed change location and that the axis of the Earth was shifted. The 360-day year was increased by 5¼ days as Mars loomed blood-red and monstrously huge in the skies. All ancient astrological records from all civilized places on Earth state that the year was 360 days long before these great Martian catastrophes, which ended about 700 B.C.

We still divide the circle into 360 degrees for no other reason than the fact that the Sun was once observed to make 360 appearances in the course of a year.

"Multitudes of terrible ones" (gigantic meteors) were seen by men to attack the Moon and the Earth. Having little or no atmosphere, the meteoric scars (called "astroblemes") on the Moon's surface still appear raw, fresh, and uneroded. From high above the Earth, our own planet still bears mute testimony to a meteoric attack. Great craters, even though softened and eroded by millennia of rain, snow, and air currents, are still visible.

Our researches into the cause of earthquakes have shown a remarkable and unexplained tendency, even today, for meteors to come streaking into earthquake-stricken areas exactly at the times of the most severe shocks. There is no scientific explanation for this.

There is nothing fixed or permanent about today's tilt of the Earth, the positions of its poles or its rotational or orbital velocity. The nations' official clock, a precise atomic device, is adjusted once or twice a year to allow for the mysterious slow-down and speed-up of the Earth's rotation. Scientists have recently learned that Jupiter does the same thing. Perhaps all the planets do. If so, there are more variables than even modern astrologers suspect. Yet they are correct in equating violence and epidemics with the red planet; but it is also an energizer, the giver and tester of our strength and courage.

After the year 587 B.C., every civilized nation was forced to recalculate its chronology, introduce new calendars, and, almost at a common signal, agreed to determine time from that date onward.

The Greeks, Romans, Aztecs, Indians, Mayans, and Chinese all looked upon the approach of Mars to the Moon quite literally as love-making. Dr. Velikovsky claims that Mars had near-contacts with the Moon and Venus and, as a result of these two "romances," Aphrodite became associated in mythology with the Moon as well as Venus. We find something of biological wisdom in the sexual assignations of the planets and their contacts.

In Homer's *Iliad*, Jupiter (Zeus) ordered Aphrodite (the Moon) to refrain from battling Mars. Great scars of this contact were shown when our more sophisticated probes sent back pictures of the old Red Warrior's battered face.

The Power of Numbers
in Your Life

6

In *We Are Not Alone,* Walter Sullivan's superb study of the possibilities of otherworld life and intelligence, he stresses the immense variety of life on our planet and the tremendous job naturalists face in cataloging all its forms.

"More significant," says Sullivan, "when the internal as well as external characteristics of these organisms were studied, it became clear that there was some form or 'system' in the plant and animal kingdoms. The situation was somewhat analogous to that confronting those who classified the stars, the basic elements, or, in our time, the subatomic particles. In each case there was clearly some *inner meaning to the orderliness of nature* (author's italics), the problem being to fathom what it was."

We perceive several areas of potential inquiry which do not seem to concern conventional scientists at all. Here too, there is clearly an inner meaning of the orderliness of different planes of nature—or of existence. *And, certainly in astrology!*

THE TREMENDOUS "NINTH POWER"

Some metaphysicians claim to perceive order and system in the *numbers* of things in nature. And in the study of *astrology,* it's almost impossible not to notice *many correlations between astronomical cycles and their significance as numbers.*

Nine, for example, seems to have a definite "power" or "vibration." It is symbolic of great planetary cycles and is intimately associated with your psychological and physical cycles. But, perhaps, it's all just "coincidental." If so, let's see how far some of these coincidences can go.

. The Bible clearly recognizes the significance and power of numbers. In *Revelations* XIII:18, for example: "Here is wisdom. Let him that hath understanding count the number of the beast; for it is the number of a man; and his number is six hundred three score and six."

Six hundred and sixty-six (666) adds to 18, the digits of which add to 9, which symbolizes (at least) a tremendous number of curiously similar coincidences.

"The Nine Cent Wonder," is the title of an item from *The Insiders Newsletter:* "Next time you're in the supermarket, take a long, hard look in your shopping cart; recent marketing surveys show you're piling it high with *superstition.* Mystifying discovery: women are bewitched by almost any item with the number 9 on its price tag, even if a similar item costs less. The finding that 9 sells a woman is now so accepted by marketers that even a book publisher decided to try the formula." A leading publisher raised the price of one of its series of books for children from 25 to 29 cents, and is now watching sales curves rise as mothers snap up the bait."

There is something of truth and wisdom in many of man's biases and superstitions. The mass subconscious recognizes the truth of astrology. If this ancient cosmic science is ever "proven," most of us will realize that we've always known the planets and stars have influenced us. This was reflected in a magazine editorial: "Lyndon Johnson was inaugurated in the full panoply of elected power while Winston Churchill lay dying in the fullness of years and fame. The stars in their courses seemed to mark the end and the beginning of an era."

A great Sidereal Year is 25,920 years. This is how long it takes for all the planets to return to their same positions *and relationships* to each other. It has to do with the *precession* of the equinoxes. This means the Spring and Fall equinoxes occur just a fraction earlier each year. It takes 72 years to complete one degree of equinoctial precession ($7 + 2 = 9$).

If you add the digits of the Great Sidereal Year, you'll find they also equate to 18—and, of course, $1 + 8 = 9$. Two and a half degrees of equinoctial precession occurs in 180 years ($1 + 8 + 0 = 9$), a period that cycle experts have shown to be extremely important in political changes.

In the monthly bulletin of the New Jersey Astrologians Association, editor George J. McCormack published many series of cosmological cycles, all of which equate to the number 9—and to man. "The added digits of various cosmic cycles," he wrote in the November, 1958 issue of *ASTROTECH*, "when reduced to 9 show a striking relation ship between macrocosmic and microcosmic cycles. The Grand Year of equinoctial precession, 25,920 years, equates to 18 or 9. The 360 degrees of the Zodiac and of terres trial longitude also equate to 9. Whether you add all the minutes in a day (1,440) or all the seconds (86,400), the digits always add to nine. *One* degree of equinoctial pre cession takes 72 years."

Any number of degrees of equinoctial precession equate to nine! Two degrees take 144 years; three degrees take 270 years; ten degrees, 720 years; five degrees, 360 years. Or . . . the entire 360 degrees of precession takes 25,920 years— both of which, as we have seen, equals 9.

The mean normal respiration rate in humans is 18 times a minute; the mean normal heart beat or pulse rate is 72 times a minute. Both equate to nine. The average number of heart beats in one hour comes to 4,320—or 9. The average number of respirations in an hour is 1,080—also 9. In 24 hours your heart beats an average of 103,680 times, the digits of which add to 18—or 9.

In this same 24 hour period, your respirations come to an average of 25,920, exactly the same number of beats as there are years in a Great Sidereal Year—9. Is all this purely coincidence?

It takes 270 days or 9 months to complete the period of human gestation. Is this also a coincidence? It hardly seem coincidental that the *harmonious* angles of 30°, 60,° 120 and 150° formed between planets equate either to 3 or 6 while the adverse or *discordant* aspects of 45°, 90°, 135 and 180° each total nine! *"The number of the beast . . . is the number of a man . . ."*

Historians and cycle experts have concluded that great political, dynastic, and historical changes occur in periodic ities which all equate to 9. These are exactly the num ber of years during which any number of degrees (or fractions thereof) of equinoctial precession take place. It takes 2,160 years for the equinoxes to precede through 30 degrees of the Zodiac, or one Sign. The equinoxes preced through 90 degrees (three Signs) in 6,480 years. It moves one half of a degree in 36 years, a quarter of a degree in 18 years, and an eighth of a degree in 9 years.

The 6,480-year period (three Signs) is kabalistically called an *Age,* and the centers of world civilization have gradually moved westward in phase with this precession. Ancient records of the cradle of Western Civilization indicate the these 6,480 year cycles are traditionally believed to end in global catastrophe. This will be detailed in a later chapter.

All these cycles are used in the World Horoscope, which the Greeks of classic antiquity learned from their predecessors, the Egyptians, Babylonians, and Chaldeans. This knowledge was probably the basis for the amazing political and scientific predictions of Michel de Nostradame (Nostradamus), and the great English astrologer William Lilly, who deciphered old Greek manuscripts which gave the key to the remaining unknown kabalistic cycles.

One of these kabalistic observations was that the reduced sum of *all* digits is 9. Thus, 1, 2, 3, 4, 5, 6, 7, 8 and $9 = 45 = 9$. *Nine is the basis of the unit value of all numbers!*

It is also most significant and symbolic for all life and civilization. The Greek astrologer Heraclitus taught that civilization is destroyed in fire every 10,800 years, the digits of which equate to 9. Another brilliant astrologer, Aristarchus of Samos, taught that the Earth is destroyed twice every 2,484 years, once by fire, the other time by water. If you add these digits, they equate to 18 or 9. This symbolism not only has deep significance, but is of dire consequence to the modern world—as we will see in later chapters.

Nine is also the fantastic number that figured in the death of Maximilian, Emperor of Mexico—and in the silver Peso that was coined in his honor. He reigned for three short years, between 1864 and 1867. When the last coinage was struck during his reign, the die broke. The last piece was badly mangled, and there hangs the thread of a fantastic story: as soon as the die broke, a tiny chip (something like a gash) appeared on Maximilian's forehead. As each Peso minted, the crack grew a little bigger and the die became progressively worse. By the time the 32nd piece was minted, the damage was clearly evident. (Maximilian was 32 years old when he became emperor.) The following three coins were badly broken, and the final (36th) piece was mangled almost beyond recognition. Indian workmen took this as an omen that the emperor would die violently of a head wound at the age of 36—killed either by a sword or bullet wound. The American officer in charge of the mint rejected the Aztec, Miztec, and Toltec superstitions of his Indio workmen, *but they were right!*

Ferdinand Joseph Maximilian, brother of the Emperor of Austria, was placed on Mexico's throne by Napoleon III on June 12, 1864. Despite appearances, Max was a true humanitarian who really wanted to help the Mexicans. But he was executed on June 19, 1867 at the age of 36. His entire body was horribly mangled by bullets, but only *one* bullet entered his head—and *at the exact spot designated by the chip* which appeared in his likeness on the Silver Peso! Was this the power of "9" operating in his life?

All cultures in all history reflect this value of 9 as inimical to humankind on this planet. The 144,000 Saints gathered from the 12 tribes of Israel equals 9. The Masonic Order of "The Elect of the Nine" incorporates 9 roses, 9 lights, and 9 knocks in the ceremony.

Ancient Jews were forbidden to wear either the Talleth or the Phylacteries on the 9th day of the month of Ab. In the story of *Kilhiveh* and *Alwen,* the castle was built with 9 gates and 9 portals beside which sat 9 dogs.

King Arthur symbolically fought an enchanted pig (his baser nature) for 9 days and 9 nights.

Receiving the Holy Eucharist on the first Fridays of 9 consecutive months is believed by Roman Catholics to be assurance of dying in a state of grace. Novenas are celebrated for 9 consecutive days.

In Grecian mythology there are 9 Muses, the daughters of Jupiter and Mnemosyne (memory). When Roman male infants were 9 days old, a Feast of Purification was held for them. Roman dead were buried on the 9th day. A "Novennalia," or feast of death, was held for the deceased every ninth year.

THE "SACRED" COSMIC NUMBER

Hipparchus was an ancient Greek scientist, philosopher, astronomer, and astrologer. He laid down some of the first rules we still regard as modern astronomy. One of his historians (Iamblichus) says, "The Assyrians have not only preserved the memorials of seven and twenty myriads of years (270,000 years—which equals 9) as Hipparchus says they have, but likewise of whole apocatastases and periods of *The Seven Rulers of the World.*

In his first book, Cicero stated that the Chaldeans had records of the stars for more than 370,000 years. Diodorus Siculus claims that their observations of the universe spanned the tremendous (according to our standards) period of 473,000 years! This is certainly a far cry from our Judaic Christian tradition of less than 6,000 years from the "Creation of the World."

And yet, we find those great thinkers and scientists of th

distant past with even longer periods of ancient knowledge than this! Thomas Taylor, in his "Notes on Julius Firmicus Maternus" (Thorndyke) tells us:

"Epigenes, Berosus, and Critodemes set the duration of astronomical observations by the Babylonians at from 490,-000 to 720,000 years!" The fact that archeologists have found the fossilized remains of a manlike creature almost 2,000,000 years old means we're going to have to revise our thinking about man's remote past. It is generally known and accepted by scientists who have investigated the subject that the Greeks of antiquity were very deficient in *original* scientific knowledge. The Greeks themselves admitted this by the fact that all their great scientists, philosophers, and astrologers traveled to Egypt and Babylon to gather new knowledge.

In those days it was tacitly understood that at some remote period in certain countries (some of which no longer existed) there were mathematicians and astrologers who knew the Earth was spherical and that it traveled around the Sun in an easterly direction—and also that the Sun was the center of this planetary system, which was but a minute particle rotating around the "Central Fire"—probably the galactic hub.

All or most of this knowledge was lost by the time the Greeks came along and attempted to explain the sciences of the Chaldeans, Babylonians, and Egyptians. The glories of Sumeria and the great city-states preceding it had long since perished. Crushed under the heel of Persian despots, the sciences of Egypt flourished no more. Nor did the scientists of Chaldea and Babylon study or write. Pythagoras and Thales were the last Greeks to visit Chaldea and Egypt before the Persian invasion.

Our knowledge of the most ancient civilization known, that of the Sumerians, indicates clearly that they were not savages or "barbarians," yet these great civilizations have been shown by archeologists to predate the Deluge. What mighty scientific systems could these proud civilizations of antediluvian times have possessed?

Josephus tells us ". . . God gave great length of life to the Antediluvians, so that they might have sufficient time to cultivate astrology; and that their lives of 600 years enabled them to make records and predictions . . ."

Syrians, Arabians, and Jews have an abundant tradition about the great astrological knowledge of their antediluvian ancestors.

In Iamblichus' reference to "periods of the Seven Rulers

of the World," he may have been referring to the fact that there were seven known celestial bodies: the Sun, Moon, Mercury, Venus, Mars, Jupiter, and Saturn. Each of these bodies exercised a certain "rulership" over the Earth; the kabalistic cycles were dependent upon them.

As far as we know, none of the ancients knew of the existence of Neptune, Uranus, or Pluto. Everything was equated to *the Seven Rulers of the World*. There seems to be only one way to reconcile this apparent contradiction between the knowledge they did have and their ignorance. *The three outer planets may not have been part of the solar system in antediluvian times or geologic epochs!*

This may seem to contradict everything we know, or think we know, about astrophysics. But consider two things: some astronomers now believe our Moon is a captured satellite rather than a planet that was born out of the body of Mother Earth. They have also speculated that Pluto, the presently outer-most known planet, was once a satellite of Neptune. But that it was previously an extra-Solarian planet captured by the gravitational field of the Solar system. For a while then, Pluto was a "moon" of Neptune before a cosmic imbalance (described in a later chapter) knocked it from its Neptunian orbit to assume its present position as the most distant known planet.

There is abundant evidence in ancient records that the planet Venus did not exist prior to the 7th Century B.C. It is at least conceivable then, that Uranus, Neptune, and Pluto are comparatively recently captured bodies in our system, and may not have existed in antediluvian times!

THE DYNAMIC POWER OF SEVEN

In any event, the original *Seven Rulers of the World* have some kind of sympathetic vibration in our superstitions—if not actually in the human collective subconscious.

We still consider seven a "lucky" number. The "age of reason" is considered to be reached at age 7. Twice seven or age 14 is the average age of puberty. Thrice seven or 21 is reflected in our laws as the age of physical maturity. At age 28, men experience the completion of a cycle of mental maturity. It happens that Saturn's approximately 28-year orbital period and its quarterly fractions synchronize with these seven-year cycles in our lives. At age 36, we reach a new level of creativity and maturity as Saturn completes the first quarter of its *second* cycle since birth. This is one of life's most important periods because the 5th *seventh* year period synchronizes with the 4th *ninth* year period. *All* the major milestones of human growth and development may be shown to correlate to celestial cycles. Some of these are so intertwined with other cycles (major and minor), that we remain mostly unaware of them.

Perhaps the Seven-Year Itch isn't a myth, and maybe there's something to the legendary seven years' bad luck.

In these post-Biblical times, we divide the month into weeks of seven days each, in conformance to the quarterly periods of the Moon. Can we really be certain that we choose to do this? It may very well be decreed by the *astronomical* influence of the Moon itself which governs the tides, women's menstrual cycles, and myriad other natural phenomena over which we have no control whatever.

Ancient Babylonian astrologers built their *ziggurats* (astronomical observatories) seven stories high. The ancients had some very good reasons for believing in the Seven Stewards of Heaven. Early Christians referred to the Seven Spirits Before the Throne. The earliest astrologers spoke of the Seven Planetary Genii; the Hindus, of the Seven Rishi; the Mohammedans, of the Seven Archangels; and the Parsi, of the Seven Ameshaspentas.

And what do we make of Mohammadenism's Seventh Heaven? Why are there Seven Deadly Sins? In music, there are seven diatonic degrees. Geographically, the Seven Seas, or the Seven Hills of ancient Rome. In those days there were Seven Wonders of the World. And what about the Greek "Seven Against Thebes"?

The Bible and history are full of references to seven. "And He had in his right hand seven stars" (*Rev.* 1:16). In a broad sense, the Bible may be considered of comparatively recent vintage in the history of man on this planet. The early Christians incorporated a blend of pagan festivities with Hebrew holy days—each of which had an astronomical correlation—in determining their holy days. At least as far back as the fifteenth century, Christianity observed Friday as a fast day—*fish day*—during the Pisces dispensation, "because Venus, which rules Friday, is exalted in Pisces, the Sign of the fish." Lent, therefore, occurred when the Sun passed through that Sign.

Furthermore, the Sun's crossing northward over the equator coincides with the approach of New Life in both the Christian Easter and the Jewish Passover. The first is at Full Moon, the latter at New Moon. Christianity and Judaism have much more in common than meets the eye. Not only is the former a direct outgrowth of the latter, but the traditions and beliefs are basically the same—and some scholars are certain that the mystical Essene sect was where the Lost Years of Jesus were spent and whence came His teachings.

Seven has always been considered the most sacred of all numbers. It governs the mystery of gestation and creation. It is "the number of perfection." There are some very good reasons for these beliefs. In Job 1:6, The Seven *Elohim* (Sons of God) created the universe: their names were Ildaboath, Jehovah (or Joa), Sabaoth, Adonai, Eloeus, Oreus, and Astanpheus.

The Seven Great Creative Rays are known to non-materialistic scientists. White light from the Sun, when broken into segments through a prism, reveals the seven colors of the solar spectrum (violet, indigo, blue, green, yellow, orange, and red).

The Seven *Elohim* of ancient Judaism were known to all antediluvian peoples. They are identical with the Seven Pitris or Fathers of India. In Phoenician mythology the *Elohim* are the Seven Sons of Sydik (Melchizedek). They are also identical with the Seven Kabiri, or in Egypt, the Seven Sons of Ptah and/or the Seven Spirits of Ra in the Book of the Dead.

The *Elohim* are the seven universally recognized powers of Egyptian, Akkadian, Hebrew, Phoenician, Indian, Babylonian, British (Druidic), and Persian lore. This is also true of the Gnostics and Kabalists.

The Jews, therefore, were not always monotheists. They worshipped Jehovah—only *one* of the Seven *Elohim*—as well as various idols.

There were (are) Seven Spirits of God . . . Seven Angels which stood before God (Michael, Gabriel, Samael, Anael, Raphael, Zachariel, and Orifiel) . . . Angels of the 7 Churches (Job 1:6, Revelations 1:4, 5:6, 1:20) . . . The seven rebel angels who made war in Heaven . . . The Seven Kronidae described as the Seven Watchers (Book of Genesis S.D. II 193).

"Seven is the symbol which refers to these Creative Hierarchies, something of their potency and power inheres mystically in it," said Curtiss in *The Key to the Universe*.

There are Seven Virtues (faith, hope, charity, strength, prudence, temperance, and justice), Seven Deadly Sins (pride, avarice, luxury, wrath, idleness, gluttony, and envy).

There are seven glandular centers of the body. "Man has 7 physical, 7 astral, and 7 psychic centers within his body in each of which is focused the force of the planet to which it corresponds. There are 7 portals having 7 golden keys . . ." (*The Voice of the Silence*).

The seven diatonic notes of the scale (true nature notes) are those upon which ancient philosophers (and Johannes Kepler) based their "music of the spheres."

The human aura is said to have seven colors. There are Seven Major Aspects of the Great Law: Order, Compensation, Cause and Effect (Karma), Vibration, Balance, Cycles, and Polarity (opposites). There are Seven States of Consciousness: Atmic, Buddhic, Higher Manasic, Lower Manasic, Astral, Desire Animal, and Instinctive.

There are Seven kinds of perception (physical, sense-perception, self-perception, psychic, vital, will, and spiritual).

There are seven natural divisions of the body, 7 parts to the human embryo, 7 great tissue systems of the body, 7 kinds of connective tissue, 7 kinds of epithelial tissue. The human body has 7 functions; there are 7 layers to the skin, 7 divisions of the eye, 7 layers to the retina, 7 divisions of the ear. The heart has 7 compartments or cavities; there are 7 natural divisions to the brain, and 7 functions to the nervous system.

The cells of your body are continually being replaced. It takes 7 months for the complete renewal of the soft tissues, 7 *years* to replace every cell and rebuild an entirely new body!

Seven members are required to form a Free Mason's Lodge. The game of dice came to us from ancient Chaldea (perhaps earlier); the opposite sides of a die always add to 7 (6:1; 2:5, 3:4).

We have "The seven gates of Thebes" (Genesis VII:2), and the golden candlestick with 7 branches (Exodus 25:31).

And so, on and on. Seven isn't the only number of mystic power, but it ranks as the most important, the most sacred and the most powerful. "The number of perfection."

ALL HUMAN AND ANIMAL LIFE IS ATTUNED TO "TWELVE"

Twelve is our final example here of the power of numbers. Christ chose exactly *twelve* men as disciples.

We note that the Earth makes one orbit of the Sun (through the 12 Signs of the Zodiac) in exactly the same time it takes the Moon to orbit the Earth 12 times. Why not eight or thirteen, or even fifteen? Is this also just a coincidence?

The great planet Jupiter, larger than all other planets of

our system combined, takes about 12 years to complete one orbit of the Sun. The number 12 also has a *terrestrial* correspondence.

To begin with, nobody quite understands why we must have exactly 12 men on a jury. Or why most big corporations have a board of directors composed of 12 men. Do we "just do it that way" because of tradition? If so, how did this tradition get its start?

The 12 sons of Jacob founded the Twelve Tribes of Israel. There were 12 princes of Ishmael and 12 Greek gods. The gods of the Greeks are believed to be the 12 kings of the legendary Lost Continent of Atlantis. The 12 disciples of Jesus were chosen from an original 72 (7 + 2=9). Osiris, the Egyptian king-god, had 12 apostles. The Aztec god-king Quetzalcoatl ("He who was born of the Virgin") *also* had 12 disciples!

There were 12 governors of the Manichean System, 12 Knights of the Round Table, and 12 apostles of the Patriarch, a well-known Jewish institution before and after the time of Christ. Guatama Buddha had 12 disciples.

There were 12 divisions of Solomon's Temple, 12 shields of Mars, 12 Altars of St. James, and the 12 Labors of Hercules. There were also 12 Brothers Arvaus, 12 Asses of the Scandinavians, the 12 Sacred Cushions of ancient Japanese cosmogony, and the 12 great Gods of the Brahmanical Zodiac.

In homeopathic medicine, there are 12 basic mineral salts, each equated to the influence of the 12 signs of the Zodiac and indicating the influence on human health of the planets in these 12 Signs. In weighing gold or drugs, there are 12 ounces to the pound. We measure 12 to the dozen and use 12 inches to the foot. Both the metric and duodecimal systems conform to the number 12. Minerals in the Earth also conform; diamonds and other pizeoelectric crystals have 12 sides or axes and must be cut along these lines.

If only human beings adhered to this system, we might ascribe it to a simple superstition of ignorant ancient people because of the Sun's apparent transit of the 12 Signs of the Zodiac, or the 12 New Moons of the Year. But non-thinking, non-reasoning, and often *inanimate* objects in nature also conform to it! How can a diamond or other kind of crystal be "superstitious"? How could the Moon realize it was supposed to spin around the Earth just 12 times for each time the mother planet orbited the Sun? In their natural, wild state, many fruits and vegetables grow in 12 sections.

In astrology, the Zodiac is divided into four triplicities:

the Fire, Earth, Air and Water Signs. Each of these four is composed of the Cardinal, Fixed, and Mutable Signs.

And in Revelations 21:13: "On the East, three Gates; on the North, three Gates; on the South, three Gates; on the West, three Gates. And the wall of the city had twelve foundations and in them the names of the twelve apostles of the Lamb."

THE POWER OF SIX AND GEOGRAPHIC LOCATION

Perhaps these assignations, which were known even in remote ancient times, are not just coincidence, but actual conformance to cosmic law. There are other correlations to *half* the number of Zodiacal Signs which seem to relate to each hemisphere of the Earth. People who have been in both the Northern and Southern Hemispheres know that water runs down a drain in *counter*-clockwise direction south of the equator and *clockwise* in the Northern Hemisphere.

Hurricanes, tornadoes and other low-pressure storm-centers in the Northern Hemisphere swirl in counter-clockwise motion, but in the Southern Hemisphere this is reversed. Even smoke spirals upward in opposite directions on each half of the Earth.

If seen from "above," (North) the planets of the solar system appear to rotate in counterclockwise motion. From the southern side of the solar system ("below"), they would be seen to rotate in the opposite direction.

No civilization of any kind has ever originated in the Southern Hemisphere; every modern nation existing south of the equator today was founded by people from the Northern Hemisphere. This dominance of the north over the south manifests itself even among nations, states, and cities. Wherever a war or conflict has arisen, either civil or international, the northern nation—or northern part of that nation—emerges victorious or dominant.

Southern Ireland is one example; both before and after the American Civil War, the North dominated the South in this country, and it still does. Although Washington, D.C. is the nation's Capital, New York is the *financial* center of the country (New York being farther north than Washington).

The United States traditionally dominates Mexico, while Mexico, in turn, dominates its neighbors to the south, except for those in the Southern Hemisphere where the situation seems to be reversed. For this reason, the European nation of South Africa will never be dominated or conquered by any other African nation. Canada, on the other hand, has not yet fully developed its potential. Yet this northern nation has always come out ahead in its dealings with the United States, a much more powerful and industrially developed land.

Canada, therefore, is the land of the future, as are other nations in the northernmost climes.

Civilization moves westward on the terrestrial sphere, and dominance moves northward. If the borders of two nations occupy the same general latitudes, then the nation whose *capital* city is farther north will always be somewhat ahead of its neighbor (or rival). Look at China's dominance over India and her rivalry with Russia.

A lot more than severe weather conditions led to the defeat of both France's and Germany's great armies in their invasions of Russia. And why is it that the mighty Soviet Union could not defeat little Finland in the late 1930s?

Distant stars, great nations, and tiny snowflakes: all are inextricably intertwined. Weather conditions are strongly responsive to the crystallizing 60° angle between planets. This 60° (hexagon) was considered by all ancient civilizations to be "sacred." Two perfect triangles of 120°, when placed together, form the symbol of Judaism, the Star of David. Each point of this star is 60 degrees from the next.

All over the world bees build hexagonal honeycombs. It's "unthinkable" that bees, of their own intelligence, consciously agree to this standard. Only recently have engineers discovered that the hexagon is the strongest, most economical storage bin imaginable. Yet bees have always "known" this —but *how?* By instinct? If so, exactly what is instinct? How does it differ from free choice?

How do bees all over the world (ever since bees were "invented") build six-sided storage bins for their honey? They've always done it, and probably will continue doing it for as long as there are bees.

Maybe it has something to do with the magnetic field generated by the Earth. Scientists might get them to build square honeycombs or octagonal ones by subjecting their hives to a strong magnetic field; a large industrial permanent magnet might even do the trick.

Obviously, small droplets of water condensing in storm clouds and falling earthward through cold layers of the atmosphere cannot "think." Yet each one of these droplets, when it freezes, forms a flat hexagonal crystal. Countless billions of them in one tiny snowfall, all with six sides or arms, and no two are ever alike. Infinite variation and endless beauty. How does this happen? Why don't they sometimes have eight or ten sides—or four?

A snowflake is a crystal of frozen water; a diamond is a crystal of "frozen" carbon. One is formed in the atmosphere, the other within the mantle of the Earth. One has six sides, the other twelve. Each seems to conform to the geomagnetic field and/or celestial magnetic fields. They cannot "think." They have no instinct, let alone reason. Therefore, they *must* be acted upon by exogenous forces!

And so is man, who believed until recently that he alone possessed the ability to think and reason. How many of *our* decisions are stimulated by "instinct" and exogenous forces—and how many by what we like to call free choice?

What if all the foregoing coincidences are *not* coincidences? Humanity has always *assumed* that it enjoys complete Free Will. But, no proof plus no evidence equals case closed.

Yet, if we do possess free choice, did we "choose" to evolve from blobs of inanimate matter? No; we didn't choose the gift of life. We didn't choose our sex, our family, our race, or our evolution. Perhaps nothing is a matter of choice after all.

Teilhard de Chardin, in *The Future of Man*, tells us: ". . . if, as history suggests, there is really a quality of the inevitable in the forward March of the Universe—if, in truth, the world cannot turn back—then it must mean that individual acts are bound to follow, *in the majority and freely*, the sole direction capable of satisfying all their aspirations towards every imaginable form of higher consciousness. Having been initially the fundamental choice of the individual, the Grand Option, that which decides in favor of a convergent Universe is destined sooner or later to become the *common choice* of the mass of Mankind. Thus, a particular and generalized state of consciousness is *presaged for our species* (author's italics), in the future: A 'conspiracy' in terms of perspective and intention."

In such a case, we have little (if any) free will, and science's blindness to "coincidences" that are not coincidental is preordained.

Your Life Cycle and the
Magnetic Tides of
the Stars

7

Four hundred million degrees Centigrade is the hottest known temperature in the universe. The surface of the Sun, which is actually a tremendous sphere of eternally roaring ionized gases, is said to be only 5,000 degrees Centigrade, and even at this temperature nothing we know of is able to exist.

Scientists are now generating ionized hydrogen gas so incredibly hot that it instantly vaporizes anything it touches. Paradoxically, it is confined in laboratories within "invisible, inside-out bottles." This is possible only because the superhot, ionized plasma generates a tremendous magnetic charge. The only force able to hold it in place and contain its deadly reaction is a wall of negative magnetic force.

In the laboratories of spaceage physicists, therefore, temperatures in excess of 800,000 times that of the Sun's surface are being kept in magnetic "bottles." The profound effects of magnetism have been detected in so many areas of human existence that magnetics may soon lay claim to being an entirely new science.

How All Living Things Respond to Magnetism

Actually, Louis Pasteur pioneered this field with his fermentation experiments in 1862. He learned that the Earth's magnetic field plays a key role in a natural ripening process and proved the theory beyond doubt by showing that the magnetic field of the Earth caused all the atoms inside the molecules of tartaric acid (from wine casks) to line up in the same direction. This caused sunlight to be deflected at different angles from different levels in a retort of the acid.

We know now that this occurs in all of nature, in *all* organic compounds. Scientists are beginning to suspect that the Earth's magnetic field activates an enzyme system in fruits and vegetables to cause natural ripening.

Drs. A. A. Boe and D. K. Salunkhe, Utah State University horticulturists, placed green tomatoes inside a magnetic field and discovered that they ripened four to six times as fast when exposed to either pole of a bar magnet or the open end of a horseshoe magnet.

Magnetism also causes seeds to germinate at many times their normal speed. Seeds and tomatoes are organic compounds with enzyme systems, and so are human beings. The Sun is a colossal electro-magnet, and so are the billions of stars which comprise our galaxy. Likewise, so are the billions of galaxies strewn throughout the known universe.

Planets are known to generate magnetic fields much like that of the Earth. And it has recently been learned that the human brain has a positive and negative magnetic polarization.

There is a great deal of speculation about the subtle differences between the sexes and the magnetic orientation of the brain. It happens that the pineal gland is almost exactly centered under the brain (at about the center of the forehead), while the pituitary is located at the base of the brain in the center of the skull.

Without our awareness, our brains might have the characteristics of radio receivers. The human magnetic field could be an invisible response-receptor or antenna which picks up signals from the electro-magnetic spectrum and translates them into emotional attitudes, moods, and so forth.

DR. BROWN'S REMARKABLE OYSTERS

Fish, animals, insects, and plants also generate magnetic charges and are subject to invisible biological influences from the surrounding universe. Oysters, for example, open and close their shells in perfect synchronization with the rise and fall of the tides.

Dr. Frank Brown of Northwestern University experimented with some oysters taken from the Long Island Sound. He transported them from New Haven, Conn. to Evanston, Ill., where he kept them alive and nourished in a tank of salt water at the same temperature and level under a steady, dim light.

The oysters, completely divorced from changes in temperature, from night and day, and from tidal changes, *still* continued to open and close their shells in phase with the tides at New Haven!

It seemed to Dr. Brown that the rhythmic opening and closing of the oysters' shells was merely an inherited characteristic—until something totally unforeseen and unexpected happened: after two weeks, the oysters clammed up and remained tightly closed during a period when they should have been open. At the end of this time, the cycle resumed, but with a profound difference; they opened their shells widest at a moment when the Full Moon was directly overhead at Evanston, Illinois, some time *after* high tide in New Haven, Conn.

Dr. Brown's oysters were obviously responding to the location of the Moon which triggered some mysterious reaction inside their "biological clocks." Here was an entirely new mystery for scientists. No one knows what the connecting link is between stars and planets and the Earthly events with which they so often correlate.

YOUR MOODS, ENERGIES AND LIFE ARE PREDICTABLE

A remarkable correlation was found during a three year atmospheric ionization study by the American Institute of Medical Climatology in Philadelphia in 1961. Police reports, fire department reports, hospital and industrial records all showed peaks and troughs corresponding to the times of the New and Full Moon.

Other recent studies suggest that the biological rhythms of all life forms are inseparable from barometric pressure changes, atmospheric electricity, ion density, sunspot cycles (as reflected in tree rings), and other little-known stellar and planetary forces.

Terrestrial forces, according to Rutherford Platt, "are affected by forces from outer space, by the phase of the Moon, by undulations in the pear-shaped, electromagnetic field that surrounds the Earth, by showers of gamma-rays, cosmic rays, and other electromagnetic forces emanating from extra-terrestrial sources that bombard the Earth's atmosphere."

Because of their simplicity, the lower life forms that inhabit our planet furnish excellent clues to the effects of cosmic influences. Man's biological complexity, rather than making him immune to these forces, seems rather to make him more sensitive.

How Magnetism Speeds Plant Growth

Since the time of Kepler and Newton, those who have sought to deduce a connection between terrestrial magnetic phenomena and celestial magnetic phenomena have been unable to exclude man's biological, mental, and emotional processes. "Magnetic vibrations" once were hypothesized as causing subtle but powerful celestial influences to act on all living things, but nobody knew what they did or how they did it.

However, a recent N.Y.U. computer study of Moon phase and rainfall supports the age-old contention that planting in harmony with the lunar phase produces the most bountiful yields.

Certain plants respond to light and move to face the source of photons from the Sun (the sunflower, for example), and they are called phototropic. Horticulturists now are aware of magnetotropic seeds and plants. The fact is, no seed or plant is known that will *not* respond to a magnetic field. Seeds show tremendous acceleration in growth when exposed to magnetism.

This same Earth's magnetism activates an enzyme system in fruits and vegetables to cause normal ripening and/or fermentation. When the field of a magnet passes through the organic compound of a tomato, apple, or peach, it triggers a loss or gain of protons which speeds up the enzyme system and causes ripening.

At a space symposium in 1962, Dr. Robert O. Becker of the VA Hospital in Syracuse, N.Y., claimed that astronauts who invade the magnetic force fields of other planets beyond the Earth's atmosphere will undoubtedly exhibit aberrations. Since then, both American and Russian astronauts have fulfilled his prediction.

Purely aside from being fried alive by the lethal radiations from a solar flare (which John H. Nelson of RCA Communications, Inc. has shown to be intimately related to planetary magnetic fields at various angles), space explorers of the future will certainly be adversely affected by strange forces.

"We have discovered," Dr. Becker said, "that the electromagnetic field in our environment has a profound effect on

behavior and biological cycles. We believe the mechanism
for its action is within the central nervous system."

Dr. Becker found a 24-hour variation in magnetism and
a 28-day biological cycle that is vital to human beings. He
has shown concrete evidence that psychotic breakdowns
correlate with variations in the Earth's magnetic field.

These changes in geomagnetism are "suspected" by many
conventional researchers to correlate in turn to the angular
distances of the various celestial bodies—the magnetic fields
of the planets. The inference seems obvious.

SCIENCE DISCOVERS YOUR MAGNETIC "AURA"

Dr. Becker, who is also an orthopedic surgeon at New
York's Upstate Medical Center, claims, "Subtle changes in
the intensity of the geomagnetic field affect the nervous system by altering the body's own electro-magnetic field. Increased activity in the Earth's magnetic field has a direct
relationship to admissions to mental hospitals."

The surgeon discovered that a direct-current electromagnetic field surrounds the human body. With highly sensitive
electrodes, Dr. Becker and physicist Charles Bachman
mapped out this bio-electrical field, which centers around
the brain and spinal cord. It has a positive charge at the
back of the brain and over the major spinal nerve groups
at the shoulders and lower back; along the arms and legs
it gradually becomes positive. These currents are connected
to the nerve cells and synapses of the brain and the spinal
column.

All man's energies and moods are determined by the
chemical-electro-magnetic changes in the brain and spinal
column nerves, which are inextricably a part of the body's
magnetic charge, which is affected by geomagnetic fluctuations. And these changes in geomagnetism are a result of
the ever-shifting magnetic patterns of the solar system.

It might be interesting to observe the results of some
serious investigation into the so-called esoteric fields. The
occultists, for example, have long reported the existence of
the "human aura," which bears a most uncanny resemblance
to the bio-electrical field discovered and described by Dr.
Becker and his colleagues.

Dr. Frank Brown, the biology professor at Northwestern
University, has proved that animals respond to changes in
the Earth's magnetism—that they find their way around by
it, thus possibly explaining the heretofore mysterious "hom-

ng instinct" of some, if not all, species. He succeeded in
confusing many animals which respond to Moonphase
changes by placing magnets where they would distort the
Earth's responses to the lunar magnetism to which these animals also respond.

BIO-MAGNETIC HEALING

Dr. Becker, who learned that the electrical charge at the
front of the brain is negative, and who knocked out test
animals by reversing this polarity, also discovered that bio-
electrical fields are primary forces in wound-healing.

In his experiments with wounded animals, he learned that
the electrical field jumps sharply from negative to positive,
then slowly returns to the normal negative state during the
healing process. By applying negative electrical stimulation
to the wounded areas, he greatly increased the speed of
healing.

Broken human bones also emit negative electrical currents
during the healing process. The mending of fractures, breaks
and open wounds in human beings, therefore, soon may be
speeded up either electrically or magnetically. There are
strong indications that, within a few short years, this sort
of treatment will become as commonplace as blood transfu-
sions in our hospitals.

Dr. Igho H. Kornblueh, of the American Institute of Medical Climatology in Philadelphia, has succeeded in rendering
completely painless the agony of third-degree burns over
the entire human body by having his patients breathe negatively charged air ions.

In a report to the AIMC, he said the treatment was also
effective when a stream of negatively ionized air was played
directly onto the burned body tissue. The blistered areas
dried quickly and healing was speeded up.

I have seen the pain of advanced, even terminal, cancer
relieved when the patient inhaled negatively ionized air; it
has been known to work even where certain drugs and
narcotics were no longer effective.

BIO-MAGNETICS IN ANCIENT CITIES

One of the most fascinating possibilities came to light as
a by-product of Dr. Becker's discovery of the bio-magnetic
field.

The ancient Egyptian, Sumerian, and Greek doctors were more advanced than we generally give them credit for; they performed tedious surgical operations and even removed cataracts from the eyes of patients. Egyptian dentists painlessly extracted teeth or filled them with gold.

The fact that Egyptian priests wore precious stones and magnetic medallions at the centers of their foreheads indicates they may have had some knowledge of the function of the pineal gland—the "third eye" of the occultists. This leads us into very strange territory indeed. Where is the dividing line between the esoteric and the scientific?

Edgar Cayce, the great psychic diagnostician of Virginia Beach who confounded medical experts by diagnosing the ailments and prescribing cures for people he'd never seen also had some experience along these lines. He showed that the Psi-faculty (or ESP ability) was vastly enhanced when a semiprecious stone was taped to the center of the forehead. His readings indicated that the use of the *lapis lingua* could accomplish this. *Lapis lingua* is described as a combination of azurite and malachite (chrysocolla).

THE ACCURACY OF ANCIENT ASTROLOGICAL SCIENCE

"There is mind in every cell of the body," Cayce said in trance 35 years before the discovery by micro-biologists of DNA and RNA, the mysterious nucleic acids which carry intelligent life-building energies throughout the human system.

There are properties to magnetism we haven't begun to guess at. Dr. Becker and Professor Brown, modern pioneers in bio-electricity and bio-magnetism, have found a host of diseases that occur in cycles; they are convinced, by practical experiment and investigation, that the bio-electrical field is *the link between the Sun, Moon, stars, and planets and human somatic and psychological function.*

The experiments with animals proved beyond doubt that the Earth's field varies in so many ways that our planet is "literally talking" in its responses to celestial magnetic forces. Animals (and quite likely humans) are known to tune in and understand this "conversation" without being aware of it.

A famous gynecologist and cytologist is the first M.D. to use an electro-magnetic activator in the treatment of advanced cases of cancer. Cancer cannot exist, he theorizes, in a strong magnetic field. The interesting side-effect of repeated exposures to magnetism on human beings, aside from

its effect as a cancer experiment, is the restoration of pig-
mentation in the hair of many patients—in most cases, from
a silvery white to its former natural color.

His discovery could revolutionize the present concept of
the aging process. For the first time, Einstein's energy-mass
equation has been applied to the practice of medicine. Ap-
plications of a magnetic field seem to relieve pain from *any*
cause and to help speed the human organism's return to
normalcy.

*There is evidence, however, that when the human organism
is exposed to two lines of powerful magnetic force inter-
secting at right angles, the effect can be disastrous.* Physicists
and electrical engineers discovered this remarkably tragic
fact during experiments with intense magnetic fields used
to energize particles in an early atomic experiment at
Holyoke, Massachusetts. According to unconfirmed reports,
several technicians died as a result of exposure to two lines
of magnetic force which were set up in X-cross fashion.

It has been found that, even at very low temperatures,
metals will alternately shrink and stretch when a nearby
magnetic field is smoothly varied.

Positive and negative magnetic polarization, an intimate
property of electrical phenomena, exists throughout the universe. All matter, organic and inorganic, participates in and
depends upon the eternal flux and flow of these energies.
Indeed, these energies are matter in motion, as Einstein pro-
pounded.

And Man, the electro-magnetic animal who dominates the
planet Earth, is approaching a revolutionary concept of himself and his place in a *magnetic universe*—as a direct result of these discoveries.

The tiny sub-atomic particles which make up your body
generate minute electrical charges and contribute these
charges to the aggregate charge of the atom, the molecule,
the cell, and the entire organism.

It is conceivable that all living things on Earth contribute
something to geo-magnetism and, at the same time, are affected by it. This may not be in the realm of what we now
call the physical sciences. *It can be considered in depth in
astrological science.*

The Creation
of the Universe

8

Nearly five centuries ago an ex-Dominican priest named Giordano Bruno was burned at the stake for the crime of teaching that the Sun is the center of the solar system. He claimed that the distant stars were as big as or even bigger than the Sun—and that many millions of these stars supported planetary systems. "Many of these worlds," he told his followers, "are even more glorious than our own."

A highly skilled astronomer and astrologer, the fiery Bruno fled the Dominican Order and disputed the right of the Church Fathers to dictate what others could or could not believe. He was the first man of his time to state in clear terms what is now the current scientific view of the universe.

EVERY SCIENTIST A POTENTIAL ASTROLOGER

Because of their courage and honesty, men like Bruno have shown that no fantasy from the mind of man can ever compare with the actual conditions existing throughout the cosmos. The New Cosmology of Copernicus, Galileo, Kepler, and Newton, now over four centuries old, has increased the breadth and depth of our understanding of the universe—and even of Creation itself!

While the world's finest scientific minds push their theories to the limit of human understanding, new frontiers are constantly being opened. Upon reaching the barrier of scientific limitation, men like Isaac Newton, Albert Einstein, Robert Oppenheimer and Fred Hoyle have been forced to adopt the tools of psychology, philosophy, religion, and even metaphysics to carry their work toward completion of a theory explaining everything we know about physical existence.

But each new discovery unveils hundreds of totally new mysteries, and it seems to many scientists that the physical universe is a deliberate plot to confound the puny mind of man. But Einstein, whose quantum mechanics and theory of relativity gave new life and broader scope to the New Cosmology, once said, "I cannot believe that God plays dice with the Universe." And on another occasion, "The Lord may be cunning, but He is not malicious."

THE STAGGERING CONCEPT OF COSMIC DISTANCE

Still, the mystery of Creation itself challenges all astronomers and mathematicians. A complete understanding of this process seems to be their real goal.

When was the universe created? How did Life originate? What is its purpose?

Questions like these are religious or philosophical rather than scientific. We should have a clear picture of what the Universe is really like.

We can start with the Earth, a sphere about 8,000 miles in diameter lying about 93 million miles from the Sun. Light from our star, traveling at 186,000 miles a second takes about eight minutes to reach the Earth-Moon system. Sunlight streaks toward Pluto, the outermost (known) planet, in about eight hours. But the more immense interstellar distances are measured in light *years* rather than miles! The solar system is four light years from Alpha Centauri, our closest stellar neighbor in the Galaxy.

The Sun's diameter is 865,370 miles, and its volume is 1,300,000 times that of the Earth. Yet it is only a medium-sized star among billions in this Galaxy (The Milky Way), ranging in size from tiny neutrino stars ten miles or less in diameter to red supergiants like Antares in Scorpio, which is thousands of times bigger than the Sun.

If our Sun were scaled down to the size of a ball only six inches in diameter, then placed in a small town in New Jersey, the Earth would be a mere speck of dust at the edge of town—*and the nearest stars would be as far away as Denver, Colorado!*

As astrophysicist Fred Hoyle phrased it, "Once let the sheer isolation of the Earth become plain to every man, whatever his nationality or creed, and a new idea as powerful as any in history will be let loose."

At about 670 million miles an hour, light takes 100,000 years to travel from one end of the Milky Way—this vast congregation of stars, planets and interstellar gases—to the other. The great disc-shaped system is turning in space like a colossal wheel. There are between several hundred million and ten billion stars in the Galaxy, tens of millions of which are believed to support a retinue of planets; and there are about a million, by conservative estimate, on which life exists.

Astrophysicists place the age of our galaxy at about four billion years but this figure, like that of the age of Life, is constantly being expanded as science learns more about Nature. On the cosmic scale it is a comparatively young group, though many of its members are older than the Sun, and many are much younger.

YOU LIVE NEAR THE "RIM" OF THE GALAXY

Rotating along with its nearest stellar neighbors, the solar system is moving at about a million miles an hour around the center of the Galaxy—except that our group of stars lies somewhere out near the rim of the galactic disc. This Galaxy of ours has rotated only about 20 times since it was formed!

The inside of the Galaxy is filled with an extremely tenuous interstellar gas, with only about an atom for each cubic half-foot of space. Yet this gas outweighs all the planets and stars of the Galaxy by about a thousand to one!

Galaxies are strewn throughout space in far greater numbers than there are individual grains of sand on the world's largest beaches. Only a few can be seen with the unaided eye; these resemble faint, blurred stars, or tiny cloudlike patches of light, each containing anywhere between a hundred million and ten billion stars. The great galaxy of Andromeda is 700,000 light years distant, but happens to be our *nearest* extragalactic neighbor. For all practical purposes it is almost a twin of the Milky Way. Studying photographs of Andromeda, we can get some idea of what our own galaxy looks like from the outside.

YOU ARE A "COSMOS" IN MINIATURE

Within all galaxies stars range in size from great super giants, thousands of times the size of the Sun, down to white dwarfs smaller than the Earth—or even Neutrino Star only ten miles or so in diameter. Neutrino Stars are so compact they can weigh billions of tons per cubic inch. Late in 1965, Dr. Anthony G. Searle of the Radio-biological Research Unit in Harwell, England, discovered that neutron radiation has a definite, powerful effect on heredity—far more powerful than anyone could have guessed. Dr. Searle used neutron radiation from atomic reactors (for *positive* control) and learned in experiments with 100,000 mice, that the change caused by this radiation in the offspring was 20 times greater than that caused by gamma rays and five times greater than with X-radiation. *All* these radiations reach us from the stars. The neutrons at the cores of fantastically dense Neutrino Stars are stripped of their electrons and crammed so closely together by the crush of gravity that the tiny particles actually *touch!*

THE CREATION OF THE UNIVERSE

Stars have a life and death cycle which astrophysicists have plotted with amazing accuracy. If all the atoms of the Earth were compressed to the density existing at the core of a white dwarf star, the entire planet would be crushed to the size of a golf ball, and a miscroscope would be needed to see the Grand Canyon. If compressed still further, say to the density of conditions existing at the core of a neutron star, the Earth would shrink from view of the naked eye! This shows us what tremendous areas of space exist between all particles of matter, whether these particles be great stars or tiny atoms.

At its core, our Sun is a neutron star about 1/100th the size of the visible Sun. While photons take about 1,000,000 years to work their way through the great mass of the Sun after their "birth," neutrinos zip right out into space from the Sun's core as if its tremendous bulk had no mass whatever. These mysterious particles interact hardly at all with any "solid" matter. In fact they "rain" upward through the Earth at midnight in as great a number as they penetrate the Earth during the day. Several billion pass through your body each hour.

Let's suppose that two farmers, each of whom is beyond effective shotgun range, mistake each other for predatory animals and fire at the same time. The buckshot from both guns fan out as the blasts fly toward each other. The particles will then merely "pass through" one another and continue along their trajectory as if neither actually existed. Roughly, this is why neutrinos, x-rays, alpha, beta, and gamma particles, as well as other cosmic radiations, can pass through "solid" objects. Astronomers have observed *entire galaxies* of stars passing through each other!

Considering the vast number of stars and galaxies in the observable universe, we might well wonder where they all came from. How did they originate?

There are at present three widely-held views of the birth of the universe: The Big Bang, the Steady State and the Pulsating Universe theories. According to the currently accepted Big Bang idea, all matter was once part of a huge mass which either exploded or expanded, creating all galaxies, stars, and planets. The fact that the most distant objects seen through a telescope are flying away from us at speeds in excess of 335 million miles an hour—more than half the velocity of light—is offered as evidence for the Big Bang or Pulsating Universe theory.

THE BIG BANG THEORY

As the galaxies move apart, their speed is measured by the degree of the "red shift" in the light spectrum reaching our telescopes. If an object were *approaching* instead of receding, this could be determined by the shift of light toward the opposite (*ultra-violet*) end of the spectrum. According to the Big Bang Theory, pieces of the primordial mass are still flying away from the center of the explosion, and the fantastic Quasars, the largest, densest, most distant objects known, are now considered as proof of this. The more distant a galaxy is, the faster it is moving and the closer it comes to the speed of light. Light speeding toward us from really distant galaxies—say, ten or twelve billion light years away—is moving at a relatively slower rate than the galaxy itself is speeding away. Therefore, at 186,000 miles per second, the light is not traveling fast enough to overcome the outward speed of the galaxy, and can never reach the Earth. Because light is necessary to our optical systems, we can never see these theoretical galaxies. It is now generally accepted that tremendous numbers of galaxies exist beyond the observable or visible universe, all speeding away from the Milky Way Galaxy faster than their light can reach us.

Another theory put forth to explain this state of dynamic expansion was that the universe only *seems* to be flying apart in all directions at once, but that this phenomenon is merely an intermediate phase of a pulsating action. Accordingly, if we were around for millions of centuries we'd be able to see all the galaxies rushing back to their common origin, to begin the expansion (or explosion) process all over again. Dr. Fred Hoyle, who devised and championed the Steady State theory for about 20 years, has now recanted and adopted the Big Bang theory, which cannot explain the origin of the Great Universal Ball of Matter that "exploded"—or is pulsating. In any event, we're almost forced to accept the belief that the Earth is at the core of the explosion, which astronomers know is not true.

If the universe was created either in a Big Bang or a pulsating condition, then all matter will eventually burn itself out and all the stars and galaxies (largely composed of hydrogen) in the universe will run down like a watch and stop. This means the end of everything we see and know and the disappearance of all matter—which is supposed to be impossible.

THE STEADY STATE THEORY

The Steady State Theory, a concept formerly arrived at by Dr. Fred Hoyle, was, until recently, the theory most commonly held by physicists. The creation of stars by the condensation of vast clouds of gas and dust was believed to be constantly happening throughout the Galaxy—until new information was provided by these immense Quasars.

Keeping in mind the existence of interstellar gas—as well as the somewhat less dense intergalactic "background material" (which outweighs all the stars, planets, and galaxies by a ratio of a thousand to one), an example may be cited from a time lapse photographic experiment I made recently.

Purely for amusement and curiosity, we set up our tripod on an isolated beach and aimed a motion picture camera at a cloud bank about 45 degress between the horizon and midheaven for several hours. At approximately 3-minute intervals, the lens was clicked and a single frame of film exposed.

When we ran off this film, it appeared that clouds were springing into existence *out of nothing* right before our eyes! The atmosphere of course, is always laden with invisible water vapor, but it was a startling sight to see huge billowing clouds just *appear!*

This is a striking illustration of what, in my estimation, occurs during the birth of a galaxy (Dr. Hoyle's recantation notwithstanding). Over billions of years, the invisible background material thickens and becomes a veil of semi-transparent dust, which then coalesces by mutual gravitational attraction into wheeling discs of primordial star material.

If a cosmic observer with a camera could live long enough to snap a single frame of this process every hundred million years he would probably see something like the time-lapse cloud formation of our experiment—except that the "clouds" would be incredibly colorful, luminous, whirling discs of ionized, magnetic hydrogen gas.

Anything less than a hundred million years in cosmology is a mere wink of the eye.

While condensing gases form a loose galaxy with rotating "arms," each galaxy's internal gases undergo a process of compacting even *more* tightly into individual stars; the increasing mass of these stars generating heat, color, gravity, and the energy they need in order to rotate.

THE COALESCING GALAXY

If you can picture this galaxy reduced to about the size of a dime, the volume of background material which had condensed into the dime-sized disc of stars and gas would measure little more than four inches in diameter and about twice the thickness of a silver dollar, according to the Steady State theory. If you placed another dime about 36 inches away, and an endless series of dimes stretching off in 3 dimensions (about a yard apart), with the outermost limit of telescopic vision about three miles distant, you'll have a *rough* picture of what the known universe is like. Just remember that light, traveling at close to a hundred million miles an hour, takes 100,000 years to speed across our galactic "dime," the Milky Way.

Dr. Hoyle's Steady State theory and his "Cycle of Creation" idea seems totally rational.

The amount of background material used in forming a galaxy is relatively much less than the colossal amounts of interstellar gas undergoing the tremendous compression necessary to create a star. The gravitational, electromagnetic field of a galaxy is duplicated in a much smaller, but more intensified scale in the condensing, compacting process that takes place during the birth of a star.

We've seen how the background material surrounding a gaseous, condensing galaxy is drawn into the forming disc of proto-stars by its own ever-increasing gravitational attraction. Individual stars are the result of even more intensely coagulant forces. Dr. Hoyle once taught that a star's gravity field draws more and more interstellar gas into its growing body, and, as the galaxy rotates, the star bores through this gas, increasing its gravity and causing the star to heat and rotate.

UNIVERSAL, ETERNAL EXPANSION

The weakness in this part of his theory seemed to be that he offered no explanation for assuming that the galaxy's gases remain stationary while stars "tunnel" their way through it, thus picking up *more* star material. One would imagine that the gases would move in the direction of the rotating galaxy *with* the stars.

In the heat and gravitational stress of a star, hydrogen is converted into helium (and many other elements), then radiated off over inconceivably long eons of time. Hydrogen composes most of the background material in the universe, except for that which is expelled by those exploding stars, the supernovae.

If the universe were static, that is, if it did not have the characteristic of dynamic expansion, then all stars and all galaxies would eventually convert their hydrogen into other elements, and after billions of years, burn themselves out, turn into black, lifeless dwarfs, and die. That would be the end of the universe, the one envisioned by James Jeans, Arthur Eddington—and much of the scientific fraternity.

But this is not what happens! The expansion of all observable galaxies, a fact discovered by American astronomer Carl Hubbell, *doesn't* originate from one central point as the Big Bang theory implies. The situation would look the same to an observer in *any* galaxy. All other galaxies are moving away, and the light from these galaxies is turning red. The degree of redness increases proportionately with the distance and speed of the receding galaxy.

In other words *everything is moving away from everything else.* The gravitational attraction within each galaxy however, prevents the expansion of its component stars.

Only those galaxies which are close enough for their light to reach the solar system can be seen. The struggle of light against expansion results in the light turning red—and this is how intergalactic distances are measured.

Cosmic background material is forever being used as it condenses into new stars and galaxies. This fact reveals something both startling and paradoxical: *the same amount of gases exist now as when the Galaxy was formed!*

THE "FIELD OF CREATION"

· Where does all this material come from? In his book, *The Nature of the Universe*, Dr. Fred Hoyle stated, "It does not come from anywhere. Material simply appears—it is created." Rather like Galileo, he has since recanted this "heresy," on the strength of Quasar evidence and professional pressure.

In spite of the obvious fact that background material is constantly condensing into new galaxies and stars, its average density *always remains the same!* New material simply comes into existence—quite literally from "nothing"! It takes about a century for a single newly-created atom to come into existence and begin vibrating in an area of about 100,000 cubic yards of "vacuum" in space. These newly-created atomic nuclei are not bunched together, but homogeneously scattered throughout the universe. It doesn't amount to much until you realize that all matter occupies only a tiny fraction of space. The universe seems to have no boundaries. As far as anyone knows, it goes on and on, indefinitely and infinitely.

With high speed computers and radio and x-ray astronomy, Dr. Hoyle and his colleagues deduced that universal background material for new stars and galaxies is being created at approximately billions of megatons per second.

The pressure of this newly-created matter causes the universe to expand, and this expansion is the cause of the galaxies flying apart through *displacement*. The apparent contradiction between the *condensation* of background material into galaxies and the *expansion* of these galaxies is completely overcome by the process of continued Creation. Roughly, about 20 to 50 new galaxies form each day, only to be pushed outward into the infinite volume of space. This process goes on and on endlessly.

If our imaginary cameraman continued taking a single frame of film every hundred million years for a billion trillion mega-years, he would be able to see galaxies being pushed apart, displaced by newly-created matter exactly as it happens now.

"One measures a circle, beginning anywhere."

If our cameraman ran his film backward far enough he would *probably* see our Galaxy dissolve into the vacuum of space. Other galaxies would apparently rush back, grow dim and disperse into the glowing background material, then disappear. Many of these "returning" galaxies would be those that had already disappeared beyond any astronomers' ability to see them—long before the Milky Way with all its stars, our Sun, Moon and Earth, had condensed into their present existence.

A Change in Scientific "Fashion"

Such a picture of the Universe seems to contradict the physical principle of the conservation of matter and energy, as well as the newly-fashionable Big Bang thesis.

Copernicus' theory was *also* in direct contradiction to certain "known" laws of his time, yet he was right and all others were wrong.

Before capitulating to the upholders of the Big Bang idea, Dr. Hoyle presented mathematical evidence supporting the Steady State theory to Britain's venerable Royal Society. In that recent polemic on the Secret of Creation, he claimed that existing matter is created from *the very energy of the universe's expansion!*

Hoyle then believed the C-Field (creation field) contained negative energy, and explained that all celestial bodies are mutually attracted by gravity. This applies to the atoms as well as the great stars, galaxies, and the newly-discovered bodies called "quasars" (quasistellar radio sources), which defy every effort to classify or explain them. These titanic, blazing objects are too massive to be stars, too dense and compact to be galaxies, and are the most powerful transmitters of radio waves thus far detected in the cosmos. They are also the largest and most remote objects known. Some quasars are 7 or 8 billion light years distant—and receding at a fantastic speed.

According to Hoyle, mutual gravitation among stars and galaxies works only if the bodies are close enough. Beyond a certain distance, they repel rather than attract. The C-Field, or "negative energy field," is produced as massive stars and galaxies burn up their fuel and contract, collapse, or pulsate.

This negative energy field is what causes submicroscopic stresses or vibrations in the vacuum of space which eventually become completely new atoms of hydrogen and are continuously being created. Even the atoms of your body and brain cells were once part of the condensing cloud of ionized, magnetized gas that became our galaxy, the sun, and the planets. It is not yet known whether the planets were formed as a result of the cooling gases of a supernova explosion or are in fact the cooled off, coagulated lumps of ionized hydrogen and other gases torn out of the Sun by another close-passing star—one that has since disappeared into the depths of space.

Although the exact method by which the planets came into existence is unknown, it is assumed that the same phenomenon of planet-formation was duplicated among other stars throughout the galaxy—and quite likely the entire universe. Among these planets, hundreds of billions must exist within the "Life Zones" of the stars, therefore making the universe densely populated with intelligent life forms.

Modestly describing his calculations as "a slight extension of Einstein's theory of General Relativity," Fred Hoyle stunned his colleagues into an awed silence with the sheer brilliance of his "parade of splendid mathematics." Then he rejected his own Steady State theory.

ALL LIFE IS RADIATION WAVE LENGTH

But a dazzled colleague, Professor Brian Flowers of Manchester University, muttered, "If you give me three months to sit down and think about it, I might come up with something."

With his new cosmological view, Hoyle believed he could explain in terrestrial terms events that take place in the most far-flung corners of the universe. But he changed his mind—or says he changed it. The Hoyle theorem clearly stated that the Sun and planets of the solar system are partly due to each other and partly due to the more distant stars, galaxies and Quasars.

Compared to the C-Field concept, the materialistic outlook of the late 19th Century is unsophisticated, cumbersome, and unable to answer any of the questions posed by new space-age discoveries—including the mysterious Quasars.

We have some idea of what matter is, but what is *Life?* Even more important, what is *consciousness*—or man's place and purpose in the universe?

All matter, even the human body, is not as "solid" as you may have been led to believe. The staid Journal of Medical Electronics points out that *everything* is composed of electro-magnetic energy fields. This conforms to the picture now emerging from universities and biomagnetic research foundations all over the world.

As Dr. Lloyd Graham of Grants Pass, Oregon, puts it: "The human body is a wonderful and orderly arrangement of electromagnetic light wave vibrational patterns in gravitational and radiational motion." He is one of a growing number of medical men who use magnetism in the treatment of illness, disease, or injury. Electromagnetic treatment is known to restore a proper balance to the body's biomagnetic field in practically all known illnesses (cases of concentrated or de-centrated energy fields). Restoring the proper balance results in a perfectly healthy organism.

THE PULSATING UNIVERSE THEORY

Light waves or photons from the Sun are particles of pure energy. Like all matter, they were created seemingly as a by-product of the universe's expansion. This is about as much as we know, or think we know, about the nature of matter. Everything we see and feel is simply "frozen" energy or electromagnetic light wave patterns "pressed" into various solid forms, both animate and inanimate. The particles (atoms) created from "nothing" which condensed into our galaxy of stars and planets are *pure energy*, oscillating at a certain wave length and phase.

This makes human existence the biggest mystery in the universe. If all life on Earth is merely an accident of evolution—as the materialists would have us believe—if life is simply a fantastically lucky "coincidence" of various chemicals, hydrocarbons, et al, which incubated in primordial seas, then animate life is little more than a myriad variety of machines, and human beings are merely complex biomagnetic animals with no more free will than a mosquito.

If we believe this of ourselves, then how are we able to think, to reason things out, to be aware of creation and to question the origin of things? What is this intangible thing we call The Mind? Is the quality of Mind a property of physical existence or is it capable of surviving physical death?

Science has found force fields existing in space, magnetic and electrical, that are totally unrelated, or at least *unconnected*, to any physical body. There could be an analogy here between Mind and brain.

WHAT ARE WE TO BELIEVE ABOUT OURSELVES?

Materialists believe consciousness lies in the physical brain. They see nothing else to account for man's character.

And yet the brain has been probed, dissected, and studied, right down to its cells and atoms, and nothing has been discovered to account for Mind, whether it is called "the soul," "the superconscious," "the subconscious," or the "Atman" of the Brahmans.

Questions like these take us a step beyond anything conventional science can tell us. Still, there is evidence that something other than materialism describes human existence and consciousness.

All over the world—even in atheistic Russia, parapsychology laboratories and psychic researchers have uncovered and presented convincing evidence that there is indeed much more about the nature of man and his consciousness than most of us suspect.

People do possess ESP; there are clairvoyants, and telepathy does exist. Healers do indeed heal—by no means known to orthodox science. Psychic and "spiritual" phenomena have been manifested; these things exist all around us as unexplainable facts of Nature.

Despite science's long record of damning such evidence into oblivion, the facts show no sign of evaporating. Instead, they keep on accumulating. And science can no longer afford to "explain it away."

Too many "otherwise responsible" people claim to remember having "lived before," and they are becoming less inclined to keep it to themselves. Such evidence must be taken into consideration when we study the Nature of Creation—whether or not it violates what we think we know of Nature.

TRUTH IS AGREEMENT BETWEEN THE MIND AND REALITY

Truth can be found anywhere. Neither science nor religion has the right to decree which path should be followed in the search for it. We can no longer afford to stick "religiously" to cold, hard, too-often meaningless and disconnected facts— or to blind ourselves to natural evidence that does not fit the prescribed groove or pre-ordained pattern; for these grooves and patterns are decreed by people with *preconceived ideas about reality*.

THE CREATION OF THE UNIVERSE

When psychologists or psychiatrists write books that flatly assume all human behavior is solely sex-or-materially-based and oriented, then they are compounding their own ignorance and committing a grave disservice to the rest of us.

It seems we have reached the saturation point with materialism. It has generated nothing but frustration, hatred, wars, and class strife. Its goal is empty and meaningless, a blind alley for humanity. We must admit the existence of new evidence, all of which points unerringly toward the sublime unity and interdependence of everything in Nature.

TO SUM UP: (1) all life and all that we see and know is composed of electromagnetic energy "frozen" into what we consider (by the five *known* senses) to be solid matter; (2) this matter originally evolved from the condensing clouds of ionized gases in the relative "vacuum" of space; (3) the atoms of this matter were "created from nothing" by a force or power whose nature is not yet even faintly understood; and (4) Man, the product of this Creative Process is capable of thinking and striving to find his true purpose in the midst of Creation.

From these data, we can ask either of two questions: (a) is the universe and all life within it an *accidental* perpetual-motion machine with infinite segments of infinite precision and infinite interdependence—even to its sub-atomic particles? or, we may ask, (b) *is the universe intelligently, purposefully, perhaps even benevolently conceived and directed?*

The answer may lie within the question itself.

The Mystery
of the Frozen Monsters

9

During November of 1930, the year Pluto was discovered, the skeletons (with tons of flesh still attached) of several huge, long-snouted beasts were discovered on Glacier Island, Alaska. These great animals were covered with hair or fur, the snouts (or trunks) were about 40 inches long, the heads 60 inches long, and the entire bodies ranged between 23 and 26 feet in length (*New York Sun*, Nov. 28, 1930).

Paleontologists studied the things in detail before deciding that they were "completely unidentifiable."

At Cape May, New Jersey, exactly 9 years before, during November of 1921, a colossal unknown animal was washed ashore. According to F. A. Mitchell-Hedges, "This mammal, whose weight was estimated at over 15 tons—which, to give a comparison of size, is almost as large as five fully grown elephants—was visited by many scientists, who were unable to place it, and positively stated that nothing yet known to science could in any way compare with it."

A World Catastrophe Can Be Predicted

So be it. Unknown creatures of every conceivable variety and size have in fact been seen, photographed, caught, cast ashore dead—they have even attacked large ships. Most of these beasts do not fit our currently "accepted" scientific classifications and are thus conveniently forgotten.

Despite our fascination with these mysterious species, our focus of attention here will be centered on the extinct, or supposedly extinct, creatures such as the mastodons and the great Imperial Mammoths—all of whom perished together, mysteriously and violently, "about ten thousand years ago"; at least this is the figure agreed upon by most experts. The fact that there is confusion and contradiction surrounding this figure will be seen.

What, you may ask, does this have to do with astrology?

Simply that in order to destroy so many life forms (in many cases entire *species!*) so quickly and so violently—as the physical evidence indicates—a terrible catastrophe of some kind must have befallen the creatures of this planet.

We are told that everyone during the time of Columbus actually believed the Earth was flat, like a two-dimensional table. Yet even the Greeks of classic antiquity had known it as a sphere suspended in space, moving in an easterly direction around the Sun! It is hard to believe that Hannibal, Marco Polo, and all those who lived in or crossed the Alps or other mountain chains could not have seen the perpendicularity of this planet's features or the curvature of its horizons.

Yet we are told that "everybody" thought the Earth was flat in those days. We are told that Life (and Man) evolved over a period of millions (some estimate *billions*) of years of peaceful, uninterrupted progress.

The evidence of geology, anthropology, paleontology, and archeology (not to mention man's own historical records and artifacts) indicate that the exact opposite is true.

Once upon a time, countless creatures, many of them entirely unknown to us, were utterly destroyed in a great calamity . . . or series of calamities.

THE FUNCTION OF ASTROLOGY IS TO UNDERSTAND AND FOREWARN

The prediction of terrible catastrophes is within the discipline of astrology. Meteorologists, geologists, and seismologists are generally of the opinion that weather, earthquakes, and volcanic eruptions are not at all connected. They also concur in the opinion that they alone (as "experts") understand the basic cause of these natural phenomena, when in fact they do not. Any good astro-meteorologist will beat the entire mighty United States Weather Bureau hands down on long-range anomalistic forecasting. The Weather Bureau *knows* this and squirms uncomfortably each time it is re-proven.

As we have attempted to show in previous chapters, astrologers through the ages have successfully predicted great disasters, a feat modern seismologists are not yet capable of duplicating. Today, astrologers are trying to rediscover those ancient rules which seem to have been suppressed by conventionalists through the centuries for religious, political, or economic reasons.

If, as all the natural evidence indicates, great disasters have repeatedly decimated the human and animal population of this planet during comparatively recent geological (or even historical) times, *there may be sufficient reason to suspect that it will occur again!* If so, then of all the rational methods of prediction, astrology may be the *only* system through which we can save ourselves. Our expression here is that we reserve the right to *try*.

THE ABUNDANT EVIDENCE OF WORLD CATASTROPHISM

In the state of California, notably in the tar pits of La Brea and Carpenteria, there are bones of thousands of camels, mastodons, rhinoceroses, super-bison, giant swine (six feet high at the shoulder), elephants, and sabre-tooth tigers.

The conventional "scientific" explanation for these fossilized remains is that "wading animals got stuck in the stuff hundreds of thousands (*or even millions!*) of years ago, and thus perished."

No mention whatever of geological catastrophism. Perhaps the theory is that by ignoring this very real possibility, it will go away, thus negating the chances of its ever occurring in the future.

Animals are not totally brainless. We're now learning that *all* species have their own highly developed methods of communication or "language." (See "Animal Communication": T. A. Sebeok, *SCIENCE*, 147/3661 26 Feb. 1965) Some animals are actually able to "reason" their way through intricate situations when pressed hard enough.

This is merely one reason why we cannot conceive of all those animals so stupidly "wading" to certain death if they could *see* and *hear* their fellow creatures perishing by the millions all around them—(allegedly).

Another point to be considered is that despite claims of great geological antiquity for the mass deaths of these animals, the highly-accurate method of carbon-14 dating of animal fossils (as well as many of the world's oil deposits) give them an age of only a few thousand years! A paradox . . . piled upon even more paradoxes.

We'll stick mostly with our mammoths in order to clarify some of this confusion. These great beasts are invariably depicted as existing contemporaneously with sabre-tooth tigers and other mammals in a frigid *Arctic* environment. Now consider that whole frozen mammoths whose flesh is still edible when thawed out have been found in Siberia, often with some very strange-looking rhinoceroses.

THE BODIES OF TROPICAL ANIMALS IN THE FROZEN ARCTIC

But elephants (or mammoths) and tigers are *tropical* animals, they do not blend with snow and ice as the polar bear does, and frozen arctic ground could not possibly have provided enough vegetation to feed large herds of these great five-ton herbivores.

Considering the fact that the frozen North is inhospitable to the majority of the Earth's mammalian population, the presence of the Alaskan and Siberian "muck" adds tremendously to the mystery of our mammoths. In these seemingly permanently frozen Arctic regions, a great layer of organic material (varying from a few yards to over a thousand feet in depth) is bound together with frozen water.

This gunk, or "muck" as it is called, is composed of sand, silt, earth, gravel, shredded trees, great masses of bones, flesh, and even whole animals. When the ice melts and the muck decomposes, the noxious gases are almost enough to flatten a strong man. This nearly homogenous mess of frozen destruction is spread all across Northern Canada to the Hudson Bay, all over Alaska, Northern Siberia and Northern Asia.

A partial list of the animals which were forced to contribute their pulverized remains to the mess includes lions, giant tigers, massive pigs, beavers and wolves, horses with claws, rhinoceroses, wooly mammoths, mastodons, ordinary horses, giant oxen, great buffalo, small squirrels—literally hundreds of species. Some are still extant, but most are extinct.

THE PLANET STOPS ROTATING—THE CONTINENTS MOVE

Many millions of creatures were seemingly ground up into varying sizes, then frozen in bits, shreds, pieces, bones, or even frozen entirely intact.

What caused it? Did the Earth itself suddenly tilt? Ivan T. Sanderson, one of the foremost authorities on the subject, reports: "Astronomers and engineers concur in stating that the axis of the Earth is a vast flywheel, and even if any force great enough to shift it could be found, it would fly apart."

The scientists of Copernicus' time were just as emphatic that the Earth was stationary and the center of the entire uni-

verse (thousands of years after ancient Greek astrologers
learned and taught that the distant stars were also Suns with
planets)!

Suppose these modern astronomers and engineers are also
wrong? What then? Is there evidence that the Earth *did*
shift?

Evidence of the Beresovka Monster

If you were standing on the bank of the Beresovka River in
Siberia about 65 years ago during the Spring thaw, you'd
have seen a fur-swathed Siberian tribesman trudging along a
familiar trail from the great Kolyma River which runs into
the Arctic Ocean. You'd have seen his almond-shaped eyes
widen in amazement when he spotted the great head of a
mighty mammoth sticking out of the frozen bank, its dead
eyes open, staring directly at him. The face of the creature is
stripped to the bone in places, mute evidence of the hunger
of wild wolves and other carnivores. The tough tribesman
cautiously unslings his axe, then realizes the thing is thoroughly dead. So he chops off the great tusks, and drags
them all the way to the trading post at Yakutsk.

Here, he sells the ivory to a Cossack, who is greatly impressed by the size of the tusks and listens eagerly to every
detail of the find. It happens that the Czar has a law which
requires that all frozen mammoths and other animal finds
be immediately reported to a government official. The Cossack
obediently complies, and within a few days the National
Academy of Sciences at St. Petersburg sends out a scientific
expedition which erects a shack over the frozen wooly elephant, builds a fire inside, thaws the great beast, and
dissects its body. Then they drag each part outside into the
frigid air, which quickly refreezes the parts, and they are
shipped by trans-Siberian railway into Russia.

This Beresovka mammoth is about to become the most
famous find of its time, for peculiar and astounding reasons
which directly relate to almost half the remainder of this
book. *These reasons include global catastrophe, the possibility of its occurring again, and how astrology may be used to
scan the future like a gigantic beacon to illuminate, to forewarn, and possibly to enable modern man to escape the fate
of his not-so-remote ancestors.*

Here is the astounding mystery for which science *still* has
no clear answer—not even after 65 years of pondering. The
Beresovka mammoth was found standing upright; its meat

was fresh and the body, except for the eaten flesh of the head, was completely intact. Most important however, was the fact that fresh buttercup flowers were found unchewed on its frozen lips, unswallowed in its mouth and undigested in its stomach—along with a couple gallons of similar vegetation from temperate and/or tropical climates.

INSTANT DEATH OF MILLIONS OF ANIMALS

Whatever had happened to this great beast had occurred in a fantastically short time! Frozen stiff, the wooly elephant was half-squatting on its hind quarters; one great hip bone was broken—either immediately before or after its death. Its very existence utterly destroyed just about everything scientists believed about the thousands of frozen mammoths they'd only heard about or had merely looked at.

You don't just casually freeze five tons of hot-blooded mammoth right down to the center of its huge torso in the wink of an eye. Yet whatever *had* happened to this specimen (typical of all others like it) had occurred so quickly that it did not have time to fall over; it did not have time to finish its last meal—or even to swallow its mouthful of buttercups, ferns, and grasses!

Arctic explorers have reported that sled dogs live quite comfortably for many hours in sub-freezing (minus 25°) gales of hurricane force. Even human beings have withstood roaring blizzards for over an hour when temperatures dropped well below minus 95°! This, however, did *not* freeze their lungs solid, as one might suspect.

THE INTENSE COLD OF ABSOLUTE ZERO

The fact is that it takes an enormous lot of cold to freeze even a small animal like a dog or a wolf, particularly if that animal is accustomed to thriving in low temperatures! There are true cases where Eskimos and Arctic explorers, in order to avoid certain death by freezing during blizzards, have shot down large animals like seals or polar bears, sliced their way into the animal's warm carcass and crawled inside long enough to sleep and keep from freezing solid!

Cold, unmoving air is one way of freezing meat that is already dead and cold—such as in a deep freeze. But the swiftest, most effective way is the "blast" method, which you get during Arctic blizzards of 115 miles per hour and

110° below zero! Humans have been known to survive even *these* conditions! The frozen tundra of the North and South polar regions are often like this, and are therefore completely incapable of providing the almost quarter-ton of vegetation a day those mammoths must have needed simply to stay alive.

Our picture becomes clear: despite their heavy coats of underwool, their thick layers of fat, and their shaggy overcoats, the great mammoths did *not* live in Arctic conditions! Neither did the tigers, lions, beavers, swine, camels, and myriad other destroyed species constantly being discovered in the frozen muck of the Arctic Circle.

The same sort of remains (without the flesh) are found throughout the temperate and tropical zones of the world; fossils of whales have been found on the tops of mountains, for example.

Ivan T. Sanderson compromises with the belief that any force capable of shifting the Earth or changing its rotation would cause the planet to break into bits and pieces. He alternatively theorizes that the 30 to 60-mile deep mantle of the Earth (of relatively "onion-skin" thickness) suddenly slipped around, moving the temperate zone into the Arctic Circle—and vice-versa in the other hemisphere.

THE ELEMENTS GO WILD

It happens that large amounts of volcanic dust are completely mixed in the Alaskan, Asian, and Siberian "muck," so it appears that many great volcanic eruptions on the scale of Krakatoa must have occurred at or directly before the horrific phenomenon which instantly froze entire herds of the great Imperial Mammoths.

In his Jan. 16, 1960 Saturday Evening Post article, Sanderson stated: "A sudden mass extrusion of dust and gases" (from all the major volcanoes erupting at once) "would cause the formation of monstrous amounts of rain and snow, and it might even be so heavy as to cut out sunlight altogether for days, weeks, months, or even years if the crustal movements continued. Winds beyond anything known today would be whipped up with violent extremes of temperature on either side. There would be 40 days and nights of snow in one place, continent-wide floods in another and roaring hurricanes, seaquakes, and earthquakes bringing on landslides and tidal waves in others, and many other disturbances. But perhaps most important may have been the gases, which probably would have been shot up highest of all . . ."

As we have seen with the gigantic eruption of the volcano Karang on Krakotoa, volcanic gases can be blasted in columns of rock, lava, steam, and dust into the thinnest reaches of the stratosphere, where it is almost instantly cooled to temperatures of absolute zero in outer space. Cold air becomes very heavy, and it was these great masses of 250° below zero air which blanketed the temperate (perhaps tropical) zone and instantly froze all the mammoths, killed entire species, and decimated all living things on the planet, according to Sanderson's theory.

"All the mammoth feels," he reasons convincingly, "is a sudden violent tingling all over his skin and a searing pain in his lungs; the air seems suddenly to have turned to fire. He takes a few breaths and expires, his lungs, throat, eyeballs, ears, and outer skin already crystallized. If he is near the center of the blob (of sub-sub-sub-freezing air), the terrible mist envelops him, and in a few hours he is a standing monument of what is virtually rock. Nor need there be any violence until the snow comes softly to pile up on him and bury him."

HUNDREDS OF MILLIONS OF ANIMALS ARE TORN TO BITS AT ONCE

Sanderson then describes what happens to another typical mammoth in Alaska: "The sky here probably does cloud over, and it may even start to snow, something he has not before encountered in September, when he is in the north on his summer migration. He starts to pad off for cover. But then comes a wind that rapidly grows and grows into something unimaginable. He is lifted off his feet and along with bison, lion, beaver from ponds and fish from rivers, is hurled against trees and rocks, torn literally to bits and then bowled along to be finally flung into a seething cauldron of water, mud, shattered trees, boulders, mangled grass, shrubbery, and bits of his fellows and of other animals. Then comes the cold that freezes the whole lot; and finally, when the holocaust is over, the snow to cover it all."

CAN IT HAPPEN AGAIN?

Sanderson's graphically horrifying picture exactly describes the conditions found in Alaska, Siberia, and Asia today. But (possibly because of space limitations) he seems to have deliberately overlooked several very important points. Assuming that his theory is correct, we are immediately confronted by some entirely new mysteries:

1. What *caused* the Earth's "skin" to slip around on its core? Did this create new continents, destroy old ones, and/or displace entire oceans?

2. Anthropologists *know* that Mankind existed at the same time as the animals which were destroyed in the cataclysm described by Mr. Sanderson. What happened to these ancient cultures? How did humans survive? What became of their civilizations?

3. What are the possibilities of such a great catastrophe occurring again in the future . . . *perhaps the near future?*

We will use astrology to answer these questions.

Your Two-Million-Year-Old
Ancestors

10

The world scientific community was electrified recently by two seemingly unrelated discoveries:

First, astronomer Alex G. Smith of the University of Florida said that beneath its brightly colored cloud bands (probably of methane and ammonia), the great planet Jupiter suddenly (and *periodically*) changes its speed of rotation.

Until recently, astronomers have always believed that the planets rotate at a *never-changing speed!* There is no explanation at all for the forces which could cause such a huge body (more than a thousand times as voluminous as the Earth) to slow down and speed up. But with an atomic clock, geophysicists have discovered the same fact about the Earth.

The second discovery occurred when fantastically ancient human skulls were found in Africa by Dr. Louis S. B. Leakey.

If we now want to hypothesize that the Earth suddenly stopped rotating, changed its speed, its orbit, or reversed its magnetic poles, the facts show that this has actually *happened many times* in the geological and even during the historical past.

PLANETS SLOW DOWN AND STOP

What's more, according to Dr. William Markowitz (director of the Naval Observatory's Time Service Division), astronomers have known for a century that the rotation of the Earth (for some unknown reason) alternately speeds up and slows down.

If our planet suddenly stopped, more than 90 per cent of

the world's population would be instantly wiped out. All the super high-power hydrogen bombs now in existence are incapable of such destruction, even if they all went off at once. The Anchorage, Alaska quake of 1964 generated the energy equivalent of more than 20,000 100-megaton hydrogen bombs.

If, in a global catastrophe, all the great cities on Earth were destroyed, what would be left after half a million years to prove that international civilization, commerce, industry, agriculture, science, and government had ever existed? It's highly unlikely that descendants of survivors of the cataclysm would have kept that knowledge alive. The few who lived through such cataclysm wouldn't be able to keep records—even if the means to do so existed. They'd be too busy burying the dead, caring for the sick and injured, and fighting off starvation, disease, and bands of fear-crazed fellow survivors to be concerned about leaving records of a dead civilization.

The cold hard fact is that after a global disaster, descendants of the survivors *would have no knowledge whatever of our existence*. Once they had re-populated the Earth and re-climbed the ladder of industrial and scientific evolution, their archeologists would be unable to find the ruins of places like New York, Tokyo, London, or Chicago. Nobody has ever built anything able to withstand the erosion of half a million years.

A DEAD CIVILIZATION DRIES UP AND CRUMBLES AWAY

In the first place, earthquakes occur at the rate of a million or more each year. There has always been enough money, material, and willing hands to rebuild places like San Francisco and Anchorage, but this could not be so after *universal* destruction. The toll of buildings and cities that were not destroyed in the initial cataclysm would mount in following aftershocks—*never to be rebuilt*. Livable areas would be leveled by numerous hurricanes, storms, cyclones, and seismic waves that follow great disasters. All existing structures would crumble into non-existence within a few decades.

During the first few months, vegetation would spread. Plant spores, carried by the winds, would take root and sprout from cracks and crevices in ruined buildings, roadways, and bridges. The deserted cities of the world with all their broken buildings, bridges, roads, tunnels, harbors, and electrical and sewage systems would be in total, almost unrecognizable ruin within 5,000 to 10,000 years.

After 25,000 years, even the ruins of great steel superstructures would have rusted and crumbled away. All ocean liners, submarines, space ships, airplanes, and land vehicles would have disintegrated. The animal population would increase as foraging lands once occupied by man again became accessible to wildlife.

Immediately following our imaginary great global disaster, human survivors would be so few in number they'd be unable to keep even a tiny area civilized for more than a few years. After the food supplies in urban stores, warehouses, and grain bins had been partially consumed, most of the remainder would simply rot away. Even canned goods would eventually succumb to rust, decay, and erosion.

A Space-Age Society Reverts to a Stone Age Culture

The survivors would naturally revert to an agricultural existence. Within several generations, the original function of the cities would probably have been forgotten (as were the ruins of the Greek temples by herdsmen and farmers).

Descendants of the original survivors, decimated by disease, would lose contact between other groups of survivors. In all likelihood, they would have slipped all the way back to the stage of making crude weapons, slings, bows and arrows, living under the open skies, and wearing animal skins against the elements.

There would be no visible sign that civilization had ever existed. Oh, a few fossilized bones would survive, but only under highly specialized conditions. They'd be buried out of sight and there'd be no science, such as archeology, to find and interpret them.

Five hundred thousand years later the descendants of the original survivors would have repeated most of the prehistory of the former race and reached a stage of international trade (and no doubt international warfare) again. After ages of superstition and ignorance the sciences would flourish once more.

Archeology would be one of them.

But in half a million years, even the sciences would be unable to detect any trace of our claim to priority of worldwide civilization.

What would anyone lucky enough to find a human skull over 2,000,000 years old be able to deduce from it? You can't reconstruct a whole world culture from a few bones and skulls.

THERE MAY BE FORGOTTEN SCIENCES FROM ANTEDILUVIAN TIMES

All previously accepted ideas on the history of man may already be obsolete, according to Professor Leakey. It may mean that certain textbooks "have got to be completely rewritten."

Professor Leakey has found evidence of a species of man more than two million years older than the most ancient man previously known.

What's even more astonishing is the fact that "homo habilis" may have resembled modern Homo sapiens more closely than the million-years-*younger* Piltdown Man, Java Man, or any other fossilized specimen of "near-man" uncovered by anthropologists thus far. One of the oldest previously recognized "men" lived in what is now Germany about 250,000 years ago.

THE 2,000,000 YEAR-OLD MAN

Though small by our standards, *homo habilis*, found in the Olduvai Gorge of Tanganyika, East Africa, was a meat eater, probably had a spoken language, and made weapons and tools. He lived more than *2,000,000 years ago!*

For the sake of comparison, let's take a look at the "almost-Man" Neanderthal, who had such a strikingly simian appearance, and who roamed Europe about 30,000 to 60,-000 years ago.

It doesn't take much imagination to detect the great discrepancy between the evolution of Steinheim Man (practically an ape) 250,000 years ago to Neanderthal (still a prototype) 30,000 years ago—and how quickly man is *supposed* to have "evolved" between Neanderthal's time and the present.

According to the anthropological view, which assumes Darwin's evolutionary theory to be a proven fact, this must mean that evolution has speeded up in the past few thousand years—a wink of the eye on the time scale with which we're dealing.

For a half a million years mankind allegedly remained little more than a naked savage, and then for some "unexplainable" reason he suddenly took an upward turn and became highly civilized during a mere 8,000 years.

Something seems radically wrong here. Let's take an alternate theory and see if there's enough substantial evidence to support it:

A Revolutionary Theory on Man's Incredible Antiquity

HYPOTHESIS: *Modern, civilized, tool-making, agricultural, scientific man has been around for more than 1,000,000 years. He looked about the same as anyone existing today. He built great cultures which surpassed anything we know of ancient Egypt, China, or India. His civilizations rose and fell many times in what we term the pre-historic past.*

In Thomas Taylor's "Notes on Julius Firmicus Maternus," he says, "Epigenes, Berosus, and Critodemes set the duration of astronomical observations by the Babylonians at from 490,000 to 720,000 years."

It isn't necessary to state that astronomy cannot be separated from mathematical skill, from writing, or from the advanced method of keeping accurate records from generation to generation necessary to check and refine the astronomical observations.

What great work then, could our proposed million-year-old civilization have left as proof that they did indeed exist? The answer would be accidental on our part, but would be incontrovertible proof.

If our civilization were destroyed today, the survivors would naturally revert to an *agricultural* or agrarian existence. An archeologist half a million years in the future might wonder how the (to him) "pre-historic" people could have developed the great cultivated cereal grains: wheat, barley and rye. Neither these grains nor maize and plantains (corn and bananas) grow anywhere on Earth in their wild state. *They must be tended by the hand of man because they haven't the ability to perpetuate themselves more than a few generations. The banana tree has no seeds and no way at all of reproducing itself;* it "should not" exist, but it does!

No one knows how it got that way, yet it has been cultivated by man (in its present form) since time immemorial.

ANCIENT PLANTS THAT CANNOT THRIVE WITHOUT MAN

The banana tree has a perennial root. The only way new banana trees can grow is to take cuttings from its roots and transplant them. Obviously, Nature herself does not create dead-end streets for her species by making them sterile. Equally obviously, the banana tree or something very much like it must once have existed in a wild, self-perpetuating state before man came along and altered it.

When we realize the Egyptians raised exactly the same kind of banana 15,000 years ago that we use today, the inference is, of course, that the banana tree was purposefully and intelligently hybridized between 20,000 and 50,000 years ago, according to the estimates of botanists.

How long the Egyptians or other unknown ancient peoples had been cultivating crops of bananas, wheat, corn, barley, and rye is a complete mystery. It could range anywhere between 35,000 to 2,000,000 years.

In a world catastrophe, nothing of our own civilization could exist in a period of only half a million years. We can hardly expect then, to find the remains of a 2,000,000 year old culture to still be around waiting to be found.

Maize (corn) is another plant that presents tantalizing evidence that great civilizations have existed not once but many times in the antediluvian past. One fact should be borne in mind—we know the human race did not suddenly just spring into existence a mere 8,000 or 9,000 years ago.

Yet the fact remains that human history, as it is currently accepted and taught in textbooks, does not go much farther back than this. Even a quick glance at ancient antifacts reveals great development 15,000 years ago. Yet the period between 1,000 and 2,500 B.C. receives the greatest attention in textbooks as though it were the most ancient.

THE DISAPPEARANCE OF MAN'S GREAT WORKS

What happened to man's records before that time? Where are his works? Considering the length of time we've been around, which even by the most extravagant hypotheses, does not seem to extend much farther than four or five million years, geological epochs, measured in the *billions* of years, gives us an infinitely greater span of time for the formation of continents, seas and mountains—and for Nature's "experiments" with various life forms such as the giant lizards—and perhaps Homo sapiens. If human beings closely resembling modern man existed 2,000,000 years ago, how long did it take for this creature to evolve—and *from what* did he evolve?

On such an incredibly long scale of time, a million-year-old civilization seems to have been a relatively short time ago. Perhaps it was.

DR. DICK'S AMAZING DISCOVERY

In 1948, Dr. Herbert A. Dick headed a group of archeologists equipped with dust masks, trowels, and whisk brooms as they dug and brushed their way through Bat Cave, New Mexico.

Deep in the lower levels, beneath crumbling layers of dry grass, dirt, and dust, one of the diggers excavated a piece of ancient vegetation. It was a large, long-stalked plant with a big pod at the end. They were seeking the beginnings of agriculture in America, a gargantuan task in view of the fast rate of deterioration of organic matter. But they actually found what seemed to be the only wild ancestor of corn in existence! It was incredibly ancient.

What it takes to transform a non-edible wild weed into a foodbearing, nourishing agricultural product is an incredible period of time and a highly-developed science.

The idea of raising crops alone presupposes a stable, agrarian society. *All* civilizations are based upon agricultural communities which evolve into centers of trade and commerce. Government, art, science, and industry are all based on agriculture.

It was not until the late 19th century that the Austrian monk Gregor Mendel discovered the secret of genetics, and mutation in plants, insects, and animals was discovered. Even so, it took many years of intensive scientific study to make practical and universal use of genetics, which had its greatest popularity in the time of Luther Burbank, the great plant breeder of the early 20th century.

TO BEAT MASS STARVATION

Despite growing population pressure and dwindling food supplies—and the fact that most of the world's growing millions are hungry most of the time—botanists haven't developed the breeding of cactus, milkweed, or crabgrass into edible, commercially useful crops.

There was an inscription at the United States Pavilion of the New York World's Fair: "Because of the wild population explosion, *we are in a race with mass starvation* (author's italics). Nothing less than a crisis effort can win it . . ."

To accomplish this requires (a) a knowledge of cross-breeding and genetics that space-age scientists cannot yet master, and (b) many thousands of years of purposeful propagation to accomplish it.

The third alternative, of course, is that by learning to write their own genetic messages into the atoms of living cells, the molecular biologists of today will eventually be able to transform some of the "nuisance" weeds into commercially useful farm crops in a few years' time.

All the farm products cultivated today must at one time have grown in a wild state. Some still do, but not the banana, not corn, and not the great cereal grains which nourish mankind.

ALL SOCIETIES ARE ESSENTIALLY AGRARIAN

Without corn, the great mound and pyramid-building cultures of ancient America could not have existed. This is equally true of beans and squash. Once the protein-rich bean became widely cultivated, hunting for meat became almost unnecessary, and agricultural communities had time to follow other pursuits: the domestication of cattle and poultry, large scale trading, etc.

The ancient Peruvians raised all of these crops more than 2,000 years before Christ. They also had one of the most glorious civilizations known anywhere on Earth during their era—it surpassed anything known in Europe or Asia during that time in human history. Of course, the Europeans knew nothing of their existence.

High in the mountains of Guatemala, near the ruins of ancient Mayan cities, archeologists discovered a tall, grasslike plant called *teosinte* or *teocentli*. It had no heavy stalk and no cobs. Yet because botanists demonstrated that *teosinte* and maize readily interpollinate, it was learned that they are distantly related. These botanists assumed the Mayans were responsible for incorporating *teosinte* into today's food plant.

But their conclusion was rejected when, after a great deal of calculation, the botanists realized that even with purposeful propagation, it would have taken the Mayans at least 20,000 years to produce corn from wild *teosinte*. Because this ancient civilization already had cultivated corn on the cob for thousands of years, and because nothing in ancient Europe had a history that old, it was assumed that nothing in the "New World" could possibly be that ancient either.

So they gave up the idea of *teosinte* and concentrated on the possibility of "pod corn" (which grows in Central and South America) as a possible ancient ancestor of modern corn.

Radioactive carbon-14 tests on Herbert Dick's Bat Cave discovery in New Mexico and on other early corn fragments found in Tularosa Cave by the Chicago Museum of Natural History, proved that edible corn existed 4,500 years ago.

Cultivated Corn Is Millions of Years Old

But the most intriguing discovery of all was made by Charles Darwin himself on the island of San Lorenzo off the coast of Chile. Darwin found many cobs of corn buried in a fossil deposit of marine animals almost a hundred feet above sea level.

Archeologists flatly (and promptly) rejected the most obvious, face-value implication of Darwin's find—that since the marine deposit was in a strata of earth several millions of years old, and was made at a time when the ocean was nearly a hundred feet higher, then corn as we know it must *also* have existed several millions of years ago. This was "unthinkable." First, because it would have taken thousands of years of purposeful propagation to develop corn from its wild ancestor, and second, because science would have been faced with a problem that threatened to upset everything known and accepted about man's early days. To explain the seeming antiquity of the fossilized corn and marine life, "experts" claimed that some Indians had "probably had a beach party a couple of centuries ago," ate roasted corn, crabs, clams, and oysters, then threw their leavings into a community garbage heap high on a hill overlooking the beach.

Now-Extinct Marine Animals Were Once Eaten by Man

There was only one thing wrong with the explanation: somebody later learned that some of the marine animals found in the "Indians' garbage heap" *had been extinct for a few million years!*

When an archeologist finds the bones of a mastodon scattered throughout the same strata of earth as the remnants of an ancient fire, some flint points, pottery, and bones of humans, his conclusion is that he has discovered an ancient camp site and that men were roasting and eating mastodon meat. Therefore, the mastodon and men lived at the same time.

In the case of the corn and seafood however, "previously established" dates (theory) caused them to discard the obvious evidence (fact).

The pre-historic Peruvians cultivated corn, beans, and squash. The people of ancient Burma, China, and other Asiatic nations also cultivated what we call "Indian corn." Some experts claim the Asiatics derived it somehow from ancient America. Other experts argue that it was originated by the ancient peoples of Asia along with rice and barley. No one has dared suggest that at some undetermined time during the pre-historical era, all the cultivated crops were known to all people, through international trade, much as they are today.

When Luther Burbank was a household name for his horticultural accomplishments, he attempted to prove that *teosinte* was the real ancestor of maize. By cross-breeding various strains, he actually succeeded in developing what appeared to be a kind of primitive corn in only 18 generations. His elation was short-lived however, when he discovered that the first generation of *teosinte* had *previously* been cross-pollinated with maize—and the hybridized Indian corn genes had been recessive during 17 generations.

Origins Veiled in Mystery

No one knows where or when corn on the cob originated Potatoes, squash, pumpkins, beans, tobacco, and many other food-producing plants were being cultivated by the ancient

Americans long before the Europeans (or Leif Ericson for that matter) had ever set foot on these shores.

Which ever way you figure it, the aboriginals (if indeed they were aboriginals) were—at the very least—far more advanced in the horticultural sciences than any European nations of medieval or ancient times. This may mean they were superior in other sciences as well.

What has been shown as evidence for the existence of corn during prehistoric times also applies to rice, wheat, barley, and rye. The earliest Egyptian dynasties from which records are still in existence were raising these cereals in their present forms between 3,000 and 15,000 years ago. Yet it is necessary to add *at least* 20,000 additional years to this civilization to account for the existence of these crops in their modern, cultivated condition.

On Egyptian bas-relief columns and on papyrus scrolls dating from 13,000 B.C., the banana is unmistakably depicted and described. Despite the fact that the banana tree will bloom and produce almost completely without care, it has its limitations as far as longevity is concerned. Yet we know that for at least 15,000 years the banana tree has existed entirely dependent upon man to survive.

This is an indication that highly developed, civilized nations probably existed and traded among themselves before the appearance of the now-extinct Cro-Magnon man.

MANY OF MAN'S EARLY CONTEMPORARIES ARE NOW EXTINCT

On the whole, it presents an entirely different picture than the one to which most of us have been accustomed. Anywhere between 35,000 and 2,000,000 years ago, early Homo sapiens coexisted with Cro-Magnon, Piltdown man, Java man, Neanderthal, and all the other tribes or species of the genus homo, each of which died out. Homo sapiens, of course, survived.

What a strange world this might have been. What was the relationship between Homo sapiens and those races of near-men with whom he lived?

If we created the present world civilization out of a purely agrarian society in little more than 7,000 years, (which we apparently did), what could we have accomplished over a period of 1,000,000 years?

Our explanation here is that prior to earliest Biblical times, man discovered the secret of genetics and developed a method of radioactive alteration of genes and chromosomes within the seeds of wild, inedible weeds, and *transformed* these wild plants into the food we know today—by purposeful radioactive particle bombardment.

This would have taken only five or ten years at most, but who would accept such a theory?

Doomsday
Revisited

11

A whole group composed of billions of Suns called
"Galaxy M-182," which exploded more than 10,000,000
years ago, was photographed by the 200-inch telescope at
Mount Palomar in 1963. In 1964, a rare supernova was photographed in another galaxy so remote it hasn't been named
or even numbered, but this single Sun was brighter than
20,000,000 stars like our own Sol. Such events are infinitely
distant and inconceivable to us. Even if our local star suddenly exploded, it would be too much for us to realize
—and we'd all be dead before we did.

But what about global disaster—Doomsday, if you will—
for a single planet? Our own planet, the Earth? We've been
living with the prospect of international hydrogen bomb
warfare for more than 20 years.

Whether this happens, or whether disaster overtakes us
by natural means, it is the job of astrology to foresee it,
and the duty of astrologers everywhere to illuminate the
future, to predict this and forewarn all humanity, if
possible.

It seems unlikely that Homo sapiens has ever decimated
itself in prehistoric times. But on several occasions human
history *has* been rudely interrupted by natural causes. The
surviving records point to something entirely different about
our remote past than we may have previously believed or
accepted.

A Series of World Catastrophes

Astrology as a door to the future cannot exist by itself.
It needs mathematics and an exact astronomy (discovered
and perfected by ancient astrologers); it also needs human

creativity and ingenuity. These are a heritage from some
dimly-remembered antediluvian past.

Once we perceive, however dimly, that our position in
this sector of space is very precarious and transitory, our
drive for survival (as the most complex and sophisticated
species currently known) may demand that we begin searching for an escape from a future world calamity. Judging
from the geological evidence, Nature seems to have tried
to erase all her handiwork and to begin all over again
on many occasions.

The Deluge was an *actual historical account* of a great
cataclysm which overtook humanity. The world prior to that
time may have been densely populated, but a great gap in
our knowledge of the era prevents our knowing this for
certain. Available sacred records however, convey the impression that the people of the times, Egyptian, Jew, Babylonian, and Chaldean alike, were "judged and found to be
sinful."

It is barely possible that the human Mass Subconscious
during that era *anticipated* world devastation and reacted
with an ancient version of our own current sexual revolution
to ensure the survival of the human species.

If so, we may speculate that the same Mass Subconscious
foresees another cataclysmic event in the near future and
has been seeking a margin of tremendous numbers to make
certain that (at least) some will survive and carry on. After
all, only one sperm out of millions that swam to fertilize
the egg in your mother's womb ever succeeded in becoming
you! Nature is profligate. Without this margin of tremendous numbers to ensure survival, man could easily go the
way of the mammoth, the mastodon, or the dinosaur—this
time on a global scale!

We are now going to see what the evidence is. At the
end, we'll have a solid foundation upon which to base some
astrological predictions about the future of our world—
with its teeming billions.

INTERPLANETARY ELECTRICAL DISCHARGES

Vitrified forts straddle the hills of Ireland, Scotland, Wales,
England, France, and Germany. Turning stone fortresses
into glass requires vast amounts of energy—either electrical or atomic energy. In *The Book of the Damned,* Charles
Fort writes: "Something poured electricity upon them. The

stones exist to this day, vitrified, or melted and turned to glass."

Only three things are capable of such terrible action: intense heat from an airborne hydrogen explosion, a meteorite of anti-matter (such as the huge object that exploded over Siberia in 1909), or, as yet inconceivable bolts of lightning from a cosmic source. This could happen only if another planet came within range of the Earth's magnetic field and an exchange of interplanetary electricity resulted. If a planet did come that close, tremendous electrical storms in the atmosphere would naturally accompany the shifting of the poles, the plane of the axis, and the displacement of great continental masses. Some of these would sink beneath the oceans while other continents rose from the depths.

Racial memory among certain American Indian astrologers has it that in distant times a "Mountain of water walked" the plains of what is now North America. This colossal tidal wave was reported by a legendary eye-witness and handed down through generations to the present day. The great wave was described as being laced with huge bolts of lightning.

Geologists know now that the site of Harvard University (the entire Boston area) was, in fairly recent geological times, 200 feet under the sea. There is truth in tradition, and in the historical and sacred accounts of ancient events. Stories of the Deluge correspond to records of all peoples about a Universal Flood. Archeologists have recently shown that the Flood occurred almost exactly as it was reported in the Old Testament.

THE FABLED CITY OF UR

Long before Columbus or Leif Ericson, the natives of the American continent told of a Universal Flood that decimated mankind. The memory of a global flood has also been kept alive by the peoples of Lithuania, the Ukraine, Armenia, Tibet, India, Kashmir, Polynesia, and Australia. It was in the ancient and fabled Sumerian city of Ur that Abraham, the son of a maker of icons, conceived his idea of One God and became the Father of Judaism.

Thousands of years passed before two modern archeologists began examining the ruins of a site along the Baghdad Railway, called *Tell al Muqayyar* by the Arabs. During six years of intensive digging at *Tell al Muqayyar,* magnificent Sumerian temples were unearthed, the work expanded to in-

clude warehouses, workshops, courts of law, and splendid villas which compared favorably with the best in vogue
today. Wholly intact jugs and vases were found, and golden
goblets, mother-of-pearl mosaic tile flooring, precious stones
and lapis lazuli were discovered within those gold, silver,
bronze, and ebony handcraft-laden ruins. A veritable treasure
was found in the adorned hair of a beautiful Sumerian "Lady
Shubad." Not even the fabulous tombs of Tutankhamen
or Nefertiti in Egypt held such riches! Yet these buried tombs
and ruins were more than a thousand years *older!* The tombs,
with their noblemen and women, accompanied by teams of
resplendent oxen, chariots, and scores of servants, held fantastic riches—and fantastic horrors—for the excavators. Each
noble took all his Earthly belongings with him, including a
retinue of up to 100 servants, into the next world.

As the layers of tombs deepened and the archeological
treasures kept appearing, scientists of the Anglo-American
team began to wonder how deep, and therefore how ancient,
their digs really were. Each time they reached a new vault or
room with a paved floor, they expected it to be the first
(or last) structure.

But as each floor was penetrated, more and more ancient
rubble, potsherds, treasures, and other artifacts kept appearing in the baskets that were hoisted out of the deepening
pit. In the summer of 1929, Sir Charles L. Woolley's party
had reached the end of its sixth season of digging at *Tell
al Muqayyar*. They had penetrated into a strata of earth that
took them back from the 20th century to 2,800 B.C.!

Woolley however, was still not satisfied. The foundations
of this latest tomb were broken into and removed. A few
thousand thrusts of the spade revealed older and older
layers of rubble from still *more* previous civilizations—each
of which had mysteriously chosen the same place to build its
culture, *an unexplainable but ubiquitous fact of Nature.*
This was true even when the geography had altered, rivers
had changed course, and there were no traces whatever of
any human habitation.

THE BIBLICAL FLOOD IS A SCIENTIFIC FACT

Shafts were sunk at seemingly the lowest level of habitation, and still *more* artifacts came up! Beneath the floor of a
king's tomb, under a layer of charred wood ash, Woolley
found numerous astrological tablets in an older and stran-

ger language than anything previously known. They were now at a depth equivalent to about 3000 B.C.

And yet beneath this there was *new* strata; new kinds of utensils, jars, pots, and bowls kept appearing. How far could this go on? The great, ancient culture of Sumeria must have reached an astonishing development at a very early age.

Finally, however, the bottom was reached. The pit was smooth and flat; fragments of household utensils were scattered around the pit's base. But a few more spade thrusts revealed sand and clay—the kind that could only have been deposited by water. Woolley surmised that it must have been the accumulated silt of the ancient Euphrates, but there were still many questions unanswered.

The excavations continued; thousands of baskets were lifted out of the ever-deepening pit. Mud and sand, sand and mud—six feet . . . seven . . . nine . . . ten feet.

Then, abruptly, the sand strata ended.

The archeologist couldn't believe his eyes. Instead of virgin soil, the artifacts of a highly advanced civilization *again* began coming up in the baskets! Strange, almost alien cuneiform tablets appeared, all undecipherable. With feverish excitement, Woolley's party probed deeper and deeper. Then, in order to double-check their discovery, they sank other shafts hundreds of yards away from the first one. The evidence remained consistent: they had not only found *The Flood,* but they had also established that civilization had existed long before the watery catastrophe! The clay shards of astrological ephemerides indicated (and probably predicted) a gigantic and catastrophic inundation of the known world.

The geological and astrological calendar indicated that The Flood occurred at about 4000 B.C. "About sixteen feet below a brick pavement, which we could with reasonable certainty date about 2700 B.C.," Woolley said, "we were among the ruins of that Ur which had existed *before* The Flood."

The search goes on, but every discovery isn't immediately announced. There is now evidence of even greater civilizations—hundreds of times more ancient than Ur of the Chaldees.

THE BLUE MEN—A FIFTH HUMAN RACE

If Australia suddenly dropped two or three miles beneath the ocean, the effect on the rest of the land masses of the world would be catastrophic. Something like this seems to have happened once upon a time.

There may actually have been a Blue Race of Men. So go the legends surrounding ancient Briton, the isles of which were allegedly inhabited by a savage people who painted themselves blue *all over*—and *all the time*. No white, brown, black, red, or yellow man was then reported in what is now the British Isles—just *Blue* people.

Where did all this blue clay or paint come from? If they were savages, they must also have been primitive chemists to produce such great amounts of coloring matter. The ancient Arabians remember a gigantic race of Blue men, but they were deferred to as a great and civilized race. The Koran alludes to their immense constructions: "built on high places for vain uses." Their "idolatry" was considered to have been tainted with Sabeism, or star-worship (astrology). These "blue giants" were quite clearly astrologers who built great observatories. Perhaps they didn't belong to this world at all. There seems to be some relationship between these "Titans" and the ancient Celts (Druids).

AMERICA'S ANCIENT GEOMETERS

Yet they all disappeared—almost as one. There is still the unfathomable mystery of the Mound Builders in the United States. The remains of great pyramidal structures greater than anything in Egypt, Peru, or Mexico (for sheer volume of Earth moved), are exemplified by more than 10,000 "mounds" in the state of Ohio alone! That's a respectable amount of work for an isolated culture with no stable agricultural system to support and feed them!

These mounds appear to be eroded by weather and/or water over long eons. There are pyramids and *absolutely perfect* geometric shapes all over the United States. No one knows how they got here. Most are full of mysteries such as cloth, beads, tools, lathe-marked metal rods, and at least one 300-pound copper axe as hard as steel! It *would* require the strength and size of a titan to wield this weapon.

There are huge boulders on the West Coast of North and South America arranged into astronomical symbols over hundreds of thousands of acres. They are so big that highways have been unknowingly built through and around them. A high-flying pilot during World War II spotted and photographed them (from about 30,000 feet) for the first time. The age of these boulders is at least 25,000 years. Somebody, therefore, must at least have known about high-flying machines 25,000 years ago! Perhaps they were "shipwrecked" blue giants from an alien world.

Things have been happening to this planet that we haven't begun yet to guess at. In fact, we're not even certain that we originated here. The North American Indians found by Columbus hadn't been here as long as the Arabs have lived in the Sahara. They had no memory of horses, so they were awed by the horses belonging to the conquering Spaniard, Cortez. Yet the areas in which they lived were fairly littered with the bones of horses, camels, elephants, and rhinoceroses!

THE GREAT MOUND OF CAHOKIA

In East St. Louis there stands the remains of the Great Mound of Cahokia. It was originally 97 feet high and had square sides, 700 by 500 feet. The top was flat and measured *exactly* 200 by 450 feet. Here was a pyramid every bit as massive as the Great Pyramid of Cheops in Egypt. The Egyptian pyramid at Gizeh was clearly constructed for astrological purposes (see "The Great Pyramid"), and this might have been, as well.

According to many sacred books *there were giants in the Earth in those days*. Dr. Ignatius Donnelly, author of *Atlantis—The Antediluvian World*, suggested that the ancient Celts (Titans) were actually a gigantic race of blue men who rebelled against the kingdom of Atlantis before its fall and the consequent devastation of the rest of the planet. Regardless of where you probe into dimly remote periods of history, you come up with dozens of perplexing stories, reports, and eye-witness accounts of devastation on a global scale.

From virtually every civilized place on Earth, we find a handful of "survivors" recording this awesome catastrophe, reporting that they considered themselves the sole survivors and were thus entrusted with the job of repopulating the world. The Ship of Babylon, or Noah's Ark (in its own peculiar version), seems endlessly reflected in the legends of all the world's people. Somebody predicted the catastrophe, built a huge ship, and salvaged everything he could. Plato gives essentially the same account—an Eden-like, idyllic existence in the early ages of Atlantis, and then the Fall from Grace and consequent destruction of the world. If this or anything like this actually happened, what advanced civilizations could have preceded it?

America:
the New Atlantis

12

The tacit agreement among the records of most ancient people is that the gods of Greek mythology were real people, and that a huge island-continent with a great race of humans was swallowed by the ocean. According to Plato, the Greeks of pre-history once battled off the colonial legions of Atlantis in much the same way that small countries in the modern world successfully resist the blandishments and armed aggression of powerful Communist nations.

Officially, few pretend to believe in this legend, but there are many astrologers who consider America to be the modern embodiment of ancient Egypt—even Atlantis!

If an island-continent of any appreciable size actually did sink beneath the sea, "mountains of water" would tear across all other continents. The Hebrew Flood legend is the same as that of the Phoenicians, those seafarers who traded with a great, thriving empire, one that is now considered a mere fable.

The Biblical Noah had no connection with Negroes, Chinese, Finns, Lapps, Japanese, Australians, or American Indians. Only the Mediterranean races are mentioned: Ayrans, Cushites, Phoenicians, Babylonians, Hebrews, Arabs, and Egyptians. The writers of Genesis probably knew nothing about other races in Europe, Africa, America, Australia, or (possibly) Atlantis. Our present world history doesn't account for extraterrestrial civilizations.

The Koran also reports a Universal Deluge. Josephus and Berosus tell the story of the Ship of Babylon which came to rest on a mountain in Armenia. The Deluge legends of all other nations seem to be derived from a single common source—ancient Chaldean astrological records.

Present world population pressures symbolize our own times, even as the Phoenix was a symbol of destruction, death and regeneration in ancient Egypt. Many American cities have ancient Egyptian names: Philadelphia, Phoenix, Memphis, etc.

In the final chapter of this book, astrology will be focused on predictions of future catastrophic events. Some earthquake and weather astrologers are convinced that the Damoclean Sword of extinction will probably hang by a slender thread about forty years from now. But during this interval, an advanced, internationally coordinated scientific effort could devise ways of averting or even avoiding a natural universal disaster.

MANY CALLED—FEW SURVIVE

Population experts now tell us that, in the future, our vast population will reduce virtually everyone to a state of perpetual want. Yet world population continually increases. It leads us to wonder if we have any truly *free* choice in the matter, or in our evolution.

Multitudes who in former times might not have survived due to lack of initiative, food, and resources, are now given every encouragement to survive and propagate. The chief aim of the humanitarian instinct of this Aquarian Age is a kind of ill-conceived and short-sighted liberalism. We don't really know what motivates the current "sexual revolution," and yet we claim to have free choice. Can we honestly say we control our own evolution any more than the ancients did?

The Egyptian Flood legend tells of mighty nations in a populous world before the Catastrophe. Many more people than Noah and his immediate family *must* have survived, but the Western world is heir mainly to the Hebrew record of the time. There are artifacts and evidence of many catastrophes—some of which occurred long before The Deluge.

135-MILLION-YEAR-OLD STAIRWAY TO THE OCEAN'S FLOOR

In 1964, when two French Naval officers descended to a depth of five miles in the bathyscaph, *Archimede*, they discovered a rocky stairway to the floor of the ocean. Their dive was made to the deepest known point in the Atlantic —off the northern coast of Puerto Rico.

"We never thought we'd have to go down a flight of steps in a bathyscaph," said Capt. Georges Houot. His asso-

ciate explorer, Lt. Gerard de Froberville, explained that the
steps were hewn by forces unknown from the solid rock face
of the continental shelf.

Nearly five miles of gigantic steps carved out of rocks
known to be 135 million years old—by "forces unknown"—
presents a mystery of staggering proportions. Some kind
of "security" lid was clamped on, and no further news releases or scientific reports were made.

If this turns out to be what it seems, we're in for some
startling reappraisals of our concept of history and of life
on our Earth . . . if, indeed, it *is* ours.

TEMPLES OF ATLANTIS OFF AMERICAN COAST

There is more evidence. When Edgar Cayce, the medical
clairvoyant from Virginia Beach said (in trance) in 1926
that the island of Bimini off the east coast of Florida was
one of the highest parts of the legendary Lost Continent of
Atlantis still left on the Earth, he also mentioned the Azores
and hinted at certain "temple building secrets of the Atlanteans."

In April, 1956, according to the Miami Herald, a father-
son scuba diving team, while searching for buried treasure
off the coast of Bimini, found the marble columns of a huge
ancient temple. Suddenly there was a hush-up job and the
principles became incommunicado.

This was reminiscent of those twin "cities of fable," Pompeii and Herculaneum, believed (by scholars and experts) to
be a myth or pure fantasy until they were discovered and
dug out of the volcanic ash of Mt. Vesuvius; but this was
on land, not under water.

For telling of these fabulous cities, the great astrologer
Herodotus earned himself the name, "Father of Liars," and
the title stuck for thousands of years. We moderns, who
are so impressed with our own technology, tend to dis-
count the great advancement of the civilizations of the Nile
and Chaldea—even of ancient America!

Now we *know* it is a geological fact that the Middle
East (and possibly a great portion of the rest of the world)
was once destroyed by water. The World Ages, in fact, are
reported in many divergent cultures (Peruvian and Hindu,
for example) to be separated by (a) storm and hurricane,
(b) flood or deluge, (c) earthquakes and volcanic eruptions,
and (d) fire. These are exactly coincident with the four "elements" of ancient astrology: Fire, Earth, Air and Water.

Therefore, if the last global devastation happened mostly by water, the next one should occur through fire. The evidence revealed by the very sciences which discredit such notions (anthropology, geology, and archeology), points to man's great antiquity and the truth of the legends concerning tremendous catastrophes. The American "Indian" supposedly knew nothing about elephants, but the Red Man has a tradition of hunting mammoth on the American continent—from the backs of camels!

We've seen how tropical mammoths were frozen by the thousands in Siberia and the Arctic. The skeletons of whales have also been found at the peaks of the highest mountains, so tremendous natural forces must have been at work.

PLANETS ON COLLISION COURSE

Dr. Immanuel Velikovsky, whose amazing ideas about planetary collisions caused a scientific furor in the 1950's, has lived to see himself vindicated in the mid-sixties by American and Russian space probes. If a global disaster occurred, it would cause great electrical discharges in the atmosphere—something on the order of high-power hydrogen bombs. This would change the planet's magnetic orientation and allow cosmic radiation to pour through on a scale which might even cause massive genetic mutation.

"The shifting of the axis," he said, "could not have been brought about by internal causes, as the proponents of the Ice Age Theory assumed it was. It must have occurred, and repeatedly, under the impact of external (extraterrestrial) forces." His conclusion is that "We are the descendants of survivors, themselves the descendants of survivors."

Some entire species were "weeded out" by the fierce competition for food in the aftermath of world destruction. The eyes of living men witnessed the raising of all the great mountain chains and the Great Rift of the African continent, according to the voluminous evidence compiled by Dr. Velikovsky. .

EARTH'S TRAGIC DISASTERS

Following these violent climatic changes, great earthquakes, and incessant tidal waves, multitudes of destitute, starving, disease-ridden, and half-mad human survivors must have wandered the globe in search of hospitable land. Only a handful could have survived these conditions; their suffering must be unmatched by anyone since then.

After several thousand years, all anyone could recall were legends of "mythical" greatness. Man turned to engineering, to the building of roads, to recapturing land from the sea, and constructing great dams and sluices. In the Alaskan muck, he found the splintered bones and tangled flesh of extinct animals in huge masses. In a Dutch village called Tegelen, beneath sand, silt, clay, wood, peat, and grape, diggers found the bones of elephants, horses, camels, hyenas, rhinoceroses and hippopotami, along with fresh water snails.

In Hawaii there is a beach 1200 feet above the present surface of the ocean! Coral cannot form anywhere except just under the surface of the sea. But on the island of Espirito Santo in the Hebrides, there are tremendous coral formations 1200 feet above sea level! This means that in comparatively recent times the ocean was well over a thousand feet higher than it is now.

Add to this the fact that there is no continuity between what we call the Middle and Late Bronze ages of human history. It takes a very long time for 12 inches of new ground to cover an old site, yet a layer of earth almost six feet thick interlards the remnants of these ages.

Geology tells us that Crete was devastated by two earthquakes within a 50-year period. At the same time, the cities of Egypt were swallowed up by earthquakes. Ancient Troy was completely rebuilt on six different occasions—and at least six times it was completely destroyed by massive earthquakes.

The barren strata of earth between the remains of every known civilization proved that an *abrupt* halt occurred. There was an end of all civilized or communal life, during which six feet of sediment accumulated. Ancient Jericho was destroyed time and time again, only to be rebuilt *on the same site* by new generations of men.

A Phoenician vase was found buried in the lava of the Sinai Peninsula, mute evidence of civilization exactly where stupendous volcanic eruptions took place. Today, there are no existing volcanoes in the area.

Etruscan vases, when pieced together, had a totally different magnetic orientation from that of the modern Earth which was thrown out of equilibrium not once or twice, but *many* times, the last time only a few thousand years ago. Each destruction of the Earth's surface was ubiquitous. World climatology changed cataclysmically and all ancient civilizations (regardless of their advancement) fell as one.

ANCIENT ASTROLOGERS WARNED OF DISASTER

Dr. Veliskovsky claims the last time it happened was shortly before the time of Christ. Now geologists are concluding
that the Sierras rose in the time of modern man—and not
gradually, but *suddenly!* During the Punic Wars (about 217
B.C.), almost 60 earthquakes hit the city of Rome. Great
meteors, comets, quakes, and erupting volcanoes seem to
have been far more numerous then than now. Thus, we can
piece together a fairly graphic picture of the *celestial environment* as reported by the astrologers of all surviving
nations. They were understandably nervous about cosmic
events and terrestrial consequences that were to follow.

Sudden geological upheavals seem to have attended the
end of every age; the irrefutable evidence is in the Earth's
mantle. Electrical currents swam over the land and heated
the rocks, which then acquired a reversed magnetism. The
intensity of this reversed polarity in some rock formations
is often 10 times stronger than the Earth's magnetism could
have produced.

Cambridge's Dr. S. K. Runcorn stated that "The Earth's
magnetism did reverse its field many times . . . North and
South geomagnetic poles reversed places several times . . .
the field would suddenly break up and reform with opposite
polarity."

The volcanic mountain chains in Japan are only *recently*
extinct. Those in the Pacific, the Andes in Peru, and the
Cotopaxi in Equador reached their present height in the
time of man. Ditto the Aleutians, the Kamchatka Peninsula, and the Kurile and Hawaiian Islands. Mauna Loa and
Kilauea are all that remain active of a great volcanic chain
—a cone built up from the depths of the ocean's floor *several miles down!*

THE CATASTROPHIC END OF THIS WORLD AGE

Only astrology, scientifically applied, can predict the time
of a future shift or tilt of the Earth. If the increasing
size of the icecaps cause the planet to wobble, we might
evacuate all coastal cities and detonate thermonuclear bombs
to melt them. All the great ports of the world would be
gone, but that's a better choice than losing the entire world
culture in one unexpected, catastrophic event.

Sooner or later, every known planet will form an adverse square, conjunction, or opposition (with respect to the Earth), with no beneficial angles to offset the catastrophe. Here then, is what happens:

The 25,000-mile-circumference of the Earth suddenly shifts and tilts. The globe shudders convulsively under a massive series of earthquakes and the planet stops rotating. But the atmosphere doesn't stop! *The oceans do not stop!* Through inertia, they continue moving at a rate of about 1,000 miles an hour. For a time, the elastic mantle, scores of miles thick, slips and slides, but when it snaps back to its former place, the atmosphere is filled with tens of thousands of roaring hurricanes, vast tornadoes, incredible twisters, cyclones, and presently unimaginable thunderstorms.

The oceans roar over the continents; mountains of sea water rake and devastate the highest mountains on Earth, depositing great marine animals in places that are quickly thrust high into the roiling atmosphere, including the corpses of whales, giant squid, sharks, and crustaceans.

Great heat develops within the Earth's core; the surface rocks melt as volcanoes rupture the planet like millions of boils. Molten rivers of lava roar forth to meet lakes, gulfs, and bays that are literally thrown out of their beds. Rivers change course radically, new mountains rise from the plains and oceans and stalk up the faces of other, older mountains.

The familiar Earth now becomes a shrieking, impossible bedlam of roaring destruction. All man's great works are wiped out. If there are high-flying satellites or spaceships on other worlds, the crews may survive, but there will be little or nothing to return to.

Large bodies of fresh water are thrown over and cascade into roaring forest fires which now become the new lakebeds—buried under hundreds of feet of sediment, sand, and gravel, are the twisted, torn shreds of men and animals alike. Great cities disappear; everything in them is destroyed in the first convulsion. The oceans rip up the land and reveal vast desert plains; the sea beds rise to become land masses.

Civilization is wiped out. Entire species of animals become extinct in the wink of an eye—some are boiled, some crushed, torn apart, smothered, or buried—all are gone.

Some manage to survive, somehow. But their suffering is inconceivable during the aftermath that lasts for years. Heat from volcanoes still erupting beneath the new oceans evaporate the seas, which rise in great, corruscating clouds of steam and fall all over the Earth as torrential rain, snow, and hail. Volcanic dust and debris is blasted into orbit around the devastated planet—possibly to float for centuries, like the rings of Saturn. Beneath all this, the Sun is blotted from view. Survivors do not know day from night, and many would freeze except for the planet's own body heat.

Down from the absolute zero of space, the moisture falls as huge hailstones and snow, but turns into a steaming inferno before reaching the ground. It is this heat from the Earth that causes a new Ice Age to envelop the Earth—not deep cold, as one would expect.

It takes decades, perhaps centuries, for this constant recycling of blizzard, thunderstorm, lightning, and cloudburst to cool the hot areas, for the planet to settle into an entirely new orbit and axis of inclination, and for the last dregs of life to cling to its last erg of courage and strength . . . and carry on.

The Earth quakes constantly for decades, volcanic eruptions occur everywhere almost hourly, all this internal, global adjustment gradually slowing down until—as in modern times—the quakes occur only when certain planetary arrangements trigger the sensitive points of the celestial compass.

There are new continents, oceans, islands, valleys, lakes, mountains, and rivers—a new geography. Life regathers its strength, the best of it, because that is what survived. But Intelligent Life gradually loses all memory of antediluvian ancestors and the great civilizations that once were. In a stone age culture, there is little time for remembering or for keeping records. Bare survival is the thing; Life must go on.

Incredible as it may seem, all this has probably happened before—many times!

Scientific Evidence of Antediluvian Culture

In 1964, the New China News Agency reported the discovery of the ruins of a large Chinese metropolis in Liaoning Province in Northeast (Communist) China. Archeologists said the city was constructed during the Han Dynasty which ruled China for a couple of centuries almost 3,000 years ago. For some unfathomable reason, the great city was completely abandoned. Like Pompeii, Herculaneum, and other such sites, its existence was regarded as mythological; even its alleged location was a total mystery for about 1500 years.

In 1939, the noted American archeologist, Professor Carl W. Blegen, discovered the remains of King Nestor's palace on the site of ancient Greece. From this point near Navarino

Bay, Nestor ordered his great armada against the glory that was Troy.

But 40 years afterward, the entire area was razed to the ground "in some mysterious fashion not known to us," wrote science writer, Dr. John Barkham.

That a schism existed between the World Ages was evidenced by the report of Sir Arthur Evans, the great British archeologist, *"scores of tablets in a totally undecipherable language,"* said Dr. Evans.

One would *expect* drastic changes in the written and spoken language over vast periods of time—or between two cultures separated by global cataclysm. The evidence of numerous gigantic catastrophes lies now in the mountains beneath oceans that once formed on land high in the atmosphere. In March, 1964, the northern tip of a new underseas mountain ridge was discovered and charted in the Pacific Ocean just south of Panama. The old legends of Lemuria re-emerged. The underwater massif is the top edge of a vast submarine mountain ridge that extends several thousand miles off the coast of South America and ends near the southern tip of Chile in the South Pacific. It is as big and broad as the Mid-Atlantic Ridge in the North Atlantic, according to spokesmen from the Scripps Institution of Oceanography and the U.S. Department of Commerce.

It is called the Galapagos Rise and is broken into huge segments by *East-West fracture zones* which still undergo many large submarine earthquakes, according to *Deep-Sea Research,* a British oceanographic magazine.

In his book *The Earth,* Harold Jeffreys states: "If we consider the axis of the Earth's angular momentum, this can change in direction only through *couples* acting on the outside." By "couples" he means two or more planetary bodies acting like tongs or pincers. His attitude is congruent with the theories of astrologers from Pythagoras and Democritus through Kepler and Newton.

Therefore, subjected to some great extraterrestrial torque, the Earth shifted, tilted—or flipped.

"What happened before can happen again," is the argument of mystics who perceive wisdom and logic in the idea of reincarnation. Thus, the fact that you were born into this life with a certain kind of horoscope is their greatest argument that it can happen again, and has probably happened before, according to the immutable Laws of Karma or Retribution.

A nation has a personality or will of its own, and its influence, however small, is felt by all other nations down through history—even if that nation's existence is subsequently denied.

CAN WE ALL BE DESTROYED?

If Karmic Law exists, as the evidence indicates, then the total extinction of *all* life forms in a final, universal catastrophe *is entirely out of the question*. Nature isn't without meaning. She does not create dead-end streets for her species.

That there are occasional global cataclysms (which we forget) only serves to illustrate some unknown, Fundamental Law by which only a few survive. It is science's job to seek out and discover the working of all natural laws—spiritual as well as physical.

By "science," we also mean *astrology*.

The United States:
A Mystical Heritage

13

Throughout every age in mankind's long history, astrologers have perceived Law and Order in the surrounding Universe; many have built or patterned great undertakings in harmony with natural astrology. This is particularly true of the birth of the United States—the greatest nation (despite its detractors from within and without) on the face of the planet. America is the most mystical nation on Earth and it was deliberately planned this way by our founding fathers, the colonial Freemasons.

THE GREAT SEAL OF THE UNITED STATES
OF AMERICA STORY

As a demonstration of this fact, you can receive from the United States Treasury Department a reprint from the Spring, 1952 issue of the magazine *Egypt* entitled "The Great Seal of the United States," written by Maury Maverick and explaining the true symbolism behind our American emblem. The Bureau of Engraving and Printing reflects the profound thinking and long-range planning of our founding fathers, those early American astrologers: Thomas Jefferson, Benjamin Franklin, and John Adams, who were appointed by the Continental Congress to supervise the striking of a distinctly American seal. Many of the members of this Congress were Masons of high degree who knew and practiced astrology. They employed these astrological principles to ensure that America would always be a peaceful yet militarily powerful nation.

This great esoteric seal was adopted by the Continental Congress on June 20, 1782 in Philadelphia. When they incorporated the Eagle (the fire bird or Phoenix symbol) and the Pyramid, an unbreakable link was forged between America and the ancient cultures of the Middle and Far East —Greece, Israel and Egypt.

Neither the Greeks nor Hebrews however, had a numerical system. They used the letters of their alphabets for mathematical and astrological calculations. This was called "gematria," from the Greek "geometria." Hence, the English noun, "geometry."

The great American seal (which, incidentally, was sent 135,000,000 miles into space when Mariner IV relayed its photographs of Mars in 1965), clearly indicates that no government that ignores or denies God can be truly American —nor can such a government exist for very long. Provided that America continues to recognize the existence of The Supreme Creator officially, it will continue to flourish and attract new states such as Puerto Rico, Guam, Cuba, and other Pacific Islands long after the present rulers of Russia, China, and other Communist nations have disappeared. Russia, as almost every astrologer knows, is destined to become the most spiritual or religious of nations—once Communism has run its course and a true democracy replaces Czarism and Communism.

Here, then, is the story behind the heraldry, mystery, and drama of the United States of America, as conceived by master astrologers—along with the occult message in our Great Seal. Each symbol in the American seal has profound significance and a definite *effect* on the national character.

THE FACE (OBVERSE) SIDE

The face (obverse) of the seal at the top signifies the Congress. The stripes on the Eagle's shield (the chief executive) represent the states of the Union. Blue is the color of the planet Earth, just as red is the color of Mars; the latter represents courage, strength, and aggressiveness, while blue symbolizes peace, vigilance, perseverance and justice. White equates to the highest aspirations and to temperance. All these qualities were decreed by law in the Act of 1782 and are incorporated in the colors of the American Seal and the American flag.

Each state is drawn toward the Chief (central Union) and helps to support it. The Eagle alone (representing the American government) supports the shield; therefore, America was meant to be self-supporting and to assist less fortunate nations of the world—even at times, our enemies.

E Pluribus Unum, the legend on the ribbon in the Eagle's beak, refers to the single nation formed by the 13 colonies ("Out of one, many"). The face of the Seal is dominated by the Eagle, ready for war because the left talon holds a bunch of arrows pointed upward. This fact signifies aim, purpose, and aspiration; the arrows are prepared for flight, thus indicating how swiftly America can gird for combat whenever necessary. But the Eagle's head is turned *away* from the arrows; it faces the *right* talon, which holds forth the olive branch of peace.

ANCIENT IDEALISM AND "LUCKY THIRTEEN"

Above the Eagle's head is a shining cloud encircled by 13 stars. The glow represents the Sun as the source of all life; the rays of light are symbols of glory, hope, and power. The (rain) cloud indicates the sustenance of Earthly life, and also stateliness and sublimity. The stars show universality and divine protection. This is the "Crown of Countless Ages," the reincarnation of an eternal ideal that once characterized Egypt, and perhaps even the legendary Lost Continent.

Despite the obvious fact that America happened to begin with thirteen colonies, there is a deep occult power behind this number; it is *not* "unlucky" as some medieval charlatans caused people to believe. The face of the American Seal shows 13 stripes on the shield, 13 stars in the circle of glory, 13 branches and 13 berries in the olive branch in the Eagle's right talon, 13 arrows in the left talon, and 13 letters in the legend, *E Pluribus Unum*.

None of this is coincidental! It was decreed by law that there must be a repetition of the number 13 in the seal's composition. Thus, the date (at the pyramid's base) was ordered to be engraved in Roman numerals (a total of nine) rather than Arabic. "Saeclorum" was made "Seclorum" on the scroll beneath the unfinished pyramid. This motto consisted of 17 letters. Altogether, there are 39 letters and numerals on the reverse of the Great Seal. This also has numerological significance, inasmuch as $3 + 9 = 12$, and $1 + 2 = 3$. Thus, 39 is merely three times 13.

THE REVERSE SIDE

Also, on the reverse side you will find 13 layers of stone in the unfinished pyramid. The legend, "Annuit Coeptis," contains 13 letters, corresponding to the 13 stripes in the American flag. According to Nora Forrest, one of the founders of the American Federation of Astrologers, "Our national birthright has been traced back to the 13th Tribe of Israel: and Manasseh was the head of this 13th tribe—to which the founders of the American dream belong." Thirteen also refers to Christ and His 12 disciples; to Buddha and his 12 apostles, and to Quetzalcoatl, god-king of the Aztecs and *his* 12 followers. Each of these Teachers, when numbered with their followers, totalled 13 in all.

During our Civil War, even though the Confederacy had only 11 states, their flag had 13 stars. General George Washington and 12 of his generals were Freemasons, and thus numbered 13. There are all kinds of odd, seemingly unrelated correlations in American history connected with the number 13. During the First World War, the first convoy to France was composed of 13 ships that sailed on June 13 (1917) and took 13 days to cross the Atlantic. Even President Woodrow Wilson's name had 13 letters.

At the exact time the Declaration of Independence was signed, the Sun was 13° in the Sign of Cancer.

INEXORABLE SIGNIFICANCE OF ASTRO-SYMBOLS

There's nothing accidental about any of this. "Thirteen harmonizes with the fundamental pattern in Nature," according to Nora Forrest. The Eagle (or Phoenix of ancient Egypt) and "13" both call for regeneration and transformation.

It happens that the Eagle is the highest form of the threefold nature of Scorpio; it is the only creature able to look directly into the Sun's dazzling brilliance. This triune nature of Scorpio is, at its lowest, the deadly scorpion, then the serpent (which represents wisdom), and finally the soaring Eagle, or Phoenix.

Scorpio in astrology and 13 in numerology have basically the same significance. Yet 13 is still considered bad luck because of backward, simple superstition. This superstition was considered fully proven when Judas betrayed

Christ (13 at the table), and is thus difficult to root out. It is so much a part of our culture that businesses kowtow to it; there are numerous hotels and office buildings in major American and European cities that have no 13th floor numbered as such—they actually skip from 12 to 14.

The Phoenix is that mythical firebird which represents the highest symbolic manifestation of our Earthly existence. In modern symbology, the Eagle is often pictured with a flame rising from its head or a flame *over* its head; this is merely our modern version of the ancient Egyptian Phoenix, the bird that rises anew out of its own ashes. It represents the endless continuity and eternal nature of the Life Force. Because of this, the most learned occultists have accepted America as the spirit of ancient Egypt reborn.

Aspiring to heights far beyond the physical or grossly material, the Eagle symbolizes the upward flight of Man's evolution, just as, in actual fact, the eagle soars to tremendous heights far beyond the range of human vision, even as our "space birds" are now doing.

This great bird has been pictured by various nations and tribes in history *without* the olive branch—or with arrows clutched in its *right* talon. Our colonial Freemasons did not duplicate the heraldry of Ancient Rome (or Hitler's Germany) in this respect. These astrologers knew that the New Order of the Ages could not be built upon force, aggression, war, or conquest, but only upon reason, good will, and (despite all appearances and arguments) upon peace, the last of which is absolutely essential to the realization of America's great destiny—her great dream.

NAPOLEON BONAPARTE'S STRANGE PROPHECY

An illustration of the potential power and wealth of the United States occurred in a prophetic statement by none other than Napoleon at a time when the central one-third of the present continental United States was part of his French Empire.

This great region, the Louisiana Territory, was called "New France" on the emperor's maps in the Tuileries. Napoleon had no intention of losing it to England, against whom he was fighting in Europe. But he desperately needed money to wage this war. So he sold us the territory of New France for a mere $15,000,000—*an area the size of India.*

But Napoleon had some misgivings: "This enlargement of its territory," he said ruefully, "consolidates the power of the United States for all time. Perhaps people will reproach me in two or three centuries when the Americans become too powerful for Europe, but I cannot take so distant a possibility into my calculations . . ."

This is a remarkable prophesy that highlights America's adherence to the tradition and symbolism of its Great Seal. We subsequently purchased the vast territory of Alaska for $7 million; we became immensely wealthy through peaceful dealings and reciprocity. But we have *never* profited or gained new territory through warfare. America has *never* plundered its former enemies as do other nations. Instead, we have always given vanquished foes a hand. America has always attempted to right whatever wrongs it feels it has committed, and so have those nations which are strongly influenced by the U.S.

The reverse side of the Great Seal was all but completely ignored by heraldry experts for 150 years. Congress made two laws, one in 1792 and the other in 1884 to omit the reverse side, but neither was ever fulfilled. The design was new, revolutionary, and truly American in composition, yet it had substantial parts of the Egyptian background, including the pyramid. On July 4, 1776, following the adoption of the Declaration of Independence, astrologers Jefferson, Adams, and Franklin were appointed to design the Great Seal.

It was Thomas Jefferson who advanced the mystical ideals of Egyptian history; then the committee decided the seal should have two sides. Today, America has the only two-sided seal in existence.

OUR ORDERED DESTINY

In 1935, for the first time, both sides of the Great Seal were printed on one-dollar bills when they were reduced in size and went into general circulation. The pyramid on the reverse symbolizes the strength and permanence of the new union and emphasizes that it was built with great care and patience. It was left unfinished after the thirteenth tier— a symbol of the fact that many new states would come to join the union. The four-sided pyramid also represents *matter*. Above the unfinished structure floats the white triangular capstone within which is the All-Seeing Eye, the emblem of Spirit.

The task of modern America is to unite spiritual development with material abundance—to establish the first Spiritualized Material Order of modern times. We've come a long way toward this goal. Our early history saw the land settled, a burgeoning agriculture and industry that accumulated vast wealth at a fantastic pace. Materialism on such a scale reached its zenith in America before it did in any other nation on Earth.

Our next step is to build a spiritualized material order, a fact already in evidence due to new, humanitarian (Aquarian Age) awareness of our evolutionary spiral upward. We are scientifically approaching the sure knowledge that matter and energy (or matter and Spirit) are merely opposite poles of the same reality. This strengthens the probability of America's Ascendant being a symbol of duality.

On the Great Seal, the motto above the capstone of the pyramid, *Annuit Coeptis* is translated: "He (God) favors our undertaking." And the motto on the scroll beneath the pyramid, *Novus Ordo Seculorum* means "A new order of Ages." When the Constitution, bylaws, and emblems were adopted, they followed the mystic Masonic-astrological patterns.

PRESIDENTS DIE—AND THE PATTERN REMAINS UNBROKEN

In his New York Daily News feature "Broadway" (October 8, 1942), the late Danton Walker devoted his entire column to predictions based upon the national seal and on its astrological significance. "The ancient triangle which had symbolized so many religio-political ideas," he wrote, "was used in building the time pattern. This trine, or triangle translated into the symbology of the Zodiac—the source of all Masonic emblems and rituals—makes a four-month interval of the 12-month year. This was believed to work out more harmoniously than other intervals. Hence, the American birthday, July 4, *is followed by two equally important dates:* The first Tuesday after the first Monday in November, when the nation elects its ruler, *and March 4, when this ruler takes office—or did until the last inaugural.*

"This triangular pattern, strictly followed from the very birth of our nation, *was completely changed* by moving the Inauguration Day from March 4 to January 20. This broke the ancient Masonic triangle and was the opening political wedge into the Aquarian pattern, since about that date (January 20) the Sun enters the Sign of Aquarius. Significantly enough, its first usage was to bring into office a

Aquarian President, Franklin Delano Roosevelt, who was born January 30.

FDR TRIES TO BREAK THE CYCLE

"This President, both from choice and from the necessities of his time, has changed one basic Constitutional law or precedent after another, the most outstanding so far being the acceptance of a third term of office and the attempted alteration of the Supreme Court. The New Deal is a forerunner of the Aquarian Age for this country, aiming at greater freedom for all and a *true democracy*, but if we had not elected Roosevelt, we would have chosen someone else fitting into the Aquarian pattern, for *Roosevelt is merely an instrument of destiny*. Wendell Willkie is also an Aquarian . . . other Aquarians who figure largely in the present picture are John L. Lewis, General Douglas MacArthur, Undersecretary of the Navy James Forrestal, General George Brett, Admiral John H. Towers and Roosevelt's confidential adviser, Justice Samuel Rosenman. The most outstanding Aquarian in American history was Abraham Lincoln, born February 12 . . ."

Almost everyone now knows of the strangely inexorable pattern formed by Jupiter and Saturn in conjunction (in "Earth" Signs) that coincides with the death of American presidents in office every 20 years. FDR had access to astrological and other occult intelligence, some of it through Louis de Wohl, a famous astrologer of the time. It is believed by many who claim to know that he changed the date of the Presidential Inaugural from March 4 to January 20 in an attempt to break this pattern and save his own life.

That he did not break the cycle is a matter of history. Both Roosevelt and John F. Kennedy knew of the tragic pattern. In fact, a veteran wire service reporter on the scene in Dallas on November 22nd, 1963, made brief notice of the fact that former Vice President Nixon was departing Dallas as the Kennedy cavalcade arrived. Fate seemed to have ordained that both men find some reason to be in Dallas on that date. The newsman reported that the President was heard to remark: "I'm going to beat this cycle."

That *he* did not break the cycle is a matter of history. President Kennedy often seemed preoccupied with the idea of his own early, tragic death.

THE FANTASTIC LINCOLN-KENNEDY "COINCIDENCES"

On the cold Washington night of January 20, 1960, after his inauguration, John F. Kennedy slept peacefully (and fatefully) in the bed of Abraham Lincoln, an act that may have been prompted by an unbreakable bond of destiny spanning a century and connecting the lives of these unusual men. An uncanny series of "coincidences" between the lives and deaths of the 16th and 35th Presidents of the United States may have been made much of, but they certainly cannot be shrugged off or dismissed casually.

Each man seems to have fulfilled his life pattern within the horoscopic destiny of the United States. Kennedy was America's first Catholic President and also its first Gemini-born President.

Both Lincoln and Kennedy were in their thirties when they married pretty, 24-year-old brunettes who spoke French fluently. Lincoln had a secretary named Kennedy who advised him not to attend the theatre; Kennedy had a secretary named Lincoln who advised him not to go to Dallas.

Lincoln had a cousin who became a U.S. Senator, and another cousin who was mayor of Boston. Another relative, Levi Lincoln, was a Harvard graduate who became U.S. Attorney General. Robert Lincoln, the President's son, was minister to London for four years.

John F. Kennedy's relatives held similar positions in government. Teddy Kennedy was a U.S. Senator from Massachusetts; Bobby Kennedy (*also* a Harvard graduate) was Attorney General and U.S. Senator from New York; John Kennedy's grandfather was Mayor of Boston; and his father was ambassador to London.

Both Presidents were elected to Congress in '47 (a century apart). Both men competed for Vice Presidential nominations (also a century apart) in '56. The campaigns of Lincoln and Kennedy were marked by dramatic debates. Lincoln with Stephen A. Douglas and Kennedy with Richard M. Nixon.

President Lincoln was elected in 1860. President Kennedy in 1960. Both were deeply involved with the Negro problem and civil rights. Both men were shot in the back of the head—and in the presence of their wives. Both men died on a Friday.

The successors to each President were Southerners named Johnson, and both Johnsons had served in the Senate. Andrew Johnson was born in 1808. Lyndon Johnson was born in 1908. John Wilkes Booth was a malcontent born in 1839; Lee Harvey Oswald, also a malcontent, was born in 1939. Both assassins were assassinated before going to trial.

President Lincoln's wife and President Kennedy's wife each lost children while in the White House. Booth shot Lincoln in a theatre and fled to a warehouse. Oswald shot Kennedy from a warehouse—and fled into a theatre. The full names of both assassins contain 15 letters.

The names of the succeeding Vice Presidents, Andrew and Lyndon Johnson, each have *thirteen* letters.

New Worlds Are Born—
Mass Consciousness
Changes

14

THEOREM: *Newly formed planets are discovered by all intelligent races within the system soon after they come into existence.*

Due to a speed-up of the space race, new astrological facts are being discovered with increasing frequency. We've shown that the Moons of Mars were seen (probably with telescopes) by astrologers during Biblical times—from 2700–3600 years ago—and it is well-known that Aztec astrologers had telescopes. On the other hand, if *all* ancient astronomers had developed high telescopic power, they would undoubtedly have known of the three outer planets: Uranus, Neptune, and Pluto. But there is no hint anywhere among ancient records that the existence of these distant bodies *was* known of, or even vaguely suspected. Like Venus, they seem to have been nonexistent prior to about 1500 B.C.

We must consider therefore, that the three "outer" planets *may not have existed* as integral parts of the solar system! Even modern astronomers didn't know about Pluto until 1930. Yet it must have been out there for centuries—if not millennia—but certainly not for billions (or even millions) of years.

It isn't simply coincidence that astrologers associate those things which happened or were in vogue at the time of the *discovery* of Pluto with the planet itself. The atomic age was born at about the time Pluto was found. Organized crime in the U.S. and abroad was rampant in 1930; groups and group activity was growing wildly in those days. Hitlerism was on the rise, and a showdown was germinating between the forces of capitalism and Communism . . . *a showdown that still hasn't reached its climax!*

TELEPORTATION TO THE OUTER PLANETS

An unknown, undiscovered planet existed beyond Neptune then. Appropriately, this most remote world was named after Pluto, the "mythical" god of the dark underworld. Coincidentally, the initials of Percival Lowell, the early American astronomer who predicted the existence of "Planet X" beyond Neptune's orbit, coincided with the first two letters of Pluto. The ligature ♇ is one of the symbols for this frigid, distant planet.

Either lunar observatories or an orbiting satellite in space will give us the answers to many of the mysteries surrounding the outer planets. It will begin in a few years and last until about 2009, when an entirely new, instantaneous method of transporting massive physical objects through space will be devised . . . like telecasting a TV picture on a light beam.

Between now and then, our rocket-launching bases will extend from Mars to the Moons of Saturn (Ganymede being the most likely), and from this point, fully automated or even manned spacecraft will land on Pluto, whose atmosphere must lie whitely frozen on its barren, rocky mantle (the Sun appearing as a bright, alien star).

Pluto is considered by most astrologers to be the ruler of Scorpio, which signifies Sex, Death, and Regeneration (or Transmutation). Considering Pluto's known astrological characteristics and significance, there must now be two more planets far beyond Pluto, their orbital periods measured in the thousands of years! These are probably the true rulers of Gemini and Taurus. Non-luminous bodies so far out cannot be seen by the most powerful Earth-based telescopes—even through our transparent atmosphere.

This double-assignation of planets to Signs is still manifested by Mercury and Venus; Mercury is now considered the co-ruler of Gemini and Virgo while Venus is believed to "rule" both Taurus and Libra. Until the discovery of Pluto, astrologers considered Mars as the ("lower octave") manifestation of Scorpio; yet Mars co-ruled Aries *and* Scorpio.

Until Neptune's discovery in 1846, Jupiter was the co-ruler of Sagittarius and Pisces. A pronounced change occurred in the mass human consciousness directly following 1846. This was the germination of socialist ideals formulated by Karl Marx in 1849 (which has divided the world). Since then, Jupiter has been the lower-octave manifestation of Pisces and the *true* ruler of Sagittarius. The same thing occurred after 1741 when another basic change in human consciousness was detected by astrologers directly following the discovery of Uranus. Until then, Saturn was considered the co-ruler of Capricorn and Aquarius. Today, Saturn is recognized in astrology as a lower-octave manifestation of Aquarius and the *true* ruler of Capricorn. Uranus is the ruler of Aquarius because the influence of both the planet and the Sign have been observed to convey the same characteristics.

SEX, DEATH AND TRANSMUTATION

Pluto is now almost universally accepted as the sole ruler of Scorpio. A peculiar physical characteristic of Pluto is its occasional passage *inside* the orbit of Neptune. During these perigee (or perihelion) transits, Pluto is closer to the Earth than is Neptune. For this reason, it is considered by many renowned scientists, including Drs. R. A. Lyttleton, G. P. Kuiper, and W. Rabe, to be an escaped satellite of Neptune. Others think it wandered into the solar system and was alternately captured and lost by Neptune or the entire mass of the solar system.

Since Pluto's discovery, few astrologers consider Mars even as a "co-ruler" of Scorpio, which in its lower (Scorpion) expression has long been associated with ruthlessness and self-destruction through physical excesses. There is also a symbolic link between Scorpio, the underworld (gangsterism), secrecy, explosive power, poisonous extremes, and indefatigable strength.

Scorpio loves mystery. But on a higher plane, this Sign can produce great research scientists, occultists, and probers of the deepest mysteries of life and of the mass subconscious. The groups associated with the recent Scorpio-born are no longer the gangster or criminal type. You do often find them in secret societies, however. They tend to express mystification at the miracle of birth, death, and resurrection (or transmutation) through sex. To one born strongly under Scorpio, the physical environment presents many imponderables. Evolved, he often discovers the existence of an Ultimate Intelligence or Guiding Force in the universe.

Physically, Pluto, the new ruler of Scorpio was thought to be comparatively small—only 3,600 miles in diameter, or less than half the size of the Earth—with a mean temperature of about *minus* 360° Farenheit! Sunlight reflected by Pluto varies periodically by a ratio of about 10 percent.

These factors are becoming increasingly important to scientific astrologers of the space age.

That Pluto may *not have existed* only 3600 years ago seems a rather wild assumption, but we're in the process of discovering many startling facts about our celestial environment. Scientific discoveries are occurring at such a rapid pace that time itself seems to have accelerated.

Radio astronomy, still in its infancy, is already revealing data we couldn't have imagined a mere 20 years ago. A man named Seyfert discovered a new kind of radio "star." For a while, these huge objects far out in space were named after him. Now they're called *quasars*—the most distant, the brightest, most violent, heaviest and most puzzling sources of light and intense radio waves in the universe! The power given off by a quasar is 100 times the total energy output of an entire giant galaxy of stars, and yet a quasar is only one-sixth the size of the average galaxy.

We are now taking close-up pictures of the Moon, Mars, and Venus. The World Horoscope, preserved by the Hindus, who have preserved the oldest records of man in existence, points inevitably to the fact that the surrounding universe is densely inhabited by all kinds of intelligent life forms. Some of these are more advanced than we could even imagine at our present stage of development. Some scientists already realize that we might not even *recognize* alien life or intelligence when we confront it! They are trying to prepare future explorers for every conceivable eventuality.

UNEXPLAINED MYSTERIES OF VENUS, JUPITER, AND MARS

Back in the 1940s, Dr. Immanuel Velikovsky was classified as a crank simply because he claimed that both Mars and Venus once made very close passes at the Earth, and that Venus was a *comet* between 2700 and 3600 years ago, before settling into its present stable planetary orbit. The thing that really shocked The Experts however, was Velikovsky's statement that Venus had been ejected from the gas body of the giant planet Jupiter!

Jupiter has a huge, mysterious Red Spot, and Venus' temperature and chemical composition are (a) exactly as high and (b) exactly as complex as Velikovsky predicted they would be. According to Dr. Gordon H. Pettengill of Cornell University, the world's largest dish-shaped antenna near Arecibo, Puerto Rico, proves that Venus is the only major planet that spins on its axis in a *clockwise* motion! All the other inner planets rotate in the same direction they revolve around the Sun—in a *counter*clockwise motion. Mariner IV proved (again as Velikovsky predicted in the 40's) that Mars has astroblemes—craters like our Moon—thus attesting to the catastrophism (catastrophes) he deduced from ancient records.

Venus, like the Earth and other planets, is a sort of "magnetic comet" with a tail stretching for millions (perhaps billions) of miles on the side opposite the Sun. This proves that astrological conjunctions have a measurable effect on earthly life and on natural phenomena, just as astrologers have always claimed.

Astronomers however, mistakenly believed that Mercury always showed the same face to the Sun, as the Moon does to the Earth. They were convinced that Mercury rotated only once in 88 days, the same interval it takes to revolve once around the Sun. Cornell's Arecibo Ionospheric Observatory cleared that up, too. Actually, Mercury rotates once every 58 days, therefore its "day" is about 46 days long. Venus rotates clockwise in 247 days; it is also hot, and has mountainous regions. Echoes of radio waves bounced off Venus in June, 1964, were *twice* as strong as those bounced off our own Moon!

Astronomers recently learned that Pluto is far bigger than they had previously believed. "Measurements of changes in the sunlight reflected from Pluto have shown the planet's light increases for about four days, then drops in about two days," according to *Science News Letter*.

This is a new and inexplicable phenomena concerning Pluto—providing eminently useful data for future calculations of Pluto's astrological effects. This outermost-known planet rotates once on its axis in 6 days, 9 hours, 16 minutes, and 54 seconds, "with a possible error of plus or minus a minute," said Dr. Robert H. Hardie, using the 24-inch telescope at Vanderbilt University's Dyer Observatory in Nashville. He concludes that *Pluto is much bigger than the Earth itself,* thus neatly demolishing the theory of many astronomers that Pluto is merely a tiny, almost insignificant (escaped) satellite of Neptune.

THE GIANT OF THE SOLAR SYSTEM
AND THE NEAR-DESTRUCTION OF EARTH

Only the Russians have claimed any success with bouncing radio waves from the surface of Jupiter. Dr. David

Morris, a radio astronomer at Caltech's Owens Valley Radio Observatory, reported that the magnetic poles of Jupiter are extraordinarily far to one side of the axis about which the huge planet rotates every ten hours. This causes the 300,000-mile-in-diameter radiation belt of Jupiter to wobble erratically as the planet rotates. The magnetic poles of the Earth are in the Arctic and Antarctic regions, close to the geographic North and South polar caps.

Because Jupiter's magnetic poles are so far from its axis of rotation, it seems as though the giant planet received a tremendous "kick" at some time during its history. Due to some unknown celestial imbalance or torque (that upset the entire solar system), Jupiter long ago ejected a planet-size chunk of gaseous matter from its atmosphere which then performed an exaggerated ellipse around the entire planetary system and made several close passages to the Earth and Mars.

Mars, affected by the change in much the same way that atomic particles leave their orbits during bombardment or chemical changes, slipped out of its orbit and headed for the Earth. Only the close passage of the great comet Venus saved the Earth (and probably Mars as well) from total annihilation.

The atmospheres of all bodies, including our Moon, intermingled—with the result that each planet still retains traces of gases we know are in the atmospheres of the other planetary bodies. The Moon clearly shows how it was devastated by meteoric debris.

The ejection of a planet-sized mass from Jupiter's atmosphere as reported by Velikovsky is evidenced by the scar it left; the great Red Spot could easily be the turbulence still existing in the Jovian atmosphere due to the ejection of Venus.

Velikovsky's data was taken from eye-witnesses who wrote the ancient records, from archeology, geology, and the sacred writings of all the world's people, including the Old Testament. Because of this unorthodox approach, his theories of catastrophism were dismissed as nonsense and Lyall's Uniformism was largely upheld. Practically every scientist who exposed himself to Velikovsky's radical theories was previously convinced that the ancient peoples of this planet were idiots, savages, or just plain ignorant about almost everything.

NEW EVIDENCE FOR THE RECENT FORMATION
OF THE OUTER PLANETS

"Since the ancients were so advanced," they asked, "where are their records of the planets beyond Saturn?"

Uranus was discovered in 1781 by Sir William Herschel; Neptune, independently co-discovered in 1846 by Leverrier and Adams, and Pluto, not found until 1930, were never mentioned in any ancient cuneiform tablet, rock carving, or papyrus now in existence.

If these planets did not exist in ancient times, then clearly no records of them could possibly exist either . . . not even if ancient scientists had telescopes as powerful as our own.

Based on new scientific evidence, it is my contention here that they *did not* exist!

Dr. Fred L. Whipple, director of the Smithsonian Astrophysical Observatory at Cambridge, claims that the three most distant known planets (as well as hundreds of comets) were once part of a gigantic "snow storm" 50 to 60 times as wide as the distance from the Earth to the Sun—covering an area of over four and one half billion square miles! Dr. Whipple dropped the following revolutionary bombshell at a Denver symposium on unmanned exploration of the solar system:

"As the huge hot cloud of gas surrounding the already-formed inner planets condensed," he said, "it began to cool, freezing first one element and then another into solids. Iron and similar elements formed dust, after which hydrogen and other gases turned into frozen vapors or snow." The resulting snow storm, 200 times the mass of the Earth, may have been almost six billion miles across. Dr. Whipple believes the snow and dust condensed into solid lumps of "dirty ice," and that the three largest lumps became huge planets and the rest comets!

Stars and other huge objects that powerfully influence Earthly life often suddenly explode for no understandable reason. Sometimes these bodies seem to "appear" almost as if from nothing, though it is now fashionable for scientists to accept the Big Bang theory of creation rather than the Steady State Theory put forth by Dr. Fred Hoyle in the 1950's.

Stars become nova or supernova and expand in titanic explosions . . . even entire galaxies of billions of stars are known to explode at once. It is therefore, well within the realm of established knowledge that the three outer planets of the solar system may not have been formed prior to the year 1500 B.C.!

Eye-witness records gathered from all over the world state that all the planets once left their courses, that Venus was torn out of Jupiter's "head," that Mars attacked the Earth, and that the Earth and Moon were devastated. The whole chronology and astrology of the world had to be recalculated.

It is conceivable, therefore, that the birth of these three outer planets could very well have been the *cause* of the violent readjustment of the solar system!

The cataclysmic end of the last World Age could well have been the result of Dr. Whipple's "snow storm."

Cosmic Freedom for
Your Will

15

When *African Genesis,* was published, some critics were appalled as were the Uniformists when *they* first heard of Velikovsky's Catastrophism. Author Robert Ardrey took a long hard look at Man and concluded that *"he (Man) is a predator whose natural instinct is to kill with a weapon."*

He did not say "reason." He did not say "judgment." His conclusion, like that of the late, great Ernest Heminway, was absolutely right—*as far as it went.* We *are* largely governed by our emotions and instincts—but not all of us, and not all the time. In many cases there is just as valid an argument for Free Will among animals as there is for "instinct" among men.

All species (even insects) *must* be able to communicate on a broader scale than we have hitherto suspected. Wide scientific studies are now going on. To convey a message, the higher vertebrates can use gestures, snorts, facial expressions, and many differences of body stance, each of which can speak volumes. Dr. Margaret Altmann of the University of Colorado, on a three-year Science Foundation grant, spent a lot of time in the rugged wilderness above the timberline around Moran, Wyoming. "With the means available to them," she wrote, "animals are able to manifest a wide range of tolerance, ingratiation, alienation, and aggression." Gorillas and baboons (and men) regard a direct, prolonged stare as a threat. When almost any species meet in passing, the smallest or weakest is the first to avert its gaze. To look directly into the other's eyes is a direct challenge. Most males "instinctively" know that you don't stare into the eyes of the stranger across the bar—especially if he is a big tough-looking hombre.

The point is simply that we take Free Will entirely too much for granted. No doubt we have some area of free choice, but objectively speaking, how much broader is it than the free choice of animals? We share with them all the influences of the surrounding *total environment;* we just happen to be more sensitive to it. There are certain fixed depths beyond which certain fish do not swim—from giant squid to tiny sardines to plankton, the basic building block of all marine life. It applies to birds in the skies and insects which always try to come to rest facing one of the four cardinal points of the compass: they *cannot* do otherwise. A high-speed electronic digital computer *must* (by its very construction) do the job it is *programmed* to do. It cannot decide to become an analog computer. The element of what we call "chance" is non-existent. Now, considering your genetic background, your social and economic environment (which can be determined by a good astrologer from your birth data), and given all pertinent facts, the laws which govern each of us can be predicted with fantastic accuracy.

"INSTINCT," "FATE," OR "FREE WILL?"

From the evidence we intend to show, there *is* a powerful case to be made of the fact that unless you *know* what your Life Pattern reveals, you haven't much more freedom of choice than a single fish in a school. What we do have is the *potential* to guide our own destinies *completely*.

In Chapter One we showed some amazing "coincidences." There are hundreds of thousands more we've been unable to cover. One other tragic example is that of George A. Blunden, Jr. and Douglas Fillebrown, who were both born in the same year, month, date, hour, and close to the same minute in the same state (Portsmouth and Gorham, N.H., on November 13, 1944). On June 22, 1964, a fire broke out in a three-story Phi Kappa Alpha fraternity house at the University of New Hampshire. A dozen young men scrambled to safety—but not George Blunden nor Doug Fillebrown. Inexplicably, both burned to death at the same time. Was this predestined? Could it have been predicted or prevented? What science other than astrology can explain why these "Astro-Twins" were attracted to the same University? Why did they choose the same fraternity? Why did they *have* to be in the same fraternity house at the exact time it burned down? Why were they the *only* ones who didn't escape?

Like frontiersmen or jungle scouts in the dark, we're going

to try to perceive something here by looking *around* it instead of directly *at* it.

In London, 78-year-old retired engineer, Henry Marsh, tried to commit suicide. He fired five bullets into his head; two missed, but three lodged deep in his skull. He remained conscious. "I don't understand," he said to the constable who found him, "I shot myself five times and I've still not finished the job."

Three days later, Henry Marsh died—*of a respiratory infection!* He probably would have died on the date he did whether or not he'd shot himself five times in the head!

What of the many strange, unexpected, and often freak ways in which people meet with accidents—and death? Americans are so accustomed to the ever-increasing statistics of highway fatalities that all we do is tally the score during week-ends and holidays.

Still, there are unexplainable cases that cannot be written off as "unforeseeable accidents." What mysterious connection can there possibly be between the man who dies of a heart attack and the people he takes with him? This is exactly what happened when 65-year-old Earl C. Russell of Jersey City, N.J. stopped for a red light. He displayed all the symptoms of suffering another heart attack. His wife got out and hurried around to the driver's side to search his pocket for the prescribed heart pills he always carried —*a fateful move on her part.* Before she could reach him, Russell collapsed and his foot solidly rammed the gas pedal. The car roared forward, caromed off the side of another car and crushed Mrs. Bernice Kelly of Park Forest, Illinois, against a lamppost. She was killed instantly.

Russell's car veered off again and crashed into Mrs. Helen Meyering of Chicago, who was violently thrown 20 feet through the air. Her body slammed into a building. She died shortly afterward. 36-year-old Cynthia Augustine was then struck (non-fatally) by the driverless car, and the vehicle finally came to a stop when it rammed a telephone booth in which a young man was making a call. Mrs Kelly was 59, Mrs. Meyering 64; both were killed in the same way and on the same day. Mrs. Russell was not injured, nor was the man in the booth. Miss Augustine suffered only leg injuries.

What strange fate called Mrs. Meyering from Chicago and Mrs. Kelly from Park Forest at exactly that time and place to meet their deaths at the hands of a total stranger from a distant state who perished with them?

If this was not an instance of Reincarnation and the Law

of Retribution as some believed, it was at least a case astrologers could have foreseen—*if both women had consulted an astrologer before traveling from Illinois to New Jersey.*

EXPLOSION, FIRE, AND VENOMOUS REPTILES

Mars figures prominently in the horoscopes of those who die suddenly, especially by metal or machinery. Mars has to do with violence, explosions, machinery, and fire.

Consider the case of 51-year-old Albert Koda, the driver of a truckload of 26,000 pounds of explosive nitro-carbonirate and 4000 pounds of dynamite. On June 26, 1965, as he drove along Route 209 in Pennsylvania, two right tires blew out at the same time. Coincidence? Koda pulled off the road and parked alongside a lot in front of a reptile farm a few miles south of the Pocono Mountain resort town of Marshall's Creek. Since the blowouts happened at night, Koda unhitched the tractor and went to sleep. He awoke before dawn and went for help, he told state police, and there was no fire when he left. Koda was on the phone talking to his boss when a mighty blast shook the earth for miles around.

The explosion instantly erased six human lives, injured at least ten more, destroyed a $300,000 school building, did $200,000 more damage, broke windows in a 2-mile radius, dug a deep crater where the truck had been standing, and killed hundreds of snakes and other reptiles. At least a hundred more snakes were released, some poisonous, and all had to be accounted for by police.

Those who died in the blast were three volunteer firemen who were hooking up hoses to fight the fire that had started, a truck driver who had stopped to help, a woman riding by in a station wagon, and a vacationing schoolteacher.

Was this just another tragic "accident"—or was there some kind of order, pattern, and inevitability to these events?

All these people had something in common, and their horoscopes, if examined thoroughly before the event, must have clearly revealed the incident.

"THRESHER" DISASTER PREDICTED

The foregoing is not mere conjecture. Astrologer Olive A. Pryor, a mundane specialist who set up a chart for the exact time of the launching of the nuclear submarine

Thresher, told her class of student astrologers in New York that unless something could be done quickly to warn the Navy, the sub was doomed and all seamen aboard would drown in extremely deep water. When the news of the *U.S.S. Thresher*'s tragedy was announced, she set up another chart for the exact moment the last message had been received.

Although she knew absolutely nothing about mechanics or machinery, let alone the intricate electrical or wiring set-up aboard a nuclear submarine, Mrs. Pryor not only interpreted the same information later revealed by the Navy's deep-diving bathyscaph, but claimed it was *sabotage,* done by a workman who rigged a tiny, electrical boobytrap device amidships that went undetected until the *Thresher's* deepest dive.

CAN WE PREVENT IMPENDING DISASTER?

Astrologers are not certain if the trends they foresee are actual events—or if they *will* occur exactly as anticipated. But the *timing* of large events is a practical certainty. The thing is, can we *prevent* the things we foresee? And the answer to that, of course, is that we just don't know yet. There doesn't seem to be any foolproof method of determining whether you've sidestepped a predicted disaster, because if you do, who is to say whether the disaster may *not* have happened after all? This is the argument of logicians, and there's something to it.

But whatever degree of free choice is given to us should be used to its fullest—and it can be enhanced by the judicious use of astrology. You have a wider range of free choice if you use astrology than if you don't.

Few of us know exactly what to expect at any given moment. Life would be infinitely more complex if we did. The unexpected, the "not-knowing," is part of our interesting existence. Without the element of uncertainty, much of the spice of life would be gone. There'd be no more sporting contests, no gambling, no stock market speculation or other forms of "chance"-taking—if there *is* such a thing. But if we live in an ordered universe of immutable Law, then things are generally mapped out for us—including your reading this paragraph at *this* moment in time. It is entirely possible that you have already received the sense of it.

Strange and wonderful things happen which can often be looked back upon as the inexorable, inevitable outgrowth of everything that preceded them—including the character and personality of those to whom the events occur. The successful prediction should be the *rule*, not the exception. Inevitability is one of the basic ingredients of fiction, as any writer will tell you.

Without a sense of the inevitable in a story, the reader feels cheated. Since fiction is but a reflection of life, a given character reacting in a certain environment results in an *inevitable* outcome. So it is with each of us in our own lives.

You *do* have free will and freedom of choice—but only within the limits defined by your sex, intelligence, heredity, and environment, and these can be determined by a detailed analysis of your horoscope. Everything in your life, therefore, seems to be subservient to the fact of the time and place of your birth.

The natal chart reveals these things to the practiced eye and mind of the scientific astrologer.

"ACCIDENTAL" DEATH BY A FALLING BODY OR OBJECT

A vacationing American girl in Paris looked up at the Eiffel Tower and saw a woman's body hurtling directly toward her; she was petrified—rooted to the spot in a kind of horrified fascination. The leaper was a Frenchwoman committing suicide. Her body slammed into the American tourist, and both were instantly killed. This was not planned, nor was it an accident or a "coincidence."

A group of large American life insurance companies are conducting an exhaustive computer study of scores of thousands of cases of the possible relationship between human longevity and the *astrological* Sun-Sign at birth. It is only a matter of time, then, before the entire horoscopes of people involved in violent accidents will be carefully compared, and some startling conclusions that will affect all our lives will be made. In advance of these conclusions, I would like to point out that it would be a folly to use the information thus gained purely for financial advantage. There's much more to these laws than mere physical cause-effect, as I will attempt to show at the conclusion.

In New York City, Frances Levin, a secretary who was watching police arrest three men for disorderly conduct in Times Square during her lunch hour, was prompted to move directly beneath a spot where, seconds later, a three-foot window pole fell from a ninth-floor office window and imbedded itself in her skull. Some of it was sawed off as she lay on the sidewalk waiting for the rescue squad ambulance. Doctors at the hospital then removed three inches of hook and wood from her head. Her condition was critical—paralysis of the right side of her body and extensive brain damage.

Here was a tragedy that *might* have been averted if an astrologer could have warned her to stay home that day. Such things have been foreseen by astrologers in the past; the astrologer then warned the client; the client then took every precaution, but in several cases had an accident *similar* to the one indicated by the transiting planets in the native's horoscope. This brings up a very fine point: Was the astrologer's warning the catalyst that *triggered* the accident, or would it have happened anyway? Or . . . would the accident have been a fatal one except for the warning?

I've talked to many level-headed, scientific astrologers; some claim they are living "on borrowed time," that they have temporarily averted a fatal illness or accident. Three astrologers cheerfully told me approximately when they expected to die. Each of the three died according to their own prediction. Mark Twain predicted his own death, correlating it to the near passage of Halley's comet.

TWO BAFFLING CASES OF DEATH UNDER MYSTERIOUS CIRCUMSTANCES

In 1964 Aida Castro, age 4, was found in a semi-conscious state on the floor of her New York apartment by her mother, Mrs. Angela Castro. The child was burned on the right wrist and cheek, but there was no sign of fire anywhere. After quick first aid by firemen, little Aida was rushed to Bellevue Hospital.

She died. "Electrocution," said the doctors.

Investigators searched thoroughly. The child was nowhere near the television set when found by her mother. The TV wasn't turned on. There were no exposed wires or flash marks anywhere in the apartment. Only a close study of the child's horoscope would have revealed the exact circumstances of her death.

The vast majority of policemen, detectives, and firemen are indefatigable and relentless in cases involving small children or helpless animals.

Such men responded to an anguished call on May 13, 1965 in Montclair, New Jersey. Forty-one-year-old Russell Holmes, a boarder, found seven-year-old Edward Steward sprawled out on a day bed in the front room when he came home in the evening. Edward didn't respond to Holmes' greeting, even though the child's eyes were open. The normally lively house was quiet as a grave. Holmes sprinted for help, and the Police Rescue Squad found four people dead and a fifth, 31-year-old Beverly Ann Branch, dying.

The victims included Eddie Steward, 46-year-old Thelma Steward, 40-year-old Elizabeth Brown, and 38-year-old Edward Watkins, who was found in the shower with the water still running. All were occupied when the tragedy (whatever it was) claimed their lives. Miss Branch died a few hours later in Mountainside Hospital.

Conventional Explanation: Experts theorized that a hot water heater in the basement *may* have burned out the oxygen in the air and that the five victims "apparently died of asphyxiation."

Possibly so, but the Weather Bureau's records for May 13 in this area prove that temperatures ranged between the high 50s and the 80s, and that there was no rain. The windows in the house were screened, but *open*. None of the victims seemed to be the least bit aware that they were slowly (or perhaps quickly) being killed.

ASTROLOGY AS A BASIS FOR WARNING OF DEATH

This leads us to one of the most "familiar" mysteries of all: What force or influence is the determining factor in bringing together people who seem almost "scheduled" to die —in a train wreck or air disaster, for example?

Even the *hint* of engine malfunction or a suspected crackpot with a homemade bomb will empty the largest jetliner and disrupt the schedule of an entire airline—yet not one major airline at this writing has ever made a thorough study of the connections in the horoscopes of those who have perished in any disaster. Such an approach would be relatively cheap, and might prove immensely beneficial.

It is interesting that two violent deaths of well-known show business personalities—although they happened years apart —each had a powerful planetary aspect to a certain fixed star that figures strongly in all deaths by decapitation, or near-decapitation. The first was Will Rogers who "almost" didn't take the fatal flight with Wiley Post. The other was the popular Ernie Kovacs, who perished in an automobile crash. Both were successful men of great wit and talent.

Sooner or later we're all going to have access to a computerized death-warning system. Of course, it may wreak havoc on insurance matters, but, on the other hand, astrology may enable you to avoid pitfalls and live a longer, happier life than ever before. Knowledge of the truth gives you immensely greater freedom of choice.

Ancient Astrology
and Prehistoric Disasters

16

In our modern museums and libraries you'll find the reproductions of original statues, biographies, and horoscopes of Plato, Socrates, and Aristotle. Like most of the Greek scholars of classic antiquity, Plato traveled extensively throughout Egypt during his studies.

PLATO'S ACCOUNT OF THE EXISTENCE AND FALL OF ATLANTIS

Ancient Egypt is believed to have been the largest colony of the great lost civilization of Atlantis. This civilization on the Nile resisted Atlantean domination, but the ancient Athenians actually succeeded in driving off the armies of Atlantis in much the same way early American colonists drove off British armies and broke the English claim to dominion in the New World. Plato reconstructed the outline of Atlantean history from information supplied by the Greek historian-statesman-philosopher, Solon, who got it directly from learned Egyptian historians. He reported these as actual events in his dialogues, *Timaeus* and the *Critias*.

Today's historians and scientists agree that Plato was a genius in every respect but two: (a) the fact that he was an astrologer, and (b) his dialogues on Atlantis.

In the antediluvian world, Plato said, there were fabulous places such as Antilla, Brazil, and the Island of the Seven Cities. All went down in a final, terrible catastrophe—the island-mainland and all nine satellite kingdoms.

Plato was one of the great geniuses of his time. If Atlantean history and the story of a universal disaster were false, he certainly would have recognized it and ignored the entire account. Yet we have scientific evidence today that a great con-

tinent did indeed sink beneath the sea—*and in the time (*
historical man!

Mysteries That Lie at the Ocean's Depths

At the bottoms of all the world's oceans, geologists expecte
to find exceedingly fine sediment that had drifted downwar
to join the accumulated silt of billions of years. They didr
expect to find granular sand, but that is what was there. O
the ocean's floor there are no winds, no tides, no current, r
erosion, and no temperature changes. It is utterly dark, ar
there is no warmth. All that *should* be present is microscop
debris. But there are mountains, volcanoes, and sharp-edge
lava formations that were formed in the air above, and the
are *beaches* that can only have been formed by the action of
sea, land, and air.

Parts of the World's Great Deserts Were Once Fertil Land

In the time of man, most of the present Sahara Desert (
land mass as large as all of Europe) was a fertile, productiv
area. Beneath tons of Sahara sands, rock pictures sculpture
in bas-relief by sophisticated artisans depicted huge herds of
cattle from remote times, grazing in shoulder-high verda
grassland. The cattle wore discs between their horns, a vogu
which became fashionable among wealthy, high-born Egy
tians *thousands of years later!* A tremendous area of th
present Sahara desert was either a great freshwater lake or
huge marshy swamp. The ancient name for this body of
water was *Lake Triton,* which emptied itself into the Atlant
Ocean during a great catastrophe. Due to huge seismic up
heavals and sharp earthquakes that sheared the land masse
the springs that fed this great lake were abruptly cut off an
the sands that formed the lake bed then became a va
desert—the Sahara as we know it today.

Tremendous earthquake fractures far beneath the onc
cultivated Gobi desert swallowed up and sealed off all th
rivers, whose beds then became arid and sterile. There wer
geomagnetic alterations deep within the Earth, and electric
currents in the ground that since then have consistently a
fected clouds that passed overhead without unburdening the
moisture content. The same phenomenon applies to the de

ert of the American southwest, and to others elsewhere in the world.

Miles beneath all oceans there now exist submarine volcanoes, lava, scored rock from glacial eras, and other conditions the causes of which geologists can only guess at. In some respects we now know more about the surface of Mars and Venus than about the bottoms of our own planet's seas.

The Hudson River canyon of New York continues for 120 miles underwater, then drops abruptly at the edge of the continental shelf, but continues for *another* hundred miles along the ocean's bed! Obviously, a tremendous valley was carved by this river at a time when it was a high and dry land mass!

Volanic ash beds and lava flows are more than ten thousand feet deep in southern Alaska, Northern California, Southeastern Maine, and New Brunswick. It takes an Earth-shattering amount of volcanic explosion to cake the surface of a planet—*any* planet—with 10,000 feet (almost two miles) of ash and pumice!

What the Modern "Atlantis" Expedition Found

In 1949, an oceanographic expedition called "Atlantis" discovered a mighty mass of mountains on the floor of the Atlantic Ocean. These mountains rival or surpass the highest peaks on the continental land masses. Soundings taken all over the Atlantic suggest that at one time a great continent existed well above the present ocean's level. There is not a single area on the surface of the Earth which does *not* show evidence of repeated upheaval, great disasters, and global cataclysm. Skeletons of whales have been found at the tops of hills in Michigan and Vermont. So far, no universally acceptable theory has ever explained the formation of mountains and the distribution of coal beds—or even the exact cause of the Ice Ages.

If all the oceans of the world had remained in their present locations for billions of years, the sedimentation at the bottom would be miles deep; but it is *not* miles deep. The sediment on the *continents*, however, is known to be thousands—even tens of thousands—of feet deep!

For some unknown reason, the level of all the Earth's oceans dropped 300 feet during the time of modern man. No one knows where all the water in the glacial cover of the last Ice Age came from. We do know it was between one and two and a half miles thick!

Geologists discovered that Lake Bonneville was once *1,000 feet* above the present level of the Great Salt Lake in Utah—and that Africa's Lake Victoria was once 300 feet higher than it is today!

NEW CLAIMS OF ATLANTIS' DISCOVERY

Atlantis appeared repeatedly on 14th and 15th-century maps. During the next 200 years, its existence was strongly defended by such men as Buffon, Voltaire and Montaigne. I was always depicted as being located in the Atlantic Ocean but new theories put forth by the Woods Hole Oceano graphic Institution and an Athens University seismologist hav tried to place Atlantis in the Aegean Sea.

Dr. Angnelos Galanopoulos and Dr. James W. Mavo collaborated in an American-Greek effort to locate the hil called "Metropolis" by Plato. The Metropolis was surrounde by a moat and thought to be the hub of Atlantean culture an government. On September 3, 1966, the team announce to the world that it had indeed found the Metropolis off th island of Thera at a depth of 1,300 feet.

"Nonsense!" retorted Immanuel Velikovsky when he hear of it. "Atlantis lies on the floor of the Atlantic Ocean just a Plato said it did."

In 1963, Tass, the Soviet news agency, said: "Using ne Soviet oceanographic techniques, the Soviet Union has foun Atlantis in frigid waters three miles deep off the souther coast of Iceland."

Oddly enough, both may be partially correct. Artifacts c ancient civilizations have been found 6,000 feet beneath th Pacific off the coast of Peru and elsewhere. Islands have rise and sunk before anyone could settle ownership rights. Th mid-Atlantic ridge is believed by many oceanographers t be part of the mountain chain that was once part of Atlanti.

A typical volcanic island rose from the depths of the se off southern Sicily in 1830. The Neapolitans, British an French sent expeditions, each of which planted its flag an claimed the island as its own. Before anyone could launc a full-scale fight over the land mass, it disappeared beneat the waves from whence it came.

The serious scientific search for Atlantis and its treasur continues. A Moscow University professor, Georgiy Lin berg, stated his convictions about the existence and technolog cal advancement of the lost continent; then he startled the Communist world with the announcement that the antediluvian world was *extraterrestrial* in origin! In fact, Russian scientists are now working on the idea that homo sapiens may have systematically exterminated some of the races of near-men found by archaeologists and anthropologists.

But not, by any means, all. An obvious analogy is the white man's invasion of the North American continent and the crushing defeat of the Red Man's culture.

GEOLOGICAL PROOFS OF A SERIES OF GREAT DISASTERS

When Mount Bandai erupted in Japan in 1888, three billion tons of Earth from one of its four peaks were blown right into the stratosphere. Even mighty eruptions like those of Krakatoa however, are piddling compared to the stupendous forces that raised the Atlas, the Rockies, or the Andes Mountains—or spread flows of lava nearly *a mile thick* over a quarter million square miles of India!

Lava also covers nearly all of South Africa, the bed of the Pacific Ocean, and the Columbian Plateau in America. Iceland has thousands of volcanic craters and well over a hundred volcanoes of *recent* origin. This island is actually the northern ridge of the great Atlantic mountain spine. Many of the glaciers there are not even 4000 years old. There was a fantastic amount of volcanic activity in Iceland not too long ago, not to mention four glacial and three *inter*glacial periods.

When the ice cover melted over what is now the northwestern United States, floods of stupendous magnitude raised all American rivers more than 200 feet above their present levels. Even the Mississippi rose almost 300 feet higher than it is today.

Human remains, human artifacts, and still-fresh (in the geological sense) bones of extinct animals have been found in Australia and various places in Florida. These remains are found in the same strata and surrounded by the same mineral deposits; therefore, they must have existed side by side.

The Quaternary Ice Age did not occur hundreds of thousands of years ago as some geologists believe. Many of the world's seas and lakes were formed during *a period in the history of ancient Egypt* . . . very "modern" when considered within geological history.

Excellent proofs of a sudden climatic catastrophe (about

700 B.C., as Velikovsky said) were provided by Scandinavian scientists who studied the seas, land, and forests, thus determining that the great disaster occurred during what they called the *Fimbul Winter*—a snowfall that lasted for many years. According to author G. Kossina, this *"Klimasturz . . .* took place with catastrophic suddenness . . ."

There are many ways of determining geological time. One is believed to be the measurement of sedimentation on the ocean floor, another is the saltiness of the oceans (measuring the amount of salt carried off the land by rainfall into the seas each year). One of the latest is the radio-carbon method of dating geological strata and artifacts (the lead content in rock, a product of radioactive decay). And there are still more accurate and reliable methods being devised by scientists.

DENDROCHRONOLOGY, ASTROLOGY AND PREDICTION

The annular rings of trees (like the strata of the Earth's mantle) can also reveal the time of climatic disturbances. This is called the science of *Dendrochronology*, and it was discovered by Dr. William O. Douglass, founder of the Flagstaff observatory, who proved that planets influence the weather just as astrologers have always claimed. He was an expert astro-meteorologist who, in 1960, predicted a 40-year drought for the Southwest and other sections of the United States.

A study of the annular rings of the oldest living things on Earth, the giant Sequoia trees, reveal titanic changes that took place in the Earth's electrical current, in the atmosphere, and in magnetic storms on the Sun in 747 B.C., 702 B.C., and in 687 B.C.

Nobody knows what abandoned ancient bronze mines are doing high in the Alps, or who dug them. But artifacts from an advanced technology have been discovered in and around the passes of these mines.

Greenland, the modern world's largest island, is slowly sinking beneath the ocean—*quite probably as a lingering result of the last global catastrophe*. Traditionally, Greenlanders do not build anywhere near the coastlines. Both American and Greenland coastlines are full of submerged forests, and there are numerous submerged cities and great sunken walls constantly being discovered all over the world— in the North Sea, in the Mediterranean, the Atlantic, Malabar, and the coastlines of Europe.

The period of history we call the Middle Bronze Age seems to have enjoyed a remarkably high degree of prosperity. Industry, art, and trade flourished on an international scale much as it does today. Then everything came to an unexplained, abrupt, and catastrophic halt.

Ancient Oriental cities have been found along the Alaskan coastline with deep trenches gouged out of the Earth by glacial ice and frozen muck. Some of these cuts or scorings are hundreds of feet deep, and many are miles long.

THE PREHISTORIC GYPSUM BEDS OF PARIS

Like the site of Harvard University and the city of Boston, the gypsum beds of Paris are solid evidence that the site of what is now the French capital sank beneath the ocean many times.

These strata of earth in France display a fascinating panorama of alternate layers of marine and land animals. The top layer contains a sea bed of fossilized extinct *and* extant crustaceans and bivalves. All shelled creatures keep their covers closed when there is danger, and this is how their fossils are found. Whatever happened in each and every case occurred with unexpected swiftness. Beneath the marine fossils lies a strata composed of many extinct *land* mammals. And under that, another layer of fossilized marine life. This layer has far more extinct species than the most recent marine layer above it. Down and down it goes—the deeper the bed, the more numerous the extinct species become.

Probably the most arresting mystery of all is the fact that scientists often discover entirely *new* species which were totally nonexistent during the immediately preceding geological past.

FOSSILS, COAL, "MANNA," AND PETROLEUM

Practically every schoolchild is taught that the Earth's coal beds and oil deposits are the result of huge piles of organic material (dinosaurs and/or microbes in the case of petroleum). The fact is that nobody really knows *how* oil deposits were formed. We do know that oil and coal did not result from the same processes. It is only fair and logical, therefore, to consider Dr. Immanuel Velikovsky's (presently) unconventional explanation: that great gouts of petroleum from the comet Venus rained vast amounts of "Manna" and fire upon the Earth as she came within range of our planet in ancient times. The sticky, yellowish substance rained down in somewhat lumpy or kernel-like form and was (suprisingly) edible—it sustained the Hebrews during their flight from Egypt's Pharoah through the desert.

When it fell into water, it turned lakes and rivers white as milk; it was eaten as a honeycomb might be eaten, Velikovsky interprets from *Exodus*, and was nourishing. The Manna fell everywhere as Venus loomed in the night sky, rivaling the Sun in brightness and cutting off Mars' headlong plunge toward the Earth.

There is physical evidence among all the civilized records available that, at the same time, "rains of fire" were falling throughout the civilized world. Whenever Velikovsky found a reference to a cataclysmic event in the Bible, the records of the Egyptians, the Toltecs, and other civilized peoples reflected the same catastrophe. The rains of fire must have gutted most of the structures; the interiors of many (then) unfinished pyramids appear to have been blackened as though by a petroleum fire. Hydrocarbons, Velikovsky theorized, must result from decaying organic matter, and the ancient records indicate a terrible plague of *vermin*, and the ancient world was inundated with insects as well as the "Manna" as Venus intercepted Mars. From these factors (which are necessarily oversimplified), Dr. Velikovsky concluded that all the foregoing phenomena were not only connected, but resulted from the mingling of the Earth's atmosphere with that of Venus; the petroleum deposits which now fuel our techno-industrial world did not originate in or on the Earth, but came from the atmosphere of Venus. And since the comet Venus was ejected from Jupiter's roaring atmosphere of methane, ammonia, and hydrocarbons, he predicts that space probes of the future will find much the same kind of life on both worlds—*insect* life!

COAL IS FORMED ONLY UNDER CONDITIONS OF CATASTROPHE

Coal is also an organic compound or residue which, like all fossils, was created under conditions of immense catastrophic pressure in the Earth's mantle. You can often find the imprint of leaves and ferns in the shale of coal beds in Pennsylvania. That which we call *lignite* is the remains of trees that were only partly converted into coal. Soft (bituminous) coal is brittle, shiny, and contains a lot of sulphur.

Hard (anthracite) coal is completely metamorphosed bitumen.

Cataclysms that suddenly buried entire forests during the Carboniferous Era are the *only way* coal can be formed! Many coal beds or seams are 50 or more feet thick. To form a layer of coal only twelve inches thick, a 12-foot peat deposit is necessary, and it takes *120 feet of plant life* to form a 12-foot layer of peat. A 50-foot seam of coal, therefore, must have been created by more than *one solid mile of plant life!*

It logically follows that almost one hundred huge rain forests were destroyed one after the other to create large seams of so many veins of coal at so many geological strata in so many locations on the Earth's surface. These living trees and green plants were *suddenly* cut off from all air and light (the only way to prevent rotting) in order to produce coal.

Some places on Earth contain as many as a hundred or more successive coal beds formed during various geological epochs. Each epoch, therefore, ended in a global or nearly-global disaster. Many of these ages seem to have occurred one after another in rapid succession. Hundreds or perhaps thousands of times, the sea has retreated from an area, leaving dry land or desert. Hundreds or thousands of times during geological history, new land formed to produce great forests, rich grazing and hunting land, and perhaps great civilizations. But suddenly the seas returned again to cover it all with billions of tons of crushing, smothering debris.

The geological evidence for this is indisputable.

> *"Below the bending crest*
> *Of your tremendous head*
> *What records do you hide*
> *Of unimagined dead?*
>
> *"Ten billion years blown down*
> *Are but a sighing breath*
> *To you, old wrinkled sea,*
> *As cryptic as death."*
>
> —ANON.

SCIENTIFIC ASTROLOGY CAN PREDICT THE END OF THIS WORLD AGE

If such catastrophism has happened before, it will almost certainly happen again, and our entire civilization will go down when it does happen unless studies and preparations are started long in advance of a disastrous geological change.

We've shown in an earlier chapter how extraordinarily difficult it is to recognize a new or unexpected fact, especially when we have preconceived ideas about it. In *The Future of Man*, Teilhard de Chardin gives the analogy that a *photograph* of a crashing surf would make it *seem* (to someone who had never seen a large body of water) that the water is actually motionless and hard as glass. We get the same impression from the pictures of mountains, yet mountains do change.

The picture represents only a micro-instant of an Earth-tide forever in motion. Our subjective view of human history, however, may be compared to the impression an ignorant savage might have while looking at the picture of a crashing surf. This latest instant, we believe, is more advanced than any in previous history; nothing that ever preceded this moment could possibly have been as great. Our styles and fads are better than any that went before. This is like *assuming* it must be high tide simply because you've just arrived at the beach.

The biologist looking through his microscope sees tremendous activity among the microbes on a slide of nutrient solution. The microbes, which, being living creatures, must have *some* kind of instinct, certainly don't have the same impression of "time" as the biologist who watches as two or three generations live and die in a very short (to him) period.

The lifespan of the entire human race, even though it will still go on evolving for billions of years, is but a micro-instant compared to the whole of geological time. And geological time is but a micro-instant of cosmic time; which, in turn, is a mere wink of the eye to eternity.

In our short passage through this comparatively peaceful geological age, the duty of astrology is to reveal as much as possible about the future.

It is flatly impossible for "Materialistic Big Science," actually a mere adjunct to our money-making enterprises and/or war-making ability, to stimulate further advances in Human Consciousness without the thorough investigation of astrological and occult phenomena. The First Science must be thoroughly studied with integrity and respect for the accumulated knowledge of all civilizations that passed before, regardless of how passionately we want to believe that the tides have never before been as high as they are now.

According to Velikovsky, *"Many of our presently existing*

species evolved in the wake of a global catastrophe, at the beginning of a new age, and were entombed in a subsequent paroxysm of Nature at the end of that age."

We all want to know if and when such a disaster will happen again. If so, we will want to use all the talent, technology, and material wealth at our disposal to prevent it; or, if this is not possible, to remove our culture until the 'storm" is past.

Chapter 16 reveals why Atlantis *must* have existed and how it was destroyed; and in the final chapter we will attempt to show (by astrological and other predictions) that America, the *New* Atlantis, could go the way of the *old*— and that after long periods of history, few would believe that any highly advanced Lost Continent such as the legendary America ever really existed, not even if future scholars recorded our history.

The Universal Deluge
Legend

17

O nce exposed to Egypt's amazingly sophisticated art, sculpture, and architecture, it is almost impossible not to get a deep impression of earliest Egypt's amazing magnificence. Paradoxically, the most ancient periods in her history were (technically and esthetically) more advanced than the later dynasties, a fact suggesting that all Egyptian culture was implanted by something even greater—a more ancient, more advanced civilization. The historical, geological, and mythological evidence further suggests that this great civilization went down in a terrible convulsion of Nature, and that Egyptian grandeur only mirrors this mysterious, vanished nation.

The gigantic and magnificent temples at Karnak represent some of the most impressive architectural feats of ancient or modern times. Colossi of Amenophis I and Thutmosis I were constructed in front of great pylons or massive gateways. These, and the statues in the "Halls of Annals" were precisely carved from Aswan granite—quarried and transported by some as-yet unknown means.

There were also great temples at Luxor, huge palaces at Amarna, royal tombs, private dwellings, monuments, roadways, chapels, government buildings, and colossus after colossus to stagger the eye and the imagination. The stupendous national temple at Karnak enclosed a great natural lake, and the Halls of Karnak could have contained several structures as large as the Cathedral of Notre Dame, none of which would have touched the walls or ceiling!

ATLANTIS—THE PREHISTORIC WORLD

Even today it has to be seen to be believed. Yet this

sample of Egyptian grandeur was only the reflected glory of something greater—*Atlantis!*

"Science," says Ignatius Donnelly in *Atlantis: The Antediluvian World,* "has but commenced its work of reconstructing the past and rehabilitating the ancient peoples, and surely there is no study which appeals more strongly to the imagination than that of this drowned nation, the true antediluvians. They were the founders of nearly all our arts and sciences; they were the parents of our fundamental beliefs; they were the first civilizers, the first navigators, the first merchants, and the first colonizers of the Earth; their civilization was old when Egypt was young and they had passed away thousands of years before Babylon, Rome, or London were dreamed of. These lost people were our ancestors, their blood flows in our veins; the words we use every day were heard, in their primitive form, in their cities, courts, and temples. Every line of race and thought, of blood and belief, leads back to them."

If true, this idea will eventually be proven—and will revolutionize our entire concept of human history.

Dr. Velikovsky, in his theories on planetary collisions, traced the last change in the world's calendars to about 700 B.C. "After (March 23) 687 (B.C.)," he wrote, "every civilized nation on Earth recalculated its chronology, introduced new calendars, and, as though at a common signal, arranged to determine time from that date onward." In 661 B.C., a new calendar was finally introduced in Japan. But as early as 721 B.C., the Chinese astrologer Y-hang pleaded with emperor Hiuen-Tsong that he could no longer predict eclipses or planetary conjunctions because the order of the solar system had been upset. Venus, for instance, had dropped forty degrees from the plane of the ecliptic to occult the fixed star, Sirius.

The French archaeologist Brasseur, in his *History of the Civilized Nations of Mexico,* says: "All Toltec histories mention an assembly of sages and astrologers convoked in the city of Huehue-Tlapallan for correcting the calendar and reforming the computation of the year, which was then known to be erroneous."

At about the same time, the Peruvian King Inti-Capac-Yupanqui ordered *his* astrologers to completely recalculate the shifted astronomical phenomena. The length of the year was changed from 360 to 365¼ days.

AMERICA'S 25,000-YEAR-OLD STRUCTURES

In China, Egypt, India, Assyria, Babylon, Israel, Mexico —in fact, everywhere—it was the same. Romulus founded the Roman Empire directly after 700 B.C. This, it appears, immediately followed a world catastrophe during which Atlantis may indeed have sunk beneath the ocean.

From the records of Assyria we know that wars of annihilation coincided with Mars' super-perigee passage, yet violent natural catastrophes claimed more lives than the bloodletting of the armies of Sennacherib, Sargon II, Shalmenesar IV, and other rulers of the time.

The same events are mirrored in the Icelandic *Voluspa:* "Dark grows the Sun . . . brothers shall fight and fell each other . . ."

Even more ominously, as Mars came on collision course: "Axe-time, sword-time, shields are sundered; wind-time, Wolf-time (*Mars was Fenris—Wolf*), ere the world falls; nor ever shall men spare each other."

It didn't happen overnight. Egyptian records indicate that about 790 B.C., the Moon was mysteriously knocked or jarred from its usual course, bombarded with great meteors (as was the Earth), and constant war was waged throughout the land.

". . . fire . . . shall devour the brier and the thorn, and shall kindle in the thicket of the forest, and it shall be wrapped in smoke ascending on high. The land is troubled, and the people shall be as the fuel of the fire; no man shall spare his brother." (Isaiah 9:18–19)

A star in the constellation of the Great Bear had been the pole star, but after this catastrophe, the pole star of the age was changed. The same catastrophe seems to have been reported everywhere. This was the beginning of the end of the last great World Age—one remarkably advanced in philosophy, astrology, and occult wisdom on one hand, and technological achievement on the other.

No one has yet been able to explain those 25,000-year-old symbols formed by great boulders on the west coasts of North and South America. Some of them were regarded by engineers as part of the natural topography. In fact, they built California's roads around and through these artifacts. But a high-flying pilot who photographed the terrain during World War II noticed that the boulders formed amazingly unnatural symbols—much like those used by modern astrologers and astronomers, which are almost identical.

How could anyone living 25,000 years ago have moved such massive weights? Given that they did, *why* were the symbols constructed? We can almost certainly eliminate human labor as the *how* of it, but the fact is that they were laid out to be seen from an extremely high altitude—one that could only be attained by aircraft—*or spacecraft!*

Perhaps a downed interplanetary ship had earthmoving equipment aboard. It's rank presumption that only the 19th and 20th Centuries are capable of deducing and engineering air and space flight. Even Da Vinci conceived it much earlier than this; so did the Greeks.

PERUVIAN GOLD, BASIS OF THE MODERN WORLD'S ECONOMY

Today, Peru seems incapable of duplicating construction on the scale achieved by ancient Egypt. But *ancient* Peru built a stone aqueduct 450 miles long that extended over rivers and mountains! If the same thing were constructed along the Eastern seaboard, it would stretch from N. Carolina to New York City!

Gran Chimu, the capitol of the Chimus nation in Northern Peru, was sacked and destroyed in a series of wars. Its ruins exist today—20 square miles of palaces, tombs, villas, shops, private dwellings, great temples and huge pyramids, some of them a half-mile in circumference! There were municipal buildings, great walls, prisons, iron foundries and other large, impressive structures. The famous "Temple of the Sun" is a pyramid 150 feet high, 470 feet wide, and 812 feet long.

Almost everything was looted by the Spaniards, who shipped hundreds of tons of gold and silver (estimated at being worth 50 billion dollars at today's rates) from Peru to Europe. The ancient Peruvians built tremendous suspension bridges to cross mountains and rivers—*centuries before they were dreamed of anywhere in Europe*. The sophisticated network of Peruvian roads surpassed anything built by the Romans in Italy, the South of France, or in Spain. The roads of Peru were actually *macadamized*—"made of pulverized stone mixed with lime and bituminous cement and were walled in by strong abutments over six feet thick." These roads, averaging 25 feet in width, rolled through the mountains from Quito to Chile, from Cuzco along the coast, and to south of the equator!

The Incas themselves admit that everything was built

long before their own time—*by bearded white men!* In Cue-
lap, Northern Peru, you can still see a solid wall of finely
wrought stones 3600 feet long, 1500 feet high, and 560 feet
wide. Built atop this mass is another—600 feet long, 150
feet high, and 500 feet wide. Inside this 300-foot-high structure, there are numerous rooms and cells.

EGYPT AS A COLONY OF ATLANTIS

The idea that Egypt was merely a colony of a greater, more
advanced culture, is strengthened by the fact that the first
king of Egypt appeared out of nowhere. With no archaeologi-
cal evidence of previous technological advancement, King
Menes is known to have diverted the mighty Nile, then built
the city of Memphis on the cleared site. He also created
Moeris, an artificial lake (or reservoir) to irrigate thousands
of square miles of agricultural land. This tremendous lake,
wrote Ignatius Donnelly: "was 450 miles in circumference,
350 feet deep, with subterranean channels, flood gates,
locks, and dams." Some feat for "primitive" people!

The entire valley and delta of the Nile, from the Catacombs
to the sea, fairly bristled with thousands of homes, temples,
palaces, tombs, pyramids, huge obelisks, colossal statues, and
pillars, yet *every stone was covered with intricate bas-relief
sculpture and inscriptions!* The ruins of the Labyrinth
astounded even Herodotus when he saw them; there were
3000 spacious chambers, half above ground and half below.
The square sides of the Temple of Karnac must have surpassed anything among The Seven Wonders of the ancient
World. It was 1800 feet wide and 1800 feet high! Archaeologists of the 19th Century estimated that the joints of the
Pyramid stones had originally been no thicker than the width
of silver paper. One way or another, the intricacy, magnificence, and prodigality of Egyptian workmanship staggers
the imagination. *Inside* the sanctuary at Karnak were lakes
and mountains—everything completely enclosed within great
walls of intricately carved stone!

The Egyptians quarried on a massive scale; they possessed
strange knowledge of a very advanced order, limitless or-
ganizational ability, and astounding wealth. Still, since its
earliest Dynasties, Egypt seems to have *degenerated* rather
than progressed. This reverse chronology suggests the im-
plantation of the entire Egyptian culture by a greater outside
source—one that no longer exists.

Everything that was great in Egypt, Sumer, or Babylon

could well have been mere copies of a mysterious Lost World. Everything the Egyptians had or knew seems to have been there at the earliest known dates, including their entire system of writing. We know this because hieroglyphic signs on papyrus rolls have been found on monuments of the Twelfth Dynasty. Later, they were found in even more refined form on Fourth Dynasty monuments (circa 2,680 B.C.), and even back to the time of Menes, the first Egyptian monarch of which there is any record.

Unsuccessful attempts have been made, and are still being made, to superimpose a crude, prehistoric beginning on Egypt, but the facts do not warrant this assumption. The Lost World reflected by Egypt's glory was of tremendous antiquity. Atlantis had colonies in Peru, Mexico, Greece, South America —even in parts of what is now the Mississippi River Valley.

Egyptian dead went to the "Elysian Fields," a place in the West where fertility and agriculture were heavily stressed. The Atlantis-Egyptian tie is further evidenced by the fact that pineapples, mangoes, papaya, bananas, corn, and all the great cereal grains were already being cultivated by Egyptians at the earliest known dates of their history. These "Elysian Fields" were the same as those of the ancient Greeks—on a great world in the Western sea. Evidently the same island known to the Peruvians, and all other "American Indians."

THE UNIVERSAL DELUGE

The Egyptians called one of the rivers of Atlantis *Uranes*, probably named after an Atlantean king called "Uranus," for whom the planet was named. The fact that Egypt furnished Solon of Sais with complete geographical descriptions of Atlantis, its islands, mountains, rivers, plains, and great cities, lends even more credence to the belief that Atlantis did exist. The most concrete evidences of all, however, are the soundings made by scores of ships during the past century. When they are superimposed, they generally confirm Plato's description of the Atlantean topography.

Practically every civilized nation on Earth has a Flood or Deluge legend: a ship, a boat, or an Ark, built by a Noah-like character, who landed on a mountain when the waters receded and then began the repopulation of a decimated planet. At the 15,000-foot level of Mt. Ararat for example, the fragments of an "ark" have been found.

Ancient astrological and religious ceremonies commemo-

rate the end of the Great Flood—the Greeks pour water
down a hole in a grotto at Heliopolis into which the Flood
waters are supposed to have drained in that area of the
world. Although there is some confusion in the chronology,
it is a scientific fact that a great Deluge did occur. We receive
strange information from rather unlikely places:

From Sumeria, we inherited the 360° circle, divided into
12 segments of 30° each. A single degree is divided into
60 minutes of arc, and each minute into 60 seconds! It's interesting that there are 1,296,000 seconds of arc in a circle—
the digits of which add up to *nine*. And there are 21,600
minutes of arc in a circle, which also reduces to nine. The
Sumerians seem to have inherited this from somewhere else.

The origin: *Atlantis!*

LEGENDS OF THE LOST

Plato said that tremendous mountains in the north of
Atlantis "exceeded all that are now to be seen anywhere."
It's a good guess however, that Plato never saw the
Andes or Rockies, let alone the Himalayas. He might, however, have seen the *Atlas* Mountains in Africa. Donnelly
claims the mountain chain was named after Atlas (Titan),
that the Atlantic Ocean was named for Atlantis, not vice
versa, and that there is profound significance among all these
similar names, which stem from the original Atlantean language. *Atalanta* was the Greek huntress in the *Calydonian
Hunt.*

Two thousand feet above sea level on the coastline of
northern Chile lie a series of dry salt basins. Once called
Lake Atacama, it is now the Chilean-Bolivian desert of Atacama. Again and again we find evidence of radically changed
geography with Atlantean names we take to be originated
by the Indians of the region. Lake *Atitlan,* in southwest
Guatemala, was raised to a height of 5,100 feet in some
prehistoric convulsive elevation. It is a volcanic lake 17
miles long and 11 miles wide, set among the mountains
with three other inactive volcanoes close by. This lake has
germinated the growth of some of the most verdant, dis-
tinctive, and magnificent scenery to be seen anywhere on
the planet. Mount *Athos,* in the southern tip of the Greek
Peninsula, is 6,000 feet high. *Athens,* the capital of Greece,
lies on the plain of *Attica,* named for *Attis,* the fertility
god of the Phrygian religion. Phoenix-like, he died, but was
resurrected each year. Orgiastic spring fertility rites were per-

formed in his honor (See *Adois, Attis, Osiris,* by James G. Frazer).

The *Azore* Islands drop to a tremendous depth—several miles to the bed of the Atlantic. Edgar Cayce (in *There Is A River* by Thos. Sugrue) believed these islands are the highest remaining peaks of the Northern mountain chain of Atlantis—the same mountains reported by Plato.

The Great Lakes Indian tradition of America has it that "The Father of all (Indian) nations originally dwelt *toward the Rising Sun.*" Nicaraguan Indians claim that the world was destroyed ages ago by a Great Flood or Deluge and that most of mankind perished. Their tradition *also* points to an origin in the Eastern ocean! The same legend persists among the Okanagaus Indians, who also claim a huge island was devastated by a series of natural cataclysms and disappeared in the depths of the ocean.

The Sioux believe that the entire Earth was once covered by water and that all men were drowned. The Chickasaws think the world was once destroyed by water—also that only one family and two of every animal were saved in a boat. The Chippewa nation's legend is that *Menaboshu* saved himself, his family, and many plants and animals (from the catastrophe) in a huge boat he built for the purpose. Menaboshu then sent forth a bird called the *diver* to search for dry land.

Plato wrote that the Kings of Atlantis controlled and ruled many colonies over large areas of *"the great opposite continent."* If there never *was* an Atlantis, we have to explain how Plato managed to guess that the American continent existed!

The Toltecs traced their origin to a place they called *"Aztlan"* (sometimes called *"Atlan"*) from which the Aztecs are convinced they once emigrated. The "Noah" of the Mexican cataclysm was Coxcox (alternately referred to as *Tezpi* or *Teocipactli*). Coxcox is reported by the historian Ixtilxochitl to have built his boat from cypress wood. When the waters receded, he landed on Colhuacan Mountain and sent out a vulture to find dry land. The vulture however, stayed out and fed on the carrion from the Flood. Much later, a surviving hummingbird returned to the ark with a leaf in its beak. Versions of this legend (with only minor variations) have been carved, drawn, painted, or recorded in pictographs by the Aztecs, Miztecs, Incas, Toltecs, Zapotecs, Mechoacaneses, and Tlascaltecs of America.

The builders of the ancient American marvels vanished without a trace. Who were they? Not surprisingly, Ignatius

Donnelly claimed: "Survivors of the great Atlantean catastrophe," and he may have been right. All Indians were not Red Men. Spanish missionaries who followed Cortez found strange paintings of the early Toltecs who were "fair, robust, and bearded." These missionaries produced evidence showing bearded men with blue eyes. Quetzalcoatl himself is described as a large man "with a big head and heavy beard." This also fits the description of the *Chinese* leader and teacher Tai-Ko-Fokee, who appeared in China after a great disaster and brought knowledge of gunpowder, ink, printing, paper manufacture, and numerous advanced arts and sciences—all of which the Chinese learned well.

Were the mysterious Quetzalcoatl and Tai-Ko-Fokee survivors of some previous global disaster? How can there be such similarity and/or contact between the Chinese, Mexicans, and ancient Egyptians—or with the cultures of Phoenicia, Babylon, Greece, and Assyria—unless a great connecting land mass no longer exists in the Atlantic ocean?

The Giants of Atlantis

In *The Book of the Damned*, Charles Fort succinctly reported: "tablets of stone, with the ten commandments engraved upon them, in Hebrew . . . found in mounds in the United States," and "Masonic emblems found in mounds . . ."

"Roman" coins by the thousand are reported to have been dug out of mounds, and are also found in every strata of the earthen digs in America. But when did ancient Romans land on American shores and penetrate west of the Mississippi? Although some Experts identified the coins as being of Roman origin, the identification must have been spurious because the inscriptions on these coins were in no known ancient or modern language. Yet they seem to have been struck from the same mint at the same time. This suggests that the coins are either part of the treasury of Atlantis—washed thousands of miles westward by seismic waves after a global disaster—or they were dropped around the country by voyagers from another world far out in space. Theories like this are becoming more and more commonplace and less likely to be regarded as science-fiction or fantasy.

The Atlantean personification of Mercury, winged messenger of the gods and ruler of the ancient Celts, was one of their divinities. He is described by Abbe F. Pezron as being associated with the Titans, a race of giants who once rebelled in Atlantis. This is reflected in the Biblical account of a heavenly rebellion of angels (winged creatures). "Their princes," said Pezron, "are the same as the giants of Scripture."

The Chinese also have a legend that the Earth was once destroyed by a Deluge. After the appearance of Tai-Ko-Fokee, another personage, Fui-hi, appeared. The latter founded the Chinese empire in 2852 B.C., introduced the custom of formal marriage, and stabilized Oriental society. Fui-hi also brought domesticated cattle with him; and, like Tai-Ko-Fokee, "Fui-hi" is *not* pictured as being an Oriental! All the men who organized and advanced the Central Americans, the Hindus, and the Asiatics, were described at various times in history as having full beards. Yet Indians and Orientals are known for the sparsity of their facial hair. The possibility that these great teachers and leaders may have been survivors of an advanced culture that suffered complete destruction is strong and distinct.

The character Tai-Ko-Fokee, therefore, is eminently worthy of closer study. Almost immediately following the cataclysmic separation of the World Ages, he appeared mysteriously on the mountains of Chin. Called the "Stranger King," Tai-Ko ruled all of China and was pictured as a bearded Caucasian—a Moses-like figure with two small horns. Tai-Ko taught astrology and pictography, he recalculated the calendar and divided time into years, months, days, and hours. The perplexing fact is that all this happened about 5,000 years ago. Nevertheless, the picture writing he introduced was almost identical to that being used by the Central Americans when the Spaniards arrived in America.

This story and description has an uncanny similarity to a find made in Copan, Central America. Here, another "horned" individual appeared out of nowhere to become a great benefactor and god-like figure to the Central Americans.

Horned creatures, even though in human form, are symbolically related to Baal or Bel, the ancient pagan god of the Semitic people. They are previously reported among Persian kings and American Indian tribes (who wore the horns of the bison), by Norsemen (horned helmets), and by Eastern potentates who evolved this practice into the wearing of twin tiaras, and, finally, a single crown. Eventually it developed into what is now the crown of royalty and the symbol of Papal Authority. The gods of the old religion often become the demons or devils of the religion that replaces it. Hence in the Hebraic-Christian tradition, Satan is a horned creature.

In each legend, the catastrophe was known by a central figure *before* it happened. These men are reported to have held communion with God or learned of it through "portents in the heavens"—or by astrology. In either case, the pre-cognition had a celestial source. The Pima Indian nation believe that an *eagle* prophesied the coming Flood on three different occasions. The eagle (Phoenix) is still regarded as the highest manifestation of the occult, secretive, astrological Sign, Scorpio.

The Pimas' record states that thunder then shook the Earth and a huge mountain of green water roared upright at a tremendous height and walked the Plains of America, being cut incessantly by gigantic lightning. The description seems to fit that of the oceanic-seismic wave that followed the sinking of a great island-continent.

India has five versions of the Deluge legend. One is called the Rig Veda and the remaining four, the Upangas.

"NOAH" LEGENDS OF THE WORLD

The "Noah" of the Indian *Bhagavata Purana* is met at the height of the flood by the god Vishnu, disguised as a great *horned* fish, who tows the ark to a mountain where a pigeon is released, then a dove, and finally a blackbird, which returns with a branch in its beak. In the *Satapatha Brahmana*, the warning of the impending catastrophe is also given by a great *horned* fish. This is clearly and simply a bastardized version of the fact that a great conjunction of planets formed in the Zodiacal Sign of Capricorn—The Sea Goat— and that astrologers knew that a watery disaster would befall mankind. (Astrometeorology of prehistoric times.)

There is a relationship between the planets and the "gods" of Atlantis, one of whom was Cronus *(Chronos,* or Saturn, the ruling planet of Capricorn, the Sea Goat, and, *in those times,* also Pisces, the watery Sign of the Fish). Much of the true significance of this knowledge was related to the Greeks by the Babylonian historian-astrologer Berossus, who lived in the 3rd Century B.C. This genius was regarded so highly by the Greeks that they erected a great statue of him —*with a tongue of solid gold!* Most of what we know of Berossus is found in the fragments of writings by Josephus and Eusebius. He is quoted as stating that after the death of Ardates, when his son Xisuthros ruled for eighteen sari, the god Cronus *(Chronos,* or Saturn, ruler of Capricorn) ap-peared to him in a dream or vision and warned that on the 15th of *Daesius* a great Deluge would destroy the world. This is another allusion to the astrological nature of the divination.

In *Ancient Fragments* (translated by Alexander Polyhistor, written in 2 B.C., and by Abydenus in 4 B.C.), I. P. Cory wrote: "He (Berossus) therefore enjoined him to write a history of the beginning, procedure, and conclusion of all things; and to bury it in the City of the Sun (*also ancient Peru's capitol*) at Sippara (an ancient "time capsule"), and to build a vessel, and to take with him into it his friends and relatives; and to convey on board everything necessary to sustain life, together with all the different animals and birds and quadrupeds, and to trust himself fearlessly to the deep . . ."

The ark of Noah is described only as a floating box without navigational ability, sails, or rudder. The Babylonians (Gilgamesh and Uta Napistim), however, built real ships when they received *their* warnings. Each had a pilot and spent over two weeks looking for land to the west, but found none.

In the *Popul Vuh*, sacred book of the Central Americans, Coxcox was warned of the impending Flood and built his boat of cypress wood. The paintings of this ubiquitous legend are found all over Central and South America. The method of the warnings are almost always celestial in origin.

Humanity could not have existed for several millions of years without having created many highly developed civilizations before the present era. Some of these World Ages may have been as advanced as the world of today; perhaps even *more* advanced. At the earliest stages of any civilization, a rudimentary knowledge of the celestial environment and its influence on terrestrial life must have been developed. This is the only logical method by which repeated World Catastrophes could have been foreseen. The legends repeated here are merely the simplest kind of mythology. In our present state of development, we are spiritually ignorant. The Phoenix symbol expresses a great message for mankind today. For out of mythology, many universal truths have been known to emerge—few of which are yet recognized or understood.

Atlantis did exist, as Plato reported. The record of the drowned world was given to his ancestor Solon (of Sais) during his journey to Egypt, by Psouchis, an Egyptian high priest. Solon's work was interrupted by his death, and Plutarch wrote his biography, *The Life of Solon*. Two centuries later Plato carried on the work, but he too died before completing it. This tremendously important record extended human history not just thousands of years before the Greek civilization, but thousands of years before the establishment of the

First Egyptian Dynasty, the Babylonian empire, or even the great civilization of Sumer (Sumeria).

ATLANTOLOGY—A NEW SCIENCE

At the end of the 19th Century the U.S. Sloop Gettysburg, commanded by Capt. Gorringe, studied all prior soundings of the North Atlantic, and discovered a great plateau on the ocean's floor connecting Madiera to Portugal. In a lengthy report, Gorringe detailed every known facet of the Atlantic's submarine topography and concluded that he had indeed found a sunken continent, but he never publicly named the invisible world he discovered.

Ignatius Donnelly dramatically states that: "The focus of all the traditions of all the great ancient nations is the universal memory of a great land that breathed its last dying gasp in the global cataclysm that drowned it beneath the waters of the Atlantic, where it lies undisturbed even to this day."

Here is the 13-point proposition Donnelly gives to support this idea:

1—That there once existed in the Atlantic, near the Mediterranean, an Atlantic island continent known to the world as Atlantis.

2—That the description of this island given by Plato is an actual historical account.

3—That Atlantis was where man first rose to a state of advanced civilization.

4—That over the ages, Atlantis, (like modern America,) became a populous and mighty nation, extending to the shores of the Gulf of Mexico, the Mississippi, the Amazon, the Pacific coast of South America, the Mediterranean, the west coast of Europe and Africa, the Baltic, the Black Sea, and the Caspian—all of which were colonized and populated by Atlanteans.

5—That Atlantis was *the focus of tradition among all ancient nations; representing a universal memory of a great land where early mankind dwelt for ages in peace and happiness.*

6—That the gods and goddesses of Greece, India, Scandinavia, and Phoenicia were the kings, queens, and heroes of Atlantis; and the acts attributed to them in mythology were only a time-confused recollection of actual historical events.

7—That the mythologies of Egypt and Peru represented Eastern and Western versions of the Atlantean religion —a kind of Sun-worship. (Be it noted that both Johann Kepler and Benjamin Franklin believed the Sun was a living, sentient Being. Franklin even suggested that we pray only to our nearest local Deity, Sol—our local star.)

8—That the oldest colony set up by the Atlanteans was Egypt, whose civilization was an attempted reproduction of Atlantis.

9—That all metallurgical science in Europe (and probably Asia) was derived from the Atlanteans, the first manufacturers of iron.

10—That the parent of all European alphabets was Phoenician, therefore derived from the Atlantis alphabet and reflected by Central American cultures.

11—That Atlantis was the original seat of the Aryan or Indo-European family of nations, as well as of the Semitic peoples, and possibly of the Turanian (Oriental) races.

12—That Atlantis with most of its inhabitants perished in a terrible natural convulsion, one that took the island-continent and its subsidiary islands to the bottom of the ocean.

13—That the few survivors carried an exact report of this appalling catastrophe to other nations, and that the story has survived to the present time in myths, legends, symbolic stories, and racial memory.

It is long past time for materialistic scientists to begin paying close attention to these reports, and to undertake the study of astrology in order to determine when a catastrophe like this will again visit our planet.

Not *if*, but *when*.

The Future History
of the World

18

Sophisticated as astrology is, no one is yet able to rule out the *psi* faculty of the astrologer. It often comes into play, unbidden, after years of intense, practical application of astrological rules that were discovered, forgotten, and rediscovered again through millennia.

Everyone has the *psi* faculty in varying degrees, so we can't dismiss the idea that astrologers often receive "hunches" that come true. All we can say is that the ancient rules are workable, and when computers are programmed with the accumulated astrological data of the ages, it will finally be proven.

In spite of all this, there are variables in astrological interpretation that leave the astrologer in a vulnerable position. But the miracle isn't that so many predictions come true, it is the fact that there aren't a greater number of complete misses! (We're discussing *astrologers*, not charlatans.)

My intention here is not to panic the reader. It's wise to remember that you've already faced and overcome all kinds of difficulty in your lifetime. We've seen loved ones die and have been at death's door ourselves. We've lost property and money, survived storms, earthquakes, volcanic eruptions, and even suffered "crushing" disappointments in love.

Would you do it differently if you had it to do all over again? Certainly not, because your horoscope would be the same. You'd experience all the same pleasures and pain because your responses to the same stimuli would be unchanged. Yet here you are—alive, hopeful, progressive, able to ignore adversity. Even if it were possible to have foreseen and *avoided* the worst of the past five, ten, or twenty years, you wouldn't be as strong as you are now by having faced the adversities and overcome them.

America is the nation it is today *because* of our Civil War, World War I, World War II, and now Asia. At the risk of seeming fatalistic, the United States doesn't seem to have been able to sidestep the foregoing (but we'd have done much better with an expert staff of White House astrologers).

Individually, you have at least a margin of free choice. Astrology enables you to use this margin to operate at maximum efficiency.

Some people, including several astrologers, were absolutely certain in 1906 that the San Francisco quake would strike. The astrologers seemed to have known the date, but the psychics knew the hour. Still, nobody listened—possibly because no one had been "programmed" to listen. Maybe it was "fated" to occur in exactly the way it did, with the same damage, the same deaths, and the same survivors with the same injuries.

But what about all those forecasts of doom and destruction that never happen? More important, how about predictions of disaster that are either minimized or *neutralized* by astrological prediction? Let's say the Sun is shining, but you know it's going to rain because the report says so. You can't prevent the rainfall. But you *can* take the necessary precautions by wearing a raincoat, carrying an umbrella, etc.

Simply put, this is the primary objective of this book. Nobody has the right to cry *"Fire!"* in a crowded theatre, we say, but he ought to report the flame he sees in the wings.

Our insistence on pursuing the physical sciences as though the Cosmos had no other purpose or meaning than that detectable to the five senses is foolhardy. Other Natural Laws (whether they be different or higher) do exist. There *is* reason, intelligence, and purposeful direction even in colossal cosmic events (and our discovery of them).

There is, for example, an overall magnetic field surrounding spiral galaxy M81. The existence of this galactic "aura" is very real and calculated to a few microgauss by very sensitive intruments. This faint feature is actually synchrotron radiation from electrons exploded by its "neighbor" galaxy, M82. This makes it quite clear that these titanic Island Universes (some containing billions of suns like our own) have a profound effect on each other. Even if the currently stylish investigation of quasi-stellar blue galaxies confirms a new theory of the origin of the Universe—it will not prove that the Cosmos is purely a random, chaotic, or accidental phenomenon.

Earthman's narrow, egocentric view of the universe is persistent. We're less interested in the pure theory of *how* it works than in the pragmatic knowledge of how it might *affect* us. Historically (for the past few centuries) astronomers have been sensitive, vague, and evasive whenever this question was raised.

THE FORTY-YEAR DROUGHT

The time of scientific uncertainty about the effect of the Cosmos on the Earth is rapidly nearing its end. Unless purification of the air we breathe and desalination of ocean water are started on a global scale, the world is faced with unprecedented famine and drought. This was the prediction of astrologer Nostradamus. It is also the forecast of one of America's most illustrious astronomers, Dr. Andrew Douglass, the late Professor Emeritus of the science he invented—Dendrochronology—at the University of Arizona.

Dr. Douglass predicted this drought in the mid-1950s. Whether it continues for another 30 years remains to be seen. But, about the end of this period, the deepest freeze in weather history has been predicted by George J. McCormack, a man who uses the same planetary (astro-meteorological) system.

By the year 2000, world population will have mushroomed to about seven billion. Even today, we cannot adequately feed a fraction of that number. By 2000 A.D., we will have consumed almost all available animal products. For example, it is already a practice in certain parts of Africa and at least one American zoo to eat roast hippopotamus. In Australia, the kangaroo is on the way out. Some "farsighted" African leaders want to kill, preserve, and export all the hippo meat they can round up. Impala, gazelle, and other creatures, including buffalo and even giraffe, are not safe from extinction by man's voracious appetite.

By 2000 A.D., the population "implosion"—that is, the mass shift of people from the country to the great cities—will be a reality. Automation will do the farming, we think, but what about meat? Even now, great schools of whale, porpoise, and dolphin (even shark!) are being hunted to extinction by the factory ships of Russia, Japan, Scotland, and the Nordic countries. Within the next couple decades—if we consume so many of our fellow creatures—we'll be subjected to virtually certain famine and pestilence.

THE "CELLS" OF WORLD POVERTY

There is an eternally unlistened-to group of scientists

predicting that our entire planet will soon slip into this un-thinkable condition unless we begin *now* to do one or both of the following: (a) start immediate, mandatory birth control on a world-wide basis, and (b) work out methods of process-ing food from materials such as petroleum and coal in a way that will not interfere with the basic organic life forms —plankton and algae. If we harvest, process, and eat all these basic micro-organisms, however, it could result in the death of all plant life, all marine and land life and the com-plete loss of the planet's atmosphere.

A universal famine afflicting hundreds of millions or even billions of human beings would be the most colossal catas-trophe in history.

Allow the present population explosion to continue un-checked and China's 800 million, scratching out a bare exist-ence in one of the world's largest dust bowls, will explode. It is likely that famine will reach serious proportions in India, Pakistan, and China in the early 1970s. They probably will be followed by Indonesia, Iran, Turkey, Egypt, and several other countries of Asia, Africa, and Latin America by 1980.

The astrological prediction is that America, while pouring forth countless millions of tons of food for these suffering nations, is itself fighting drought and pestilence, natural dev-astations of unprecedented proportions, and the fires of mob rule, and will slide down the scale of world power—unless exceptional leaders and exceptional measures soon begin to employ the tools of astrology to prevent it.

Only extreme foresight and action at long range can prevent the dangers that lie ahead for our nation and for the world at large. There is no astrological lobby in Washington; astrology has no unified voice. Yet we should at least make an attempt to forestall these coming events by careful, serious, impartial study of the phenomena.

DESTRUCTION OF THE AMERICAN COASTLINES

It is the studied, conservative view of everyone who predicts future events regularly and accurately that the Earth is rapid-ly approaching the end of this World Age. Both the Eastern and Western coastlines of the continental United States sink-ing beneath the oceans is a common prediction. Even ortho-dox scientists now expect that people living in the Southeastern section of the U.S. will witness a large land mass rising from the depths of the ocean. A series of calamitous earthquakes will gradually break apart the state of California and cast

234 THE FUTURE HISTORY OF THE WORLD

the pieces beneath the waves of the Pacific. There will be ample warning when the magnitude and intensity of the earthquakes increase.

It won't happen immediately, but there is sound reason for deeper probes into the reasons some astrologers believe that, between 1999 and 2001, the axis of the Earth will change, the poles will shift, and a radical new cycle will begin. When this occurs, the waters of the Great Lakes will empty into the gulf of Mexico. South America will be shaken from end to end, and water will rush from the present Antarctic off to Tierra del Fuego (an archipelago south of South America).

In the Caribbean, new dry land will appear out of the ocean's depths. *"And ye shall hear of wars and rumors of wars . . . nation shall rise against nation, and kingdom against kingdom, and there shall be famine, and pestilences, and earthquakes in divers places. But all these things are the beginnings of sorrows. (Matthew 24:7–8)*

And yet, according to a prominent astrologer-scientist-philosopher, Manly Palmer Hall, the 14-year period between 1966 and 1980 is a Sagittarian cycle which brings a great emphasis to the United States—a time of fantastic national progress when America will lead the social and intellectual life of the entire planet. This interpretation of the Sagittarian cycle suggests that American leadership *will* have adopted the tools of astrological analysis and insight as a policy-making device. But between 1969 and 1974 (according to the theory of geodetic equivalents), there will be a heavy astrological emphasis on Asia as well. America will have to deal with the unification of Eastern Asia, the East Indies, Japan, the Philippines, and even our own Pacific outposts. Between 1975 and 1980, however, the re-emergence of a totalitarian dictatorship will cause the coalition of Asian groups with the danger of all-out war in South Central Asia.

Geographic Realignments to Come

The time for a land mass to rise from the Atlantic is within the next decade. Edgar Cayce called it *Poseidia*. There will be a mass exodus from the Eastern coast. The safest parts of the continent, Cayce said, will be the eastern parts of Canada and South Central Canada, much of Ohio, Indiana, and Illinois. The American West Coast, he added, will be rent asunder and drown beneath the sea.

Huge sections of the Eastern United States, including New York, will disappear—probably by the turn of the century.

There will be ample warning, however, when the southern parts of Georgia and the Carolinas experience tectonic movements and seismic waves resulting from the beginning of the rise of a land mass in the Atlantic. Even so, the greatest geographic changes will occur along the North Atlantic coast.

Ample warning of the impending World Change will be the early breaking up of islands and chains of islands by volcanic action and earthquakes in the South Pacific and in the Mediterranean. When regular, massive eruptions begin in the area of Mount Etna, these changes (which will alter the planet's geology) will have seriously begun. Nostradamus' astrological prediction was that by between 1999 and 2001, the Earth's axial tilt and its poles will have violently shifted.

FIRE, EARTH, AIR AND WATER

There are Mexican ephemerides (planetary calendar stones of the Maya, Toltec, and Aztecs) which count Seven Earths and Seven Heavens separated from each other by various catastrophes—fire, earthquakes, hurricanes, and inundations of water. The Armenians and Arabs, geographic neighbors, have similar traditions relating the duration of each World Age. Chinese and Tibetan tradition insists that four Ages of Mankind have already been destroyed in world-wide cataclysms. Zoroaster (Zarathustra), the prophet of Mazdaism, the religion of ancient Persia, states that there are Seven World Ages. He described: "The signs, wonders and perplexity which are manifested in the world at the end of each millennium."

The Hindu "Visuddhi-Magga" also states that Seven World Ages exist, and that each must end in a world catastrophe. In almost every instance, this knowledge is based on the most ancient celestial cycles known to man: the Yugas preserved from prehistoric India. It is most remarkable that such divergent cultures as those of Iceland and the Polynesian Islands, including Hawaii, share almost identical traditions of great World Ages ending in universal destruction. Each of these Ages is violently concluded "with a different sky above the Earth."

If our planet's people raised themselves from a Stone Age culture on five different *antediluvian* occasions to a condition equal or superior to our present stage of development, evidence of it may be found in the very near future.

If the Earth shifted, tilted, and began rotating in a new

direction around a new axis, survivors would naturally see and report that entirely different constellations of stars rose and set in different areas of the heavens. Unfortunately, there'd be no presses to print books about it, and many of the rock carvings would have eroded or become undecipherable through the ages.

But the legends would persist!

PREHISTORIC SATELLITES WILL BE DISCOVERED

The American and Russian space programs aren't reporting everything they discover. If they haven't already been found, our probes will eventually discover "alien" satellites in orbit around the Earth—satellites which were not put up by either American *or* Russian rockets! The inscriptions will excite the most mundane academic mind because they'll be most similar to the oldest known languages ever devised on the Earth. They will not belong to some alien planet unless they're very recent (unknown) satellites of the Earth.

Immanuel Velikovsky reported that the ancient Chinese encyclopedia, *Sing-li-ta-tsiuen-Chou* recorded many destructions of mankind that ended each World Age. An ancient Greek writer named Hesiod however, told of five previous World Ages and the destruction of each with whole generations perishing before the repopulated Earth could resume its interrupted history. The Fire Bird of Atlantis and Egypt was the symbol of destruction and regeneration of the Ages of the World—as well as the endless reproduction of life itself.

Aristotle, who was an astrologer, also knew about the Supreme Year (the Great Sidereal Year). He said that at the end of this Great Year the Sun, Moon, and planets lined up in their original positions and relationship and life on the Earth was destroyed before the cycle resumed. In the year 300 A.D., Censorinus said, "Men thought that different prodigies appear by means of which the gods notified mortals at the end of each age. The Etruscans were versed in astrology, and after having observed the prodigies (*positions of the stars and planets*) with attention, they recorded these observations in their books."

UNIVERSAL UNDERSTANDING OF THE WORLD AGES

Philo of Alexandria repeatedly proved that the Greeks had a remarkable understanding of the nature of reality: "Democrates and Epicurus postulate many World Ages, the origin of which they ascribe to mutual impacts and interlacing of atoms (!), and their destruction to the counterblows and collisions by the bodies so formed."

The Greeks clearly understood the atomic structure of matter and the likeness of celestial systems to the atom. They understood the destruction of atoms as well as of entire planets! Their knowledge was derived from the Egyptians. In his work, *On The Eternity of the World*, Philo explained why the exact knowledge of these titanic events did not survive the ages: "By reason of the constant and *repeated* destructions of water and fire, later generations did not receive from the former the memory of the order and sequence of events."

Heraclitus, another Greek astrologer-mathematician, taught that all civilization ends in fire every 10,800 years. Aristarchus of Samos taught that the Earth is destroyed twice every 2,484 years; once by fire, once by water. Although there is some doubt about the exact number of World Ages preceding our own, the general opinion among astrologers is that it was *five*. In his *History of the Civilized Nations of Mexico*, however, C. E. Brasseur de Bourbourg wrote that: "Man had been created and life had manifested four times."

But the Sibylline Oracles, now classified by both Jewish and Christian authorities as *"pseudipographa,"* prophesy that *two* World Ages are yet to come. After each great catastrophe (or Sun Age), the Earth shifts its axis and the Sun appears to change its course through the sky.

There is something remarkably similar and universal about these reports. Obviously, *something* catastrophic happened to this Earth and its people not too long ago—something so horrendous and terrifying that only a few scholars have dared face up to the facts of history. Dr. Immanuel Velikovsky is one of these scholars. He saw in the atom's activity a rule that applied equally to the outer cosmos, the planets. We reported that these are not mere accidents of celestial traffic, but normal phenomena like birth and death.

LIFE IS CYCLICAL, NOT LINEAR

Obviously, neither your life nor anyone else's can proceed without interruption or change; nor can any city, state, or nation continue forever. India, one of the poorest of nations, was once one of the richest and mightiest. America and Russia may one day be a mere wisp of historical legend, existing in mythology as a dreamlike Troy or Atlantis.

Nothing that exists—not even our Galaxy of Suns—can exist in its present form for all eternity. Every advanced, intelligent species probably realizes this simple fact, and yet a few thousand years seems immensely long to us. Cycles exist within cycles—for you, for the Earth, for every atom in the Universe. In the more profound study of Mundane Astrology, the World Cycles seem to represent a puzzle impossible for us to decode and understand, *until we fully realize that they actually exist.*

If all Earthmen continue to plunge blindly along the present course, the impending shake-up will again envelop the world in violence and destruction. Perhaps it is unavoidable; and perhaps we have only seven chances to learn our Cosmic Law before total extinction. True, this is an "iffy" proposition, but we've nothing to lose by *trying.* Whatever pitiful survivors may exist a few centuries hence may have to start blindly all over once more, with only a few sadly misunderstood legends of former world greatness and the destruction which ended it all. And all the while there may be electronic satellites whirling around overhead as Mankind goes through the painful process of climbing the ladder of evolution; slavery, human sacrifice, superstition, feudalism, "new" inventions, the arts, sciences and, finally (if they are lucky) enlightenment.

According to Gina Cerminara in *The World Within:* "If we are to take Edgar Cayce's prophecies with regard to our planet seriously, we can prepare for drastic upheavals, but not for total extinction. Civilization will go on, and we could well build a superb new global civilization upon the mud and muck of the old."

THE KALI YUGA WORLD CYCLES

About 20 years ago a blind man named McDermott gave a written interpretation of the Kali Yuga World Cycles to Nora Forest in Pittsburgh. This was a 5,000-year Kabalistic cycle divided into seven-year periods extending from 1912 to the year 2010. McDermott had received the antique record from an Indian national sometime after World War I.

I first saw it in 1960 and can vouch for what it said. The predictions about J.F.K. and Pope John XXIII alone make it a most remarkable document:

1912–1919 MARS/positive. It is the first of three septenarians of war-woe in this country since 1775. Mars in

Europe means the Balkans, Central Europe, and Northern Italy; all three are involved.

1919–1926 URANUS/ negative. This period sees a psychology fad, wireless radio, popularizing of the automotive mode of travel, the beginning of a great advance in air flight—all very Uranian. The United States and Russia are negative in world affairs.

1926–1933 JUPITER/ positive. A Jupiter cycle always has two phases. The first half of this phase is too optimistic and over-expansive in all directions. Jupiter, ruler of organized religion, gives so much prosperity during the first phase that people are not interested in the higher life and an economic crash ensues. Jupiterian optimism fades during the second phase and a truly serious depression follows. As worldly opulence dissolves, interest in religion increases.

1933–1940 SATURN/ negative. This is a very Saturnine time, giving the general public fears, depression, uncertainties, restrictions, and then teaching them to live frugally. The Jews again feel the terror of persecution, and great unrest is felt in Europe.

1940–1947 NEPTUNE/ positive. The second of the seven-year war cycles. During the Neptune sub-period of a thousand years ago (820 to 1072) the terror came from the sea. (Now it comes from the air.) In this period, the Orient looms larger and larger and the world grows smaller in general observation. The entire world is troubled.

1947–1954 MERCURY/ negative. This is a time of restlessness and mental unsettlement; many new fads and all sorts of movements are introduced. The more thoughtful will say and write that the world has learned nothing from the second war, but all the time a new religious wave will be spreading. Ireland may produce a child that will develop a new literary form and France will very likely have a new or different kind of government.

1954–1961 VENUS/ positive. This being the first Venus influence since the Mansions of Libra came into the world, this would be a time of peace and yet a war that is not a war is being waged. The emphasis on art and beauty receives recognition as a cultural trend. The institution of marriage swings almost too far towards secularity but will swing back to being a ceremonial natural law. Racially, the Nordic and Western European peoples have strong urges toward coalescing, probably the formation of a United States of Europe.

1961–1968 SUN/ positive. There is an old prophecy that

the greatest of the Popes is to arise in this century and this seems to be the time for the "Flower of Flowers" as he is called. It is to be the last Glory of the Catholic Church as changes in the Church rules are indicated. This is the period in which the United States of America would have the first Catholic President. Racially, there is a decided coalition among the nations. Asia and Africa may be unfriendly to the United States.

1968–1975 MOON/ positive. Wide changes in ideas are instituted about property, and taxation will be more reduced than economists thought possible so soon. Racially, the Arab peoples will be feeling the strength of unity and it will take statesmanship to keep the new power within bounds.

1975–1982 MARS/ negative. Rumors of wars and dissatisfaction with world-governing body's restraints on nations are indicated. Possible war will threaten from Arabs and from Eastern Asia. Since this is a negative Mars cycle, the period of peace will not end entirely. This is the time in which natural cataclysms will take place. Disunity in the Balkans and restlessness in Central Europe and Africa are still problems in the world.

1982–1989 URANUS/ positive. The 1920's negative Uranus cycle popularizes the subconscious mind. This period will bring forth a science of the super-consciousness. This is a wonderful time for a new super-psychology, the spread of occult wisdom and vast voyages into worlds hitherto unknown. The United States and Russia dominate the world and their policies may still be at cross purposes that will end in disaster. This will be a period of great explosion in many ways.

1989–1996 JUPITER/ negative. This is very bad for organized religion. Jupiterian optimism and belief in goodness and peace may lead to a blindness about troublous things people do not want to see or believe. During the second half of this cycle comes the Third woe, with worldwide calamities.

1996–2003 SATURN/ positive. (Some scholars have placed the date of the beginning of the Millennium here. But it seems unlikely this would be born in a Saturn cycle.) Yet, the Great War ends in this period. The Jews will be the most fortunate people of the time.

2003–2010 NEPTUNE/ negative. Time of the "Thousand Years of Peace" is indicated. If an ephemeris for those years were available today, astrologers could find the time for the beginning of the Millennium and the Aquarian Age.

It would certainly have to be a powerful and most benign
configuration to justify the optimistic prophecies of the past
5000 years of darkness. (author's italics.)

The fact that this interpretation of the Kali Yuga Cycles
coincides in the most astounding way with the events of
the world since 1912 indicates that a closer study of this
document will eventually prove the validity of the World
Cycles.

THE DREAM OF REINCARNATION

"Immediately after the tribulation of those days shall the
Sun be darkened, and the Moon shall not give her light,
and the stars shall fall from heaven and the powers of
heaven shall be shaken . . ." (*Matthew* 24:30)
Was Matthew referring to something that had already
happened, or was yet to happen? If this prophesy lies in
our future, *when* will it take place?
There may be an answer from the great American prophet
and clairvoyant, Edgar Cayce. In a trance-state from which
he emerged with absolutely no memory of what he'd said,
Cayce was able to diagnose the ailments of thousands of
people *accurately*. Most of his "readings" were of people
he'd never seen or heard of, but he described them as
though through the eyes of non-physical beings. According
to the A.R.E records, the essential part of your Self—in a
way scientists do not yet understand—is continually being
reincarnated in one life after another.
The year 1968, according to the horoscope of the United
States, will be the most difficult, soul-wrenching time for
any President in America's history. Either in spite of or
because of all this, spiritualism, mediumship, ESP, and
clairvoyance will become routine, matter-of-fact realities.
Madame Blavatsky, one of the world's best-known mystics
is reported to have said that every century the Masters of
Wisdom send a messenger, and the next one is to appear
by 1975.
If her prophesy works out, the new Teacher will then be
only about 12 years old. Astrologically, he is predicted to
have been born either in Asia or South America in 1962.
All children born around the time of the great Aquarian
eclipse-conjunction of Feb. 4, 1962 are the crystallization
of this Aquarian Age we're entering.
Astrologer Mary Forbes described in a West Coast news-

paper in 1925 that Ecuador would become a great point of spiritual illumination. "A new continent," she predicted, "will arise in the Pacific."

FUTURE LANDS OF SAFETY

It happens that the northernmost nations of the Earth (particularly the latitudes of their capitals), according to astrology's geodetic equivalents, will always be dominant over their southern neighbors. This holds true even within national boundaries—the Civil War being a classic example. Accordingly, Cuba will again have a free, stabilized government when Castro (a Leo like many previous dictators: Caesar, Napoleon, and Mussolini, for example) disappears into history.

Canada and Alaska will become the land of the future. The capital of America will be moved from Washington to Fairbanks (Latitude 65° N.), thus enabling the U.S. to gain political and military supremacy over Peking (39° N.) and Moscow (55° N.). Washington, D.C. is now at 38° N. Latitude.

Edgar Cayce had this to say about the end of the present World Age: "The Earth will be broken up in the western portion of America . . . the greater portion of Japan must go into the sea . . . the upper portion of Europe will be changed as in the twinkling of an eye . . . land will appear off the East coast of America . . . there will be open waters appear in the Northern portions of Greenland." The latter statement indicates a global tilt when North Greenland again becomes temperate or even tropical.

Three months after Vesuvius and/or Mount Pelee explode as mightily as did Krakatoa in 1883, a great spate of subterranean and surface earthquakes will raise tidal waves to inundate the lower coastline of California, and the vast expanse between southern Nevada and the Great Salt Lake in Utah.

G. J. McCormack predicts what may well be the shifting of a polar region in the year 1981, when temperatures in America will drop to their lowest in man's memory.

Nostradamus predicted that the eclipses of July and August of 1999 would be followed in October by the flip of the Earth and the changing of its polar regions.

THE NEXT MARTIAN INVASION

Even though these geological changes will be caused by the shifting globe, and ultimately by extremely adverse configurations between the planets, it is interesting that many ancient and medieval astrologers predicted the conquering of all Northern Europe and America by a terrible Mongol-like invader. Here is what Nostradamus predicted in his 72nd astrological quatrain:

> "*Like the great king of the Angolmois* (Mongolois, or Mongol-like),
> *The year 1999, seventh month,*
> *A great king of terror will descend from the sky,*
> *Around this time Mars will reign for the good cause.*"

On the surface, it appears as though we'll be invaded by Mongol-like Martians or we will have an interplanetary war with the inhabitants of Mars (perhaps by then an Earth colony fighting for its liberty—a "Good Cause"). If so, alien troops could invade and dominate all the nations of the Earth, according to the *interplanetary* extrapolation of the theory of Geodetic Equivalents, wherein the Northernmost or coldest areas are dominant. If this "great king of the Angolmois" comes from Mars, the Earth could well be invaded by Alien Beings with superior technology. Be it noted that Nostradamus accurately predicted air flight by means of lighter-than-air craft. He even gave the name of its inventor—Montgolfier—who devised the first balloon!

THE DESTINY OF GERMANY

One of the most versatile men of our times—writer, reporter, and philosopher,—Pierre Van Paassen published a book called *Days of Our Years* about three decades ago. In this work he gave astrological figures obtained from the writings of a gypsy astrologer in Germany in 1849. These long-range astrological predictions clearly foretold Germany's ultimate destruction beginning with World War I, then followed by World War II and the division of Germany by its enemies. Nobody in Germany listened. At the time, Hitler was killing Czechs, Jews, Gypsies, and others—including a few astrologers whose advice he didn't like.

The world, Van Paassen says, is heading for disaster. This statement, from a man who predicted in the 1930s that Germany "will lie in ruins in 1946," must be accorded its due attention, if not full respect.

VAST EARTHQUAKES AND AMERICAN POLITICAL UPHEAVALS

Long before there is any repetition of celestial cataclysm, there will be radical changes on the Earth—both natural phenomena and political changes—most of them violent.

By foreseeing these natural cataclysms, which many astrologers are convinced are going to spell finish to this World Age, Olive A. Pryor concluded: "The imagination is staggered by the many geological and political changes evident in the horoscopes of all nations between now and the end of the century."

MAN'S WAY OUT—NEW HOPE FOR THE FUTURE

Will this World Age soon end—with no continuous history and no accurate memory of what preceded it? It need *not* happen if we honestly apply our resources to the study of the great discrepancy existing between man's obviously advanced physiological state and his extremely short history.

No one can avert a New World Age, but with the use of astrology it is perfectly within the realm of possibility to make the transition smoothly. Your future and that of your children and your children's children can be assured with ancient astrological wisdom.

Now is the time of the new prophets, the modern astrologers. These prophets can be *you*, your *children*, and *their* children. It is time scientist-astrologers were heard in our universities, high schools, and elementary schools.

The Aquarian Age is already upon us. Whether we meet it in a universal disaster or whether we employ astrology to foresee and avoid the disaster is a decision the current World Age will have to make.

Astrology, the Mother of all sciences, is our way out of this endless cycle of world destructions. With it, we can save the best that is in the world, the best of man's creative genius and the countless multitudes of living creatures who share this existence with us and who (except for our efforts) might go the way of all extinct species.

You and I can not only preserve everything we've built and

earned, but we can also add to it. We can learn to recognize every man's distinctly characteristic image—*his horoscope*—as his unique and indelible cosmic "stamp." In the
process, we can learn to value and respect each representative of the Twelve Signs, because all Earthmen share something far greater than fractional nationalism, racism, or
religious ideologies. We all have the same Zodiacal Signs in
our horoscopes, the same planets but in different positions
and relationships and "houses")—in short, Earthmen are in-
vitably bound by the same *astrology*.

OUTWARD TO THE STARS

The reason seems clear: if we learn enough, we'll be quali-
ed to survive, and to meet with so-called Alien Life—intelligent Beings from other worlds, other star systems, per-
aps even other galaxies! Each planet, like each human being,
as its own astrological system. The truly advanced civiliza-
ons out there at this moment must know this, and there-
ore must conform harmoniously with the inhabitants of
other worlds.

Our scientists are now learning that there are superciviliza-
ons encompassing entire solar systems—whole groups of
tellar systems and entire constellations of stars! At this
riting, several of them are signalling to us from the
epths of interstellar space. Beacons of incredibly powerful
rtificial radio emissions are bombarding the entire gamut
f Earth's radio-astronomy antennae—the grid-like "bowls"
ith which radio-astronomers around the planet constantly
sten to a regular series of messages no one has yet been
ole to decipher.

One series of coded signals are being transmitted in all
rections at once on a scale equivalent to thousands (per-
aps millions!) of megacycles. This is more radio power than
ur own blazing Sun is capable of emitting, even if it were
ultiplied many times!

The regularly-spaced emissions have been discovered in
e direction of Aries and Pegasus by most of the world's
dio astronomers.

I'm convinced that someone who has been through it
l long before we came into existence are trying to tell us
mething. Just learning what that message is must be worth
ery conceivable expense and effort we can muster to sur-
ve the coming World Change.

Only through the universal re-evaluation of astrological wisdom will we be able to live through the next few decades and accomplish that which none of the antediluvian peoples were able to achieve.

Index

M